China's Soft Power
Diplomacy in South Asia

China's Soft Power Diplomacy in South Asia

Myth or Reality?

B. M. Jain

LEXINGTON BOOKS
Lanham • Boulder • New York • London

Published by Lexington Books
An imprint of The Rowman & Littlefield Publishing Group, Inc.
4501 Forbes Boulevard, Suite 200, Lanham, Maryland 20706
www.rowman.com

Unit A, Whitacre Mews, 26-34 Stannary Street, London SE11 4AB

British Library Cataloguing in Publication Information Available

Library of Congress Cataloging-in-Publication Data

Names: Jain, B. M.
Title: China's soft power diplomacy in South Asia : myth or reality? / B. M. Jain.
Description: Lanham : Lexington Books, [2017] | Includes bibliographical references and index.
Identifiers: LCCN 2017009339 (print) | LCCN 2017030252 (ebook) | ISBN 9780739193402 (elec-
    tronic) | ISBN 9780739193396 (hardback : alk. paper) | ISBN 9781498559478 (pbk. : alk. paper)
Subjects: LCSH: China—Foreign relations. | Diplomacy.
Classification: LCC JZ1734.A5 (ebook) | LCC JZ1734.A5 .J35 2017 (print) | DDC 327.51—dc23
LC record available at https://lccn.loc.gov/2017009339

Contents

Acronyms

ASEAN	Association of Southeast Asian Nations
BIT	Bangladesh Institute of Technology
BDCA	Border Defence Cooperation Agreement
BRICS	Brazil, Russia, India, China, South Africa
CBM	Confidence Building Measure
CIs	Confucius Institutes
CIKU	Confucius Institute at Kathmandu University
CPEC	China-Pakistan Economic Corridor
CPN	Communist Party of Nepal
EEZ	Exclusive Economic Zone
GDP	Gross Domestic Product
IMF	International Monetary Fund
JeM	Jaish-e-Muhammad
J&K	Jammu and Kashmir
JWG	Joint Working Group
LAC	Line of Actual Control
LoC	Line of Control
LTTE	Liberation Tigers of Tamil Eelam
MNDF	Maldives National Defence Force
MoU	Memorandum of Understanding

NSG	Nuclear Suppliers Group
OBOR	One Belt, One Road
PLA	People's Liberation Army (China)
PoK	Pakistan-occupied Kashmir
PRC	People's Republic of China
SAARC	South Asian Association of Regional Cooperation
SED	Strategic Economic Dialogue
SPA	Seven Party Alliance
SR	special representative
ULFA	United Liberation Front of Assam
UN	United Nations
WTO	World Trade Organization
ZTE	Zhongxing Telecommunication Equipment

Acknowledgments

This book is an outcome of various courses I taught on India and China, China and the United States, and China and South Asia at SUNY, Binghamton, New York, in 2006–2007; Jaume 1 University, Castellón, Spain, in 2008; and Cleveland State University, Cleveland, Ohio, in 2013. I must acknowledge that I have enormously benefitted from comprehensive and intensive discussions with the faculty, colleagues, and students at those schools. More often than not, informal interaction over tea or coffee in universities' cafeterias proved extremely fruitful in crystallizing my thoughts on China's soft power instruments in its foreign policy.

It was just a sheer accident that the idea of writing this book synchronized with an official launch of the Chinese government's soft power project in the early twenty-first century. Since then my interest grew deeper and sharper in understanding the rationale and motivation behind China's soft power diplomacy. Moreover, a huge amount of source material available in the form of books and articles at the aforementioned universities and various institutions went a long way toward helping me complete this book project. During the course of writing, a large number of individuals contributed in several ways. It is not possible to thank each individual personally. But I owe my thanks to all of them for their valuable time, energy, and suggestions.

For reading through the manuscript and for writing endorsements to the book, I am deeply grateful to Joseph Tse-Hei Lee, professor at Pace University, New York; Zhiqun Zhu, professor at Bucknell University, Lewisburg, Pennsylvania; and Rajesh Basrur, professor at Nanyang Technological University, Singapore. Indeed, this was a stupendous task.

I am deeply thankful to acquisition editor Justin Race, formerly with Lexington Books, for expediting my book proposal. Having sensed its importance, he presented it to the members of the editorial board, who readily put their final stamp of approval on the proposal. I wish to thank them also. I will be failing in my duty if I do not give my sincere gratitude to Joseph Parry, senior editor at Lexington Books, for his patience and cooperation. Also, I must mention that Parry extended the deadline for submission of the manuscript and accommodated my genuine concerns ungrudgingly. I am thankful to Emily Roderick, Jessica McCleary, and all other members of the editorial team for their understanding, patience, and cooperation throughout the process of publication of this book.

Last but not least, I cannot forget the great deal of cooperation and support I received from my daughter, Romi (Cleveland State University, Cleveland, Ohio), for her incisive editing and from my son, Rahul (Kelowna, Vancouver, British Columbia), for typesetting the manuscript. My special thanks go out to my wife, Manju, for her understanding, patience, and encouragement.

Introduction

There has been a remarkable shift in China's foreign policy with the dawn of the twenty-first century. The country transitioned from Deng Xiaoping's low-profile and "hide-our-capacities" approach to a strategy of power projection and assertive diplomacy at global and regional levels. In hindsight, the roots of China's rise can be traced to the Nixon-Kissinger team's instrumental role in ending China's long international isolation in the early 1970s by supporting the entry of the People's Republic of China (PRC) into the United Nations (UN) in 1971 while simultaneously expelling the Republic of China (ROC)—its longtime ally.[1] This was interpreted as one of the egregious episodes in US foreign policy in the twentieth century.[2]

A similar narrative was repeated by President Bill Clinton's fatuous estimate that China's integration into the global economy would transform it into a peaceful and responsible stakeholder in an interdependent world order. For that, Clinton vigorously campaigned for China's entry into the World Trade Organization (WTO). The PRC's admittance into the WTO in 2001 opened floodgates of opportunities to establish its economic footprint through massive trade and investments across the globe.[3] These two extraordinary developments—a permanent seat in the UN Security Council and WTO membership—elevated China's stature, image, and prestige in the international system.

While gradually building on its economic might, China began to play an assertive role, in contrast to Deng's lay-low strategy in global and regional affairs, whether it be energy and environmental security or the crisis in the Korean peninsula over North Korea's nuclear threat to its neighbors. In order to achieve and consolidate its foreign policy objectives, China adopted a two-pronged strategy. First, the post-Deng leadership embarked on the globetrotting strategy to spread its strategic footprints worldwide. Second, the Beijing leadership sought to vigorously promote Chinese language and culture as a tool of its cultural soft power. It has established 500 Confucius institutes and 1,000 Confucius Classrooms in 134 countries and regions, with an enrolment of 1.9 million students as of December 1, 2015, to promote "cross-cultural exchanges."[4] Also, there is a widely shared perception among Mainland academia and intellectuals that the Beijing leadership's proactive pursuit of soft power is a political strategy to deal with the simmering domestic discontent in order to maintain its authoritarian control over society.[5]

Interestingly, the official Chinese discourse on soft power began in 2005/ 2006, with an idea to present a Chinese alternative model to the Western liberal order, or the replace the Westphalia-based international system with a Sino-centric world order based on Chinese characteristics. With the publication of Joshua Kurlantzick's book *Charm Offensive* in 2007, Chinese leaders recognized the value of soft power to safeguard, sustain, and promote its core national interests in the Asia-Pacific region.[6]

Given this backdrop, I have attempted to examine the potency and relevance of China's notion of soft power in general, albeit mixed with the nuances of Joseph S. Nye's connotation of soft power, and to apply it to South Asia in particular. While tracing the genesis of China's foreign policy from a historical perspective, the book first discusses the term "soft power," which was coined by Nye, of Harvard University, in 1992, in the context of hard-boiled realities of international relations in the age of information technology. Having recognized limitations of American power, Nye urged the United States to employ soft power as a means to obtain the "preferred outcomes" through "attraction" and "persuasion" rather than through military force or coercive measures. Nye insisted that given the declining power of the United States and its increasing vulnerability to a new set of threats and challenges in an anarchical world order, American policy makers garner cooperation of nations through persuasion premised on a "community of interest."[7] Second, the book investigates not only the Chinese version of soft power based on Chinese characteristics but also its institutionalization in dealing with neighbors. In this regard, a host of questions have been examined. For instance, what factors have impelled the Beijing leadership to embrace and promote soft power through multiple windows of Chinese language and culture and Confucian thought? What were the overriding reasons behind reinventing Confucianism as an integral component of China's soft power diplomacy?

In an attempt to project China's image as a benign and responsible international actor, China's political heavyweights made a fervent appeal to indigenous intellectuals and Chinese diaspora to propagate and popularize soft power as a means of increasing China's influence globally. The political vision of the leadership to replace the US-centric unipolar world prompted it to popularize the soft power approach to the international system. Apart from this, the Beijing leadership perceived a strategic value in propagating soft power to forestall the brewing discontent in society, wading through abject poverty, poor healthcare, and unemployment. With an intent to conceal its failure on the domestic front, China launched the soft power project as a political renaissance in the early twenty-first century.

AIMS

This book has multiple aims. The first is to explain the ongoing intellectual discourse on cultural soft power and the "harmonious world" as instruments of China's foreign policy in an attempt to offer a Sino-centric world order opposed to the hegemony of the West in realms of peace, development, and global governance. Second, the book aims to illuminate and explore whether China's ancient cultural norms and social values and its philosophical underpinnings based on the Confucius thought have the potency as sources of soft power to attract others to embrace China's worldview. Third, it aims to examine the underlying motives behind China's drive for using soft power instruments such as foreign aid, grants, scholarships, and diplomatic support to South Asian countries. Fourth, it purports to examine a host of research questions to decipher motivations behind China's launching of soft power diplomacy in South Asia.

METHODOLOGY AND THEORETICAL FRAMEWORK

A simple analytical approach has been adopted to examine the extent to which China has been able to use its soft power instruments, mainly providing development assistance and economic packages, building cultural links, promoting people-to-people contacts, providing research fellowships, and supporting linkages with think tanks outside the country, especially neighboring countries. For the source materials, contemporary and current literature in the form of documents, books, journals, magazines, newspapers, and content from official and unofficial websites were widely consulted to collect the relevant materials and analyze them in an objective and scientific manner. As regards the theoretical framework, the book's title itself suggests that the soft power theory developed by Joseph Nye has been used as a point of reference, mixed with the Chinese version of soft power, in application to South Asia. Its analytical value, as well as its limitations, has been clearly spelled out to remove any confusion in the minds of readers and reviewers.

WHAT IS DISTINCT ABOUT THIS WORK?

The book entails a couple of unique features that make it a study distinct from the vastly available literature on China's soft power. First, this book deals with China's soft power diplomacy in South Asia, especially in the context of smaller states such as Bhutan, Nepal, and the Maldives. Second, the book traces the origin of China's engagement with South Asian states from historical, ethnic, cultural, and societal perspectives in order to better understand the dynamics of its South Asia policy. Third, the book addresses the underlying reasons to explain why China's soft power diplomacy in South Asia is neither appealing nor attractive to its biggest player in the region: India. Fourth, an array of factors have been outlined to thoroughly discuss why Pakistan figures as an exceptional entity in the region in Chinese perception, as manifest from President Xi Jinping's description of China's relations with Pakistan as "sweeter than honey," "higher than the Himalayas," and "deeper than the oceans."[8] Is this expression mere political rhetoric or a reality? Given the special category of the relationship between Beijing and Islamabad, this book illuminates the relationship's wider implications for South Asian security and stability as well as its impact on China's relations with India, while spelling out the future of Sino-Indian strategic partnership. Fifth, the book addresses the complexities and nuances of China's soft power approach to South Asia in light of the psychocultural and geopsychological peculiarities of South Asia, which might prod scholars of South Asian studies to flesh out the importance of these complexities and peculiarities in conflict resolution mechanisms in future research. Finally, findings of this study are likely to further advance and refine research in the domain of soft power.

ORGANIZATION OF THE BOOK

This book is divided into six major chapters, apart from a brief concluding chapter. Chapter 1 defines and elaborates on the term "soft power," as coined by Joseph Nye. While building on Nye's concept of soft power, China has sought to introduce it in its diplomacy, based on Chinese characteristics. In this chapter, a modest attempt has been made to relate and apply China's soft power model to South Asia with the motivation to evaluate the model's feasibility and relevance in the case of smaller countries of South Asia like Bhutan, Nepal, and the Maldives. It further offers scientific explanations through examples and evidence as to why China's soft power approach has been very appealing to smaller nations of South Asia but not to India.

Chapter 2 examines and evaluates sources of conflict and cooperation between China and India within the framework of their respective worldviews and also each country's perception of the other, which emanate from the influences of intermeshing variables such as history, geography, culture, nationalism, and geopolitics. An attempt has been made to locate sources to determine whether or not China's soft power strategy has been successful in eroding India's influence in the region. In this regard, the chapter delves deeply into establishing conjunction or disjunction between China's soft power initiatives and the influences they produce. The chapter argues that core irritants such as the unresolved boundary dispute between China and India, which has been ongoing since 1962, and the Sino-Pakistan strategic nexus vis-à-vis India are by-products of the ruling class's cognitive dissonance in both countries. Moreover, lingering problematic issues such as these make it much harder for China to attract and influence India with its soft power initiatives in South Asia. Simultaneously, India, while embarking on its multiple programs of defense modernization, has been seriously engaged in strengthening and deepening its military and security ties with the United States to balance off China. India has also been keeping a low profile in China's backyard of Southeast Asia so as not to antagonize it, although India pushed through its strategic presence in Vietnam temporarily.

Chapter 3 notes that despite the absence of commonality between China and Pakistan in terms of social, cultural, and political outlook and values or ethnic and religious affinity, Beijing and Islamabad have been able to consistently maintain friendly and stable ties without any hiccups. The chapter examines the core factors that have contributed to their all-weather friendship. The most plausible explanation offered in this respect is the persistence of their shared geopolitical interest in keeping India's rise in check, though with divergent goals and objectives. China has three main objectives. First, it aims to garner Pakistan's succor to realize its strategic goals in Pakistan-occupied Kashmir (PoK): namely, building an economic corridor to link its Xinxiang province to Pakistan's Gwadar port. Second, its objective is to enlist Pakistan's support to weaken the secessionist movement of Uyghur Muslims in Xinxiang. Third, China aims to project Pakistan as a military bulwark against India through a transfer of massive military hardware and assistance to Pakistan's nuclear weapon and missile programs.

To Pakistan, first, China is a reliable source of military hardware to meet an impending Indian threat to its national security. Second, Islamabad perceives Beijing as a sure shot to block India's permanent membership to the UN Security Council, including several other multilateral institutions like the Nuclear Suppliers Group. Third, Pakistan considers China's diplomatic succor indispensable for defeating any Indian move at the UN that impinges on its national interests. For instance, China has twice foiled the Indian move at the UN to declare Jaish-e-Muhammad (JeM) chief Maulana Masood Azhar a terrorist.

Chapter 4 traces the history of China's relations with the Himalayan states from geopolitical and geostrategic points of view. The chapter argues that China's expanding strategic footprint in Nepal, for instance, has been facilitated by the Maoist regime since August 2008. The chapter further argues that the compulsions of infrastructure and economic development have prodded Nepal and Bhutan to welcome China's soft power instruments such as foreign aid and grants, which they consider indispensable for the nation-building process. Besides, there is a greater sense of realization on the part of Kathmandu and Thimpu that since the gravity of power is fast shifting toward China, they should not miss the opportunity to come closer to China to minimize the age-old dependency on India. On the other hand, China believes that its massive economic aid might go a long way in solidifying its strategic presence in the Himalayan region.

Chapter 5 explains and reviews China's soft power projection in Sri Lanka and the Maldives through expanding and strengthening its economic and trade ties with them. China's soft power initiatives in Sri Lanka in the form of major infrastructure projects, such as development of ports, airfields, and roads, contributed to expanding China's strategic presence in Sri Lanka, especially during the Rajapaksa regime. The chapter argues that China's massive supply of military hardware to Sri Lanka played a potential role in defeating the Liberation Tigers of Tamil Eelam (LTTE), bringing China much closer to Sri Lanka, while at the same time India's role in Sri Lanka was hugely marginalized. The fallout for India was noticeable. To restrict China's strategic influence, the South Block in New Delhi was forced to rebuild its ties with Sri Lanka by initiating defense cooperation with Sri Lanka, beginning with joint naval exercises in 2011.

Chapter 6 examines how Sino-Bangladesh relations, initially characterized by mutual suspicion, were transformed into an intimate friendship between the countries. The chapter discusses multifaceted ties between China and Bangladesh from a holistic perspective. It also evaluates whether or not China's strategy of drawing Bangladesh into its strategic fold through its soft power instruments has succeeded in weakening the Dhaka–New Delhi relationship in light of their shared commonalities in terms of historical legacy, culture, language, and ethnocultural affinity. The chapter finally evaluates China's underlying motivations in Bangladesh by focusing on its heavy investment in infrastructure development in Bangladesh, including provision of soft loans and military assistance.

Chapter 7 summarizes the discourse on the conceptual and application components of China's soft power diplomacy in South Asia in sync with exploring the role and effect of the Chinese model of a harmonious world in reordering the international system. It is true that there is no precise yardstick to measure the extent to which Chinese cultural norms and historical narratives of its civilizational greatness have contributed to reshaping the international order in general or South Asian political order in particular. Nevertheless, this study offers some tangible clues that China's soft power instruments have exercised considerable influence over foreign policies of smaller countries of the region. For this, three main reasons can be cited. First, China is a principal source of foreign aid and grants for infrastructure development in less developed South Asian countries, whereas India is unable to match the quantum of aid that China offers to them. Second, while recognizing the shifting of gravity of power toward China, smaller nations of the Indian subcontinent do not want to remain under an Indian tutelage. Third, Indian foreign policy's hegemonic demeanor toward smaller countries like Nepal, Sri Lanka, and the Maldives is a major factor drawing those countries closer to China, who is squarely sensitive about their national pride and national sovereignty.

However, China's aggressive nationalism regarding territorial disputes— for instance, in the South China Sea—undermines not only its claim that it's a peaceful and law-abiding nation but also the legitimacy of its soft power. China's flexing of military muscles on the issue of the territorial dispute in the South China Sea, as well as its rejection of the tribunal's verdict in July 2016, has created doubt about the credibility of China's soft power approach. If China is really serious about improving its image in the perception of its neighbors, it will need to exercise restraint in dealing with them. In a larger context, China's soft power resources have not proved adequate at producing satisfactory outcomes in cost-effective terms. On global commons, China's overall record on compliance with international laws and treaty obligations is scarcely impressive. China's double standard on global terror is clearly manifest from its twice blocking the Indian move at the UN to designate Pakistani Masood Azhar as a terrorist. The book leaves more questions to be answered. What will China do with a Sino-centric world order? Does China's notion of a harmonious world enchant the global audience? What is the precise roadmap of the China-led world order in contrast to the Western system?

New findings and interpretations in this book are likely to provoke future research in the field of China's soft power structures and processes. They might also lead to a fresh discourse on the rationale and legitimacy behind the Chinese school of international relations. Scholars who are already engaged in soft power research will be further tempted to prove or disprove the veracity and efficacy of soft power as a means to achieve foreign policy goals.

Last but not least, I alone am responsible for all interpretations and any lacunae in the book. As far as I know, this is the first-ever full-length book on China's soft power diplomacy in South Asia.

I am sanguine that this book should provoke more critical and creative debate on the implications of China's soft power diplomacy in South Asia and beyond it.

NOTES

1. Peter Hays Gries, *China's New Nationalism: Pride, Politics, and Diplomacy* (Berkeley: University of California Press, 2004).

2. Edward C. Keefer, *The Nixon Administration and the United Nations: "It's a Damned Debating Society,"* http://www.diplomatie.gouv.fr/fr/IMG/pdf/ONU_edward_keefer.pdf.

3. Zhiqun Zhu, *China's New Diplomacy: Rationale, Strategies and Significance*, 2nd ed. (Surrey, UK: Ashgate, 2013).

4. "China Has Established 500 Confucius Institutes Globally," *Hanban News*, December 14, 2015, http://english.hanban.org/article/2015–12/14/content_626902.htm.

5. Joseph Tse-Hei Lee, Lida V. Nedilsky, and Siu-Keung Cheung, eds., *China's Rise to Power: Conception of State Governance* (New York: Palgrave Macmillan, 2012).

6. Hongyi Lai, Yiyi Lu. eds., *China's Soft Power and International Relations* (New York: Routledge, 2012).

7. Richard Javad Heydarian, "Is China's Soft-Power Bubble about to Burst?," *National Interest*, August 25, 2015, http://nationalinterest.org/feature/china%E2%80%99s-soft-power-bubble-about-burst-13683; also Joseph Nye, *The Future of Power* (New York: Public Affairs, 2011); Joseph Nye, *Soft Power: The Means to Success in World Politics* (New York: Public Affairs, 2004).

8. BBC News, "Is China-Pakistan 'Silk Road' a Game-Changer?," April 22, 2015, http://www.bbc.com/news/world-asia-32400091.

Chapter One

China's Soft Power Diplomacy

Theoretical Discourse and Application to South Asia

Discourse on China's soft power policy has captured the attention of academia and intellectuals across the globe. In particular, an intensive debate has ensued among Chinese academia and political leadership as to whether China's charm offensive will be able to reverse the perception globally that China's rise poses a threat to peace and stability. Given this, nuances and rubrics of soft power need to be excogitated, especially when China has begun playing a more active and assertive role in international affairs, contrary to its passive role in world politics before the onset of the twenty-first century.[1] China is in need of a peaceful and conducive environment at global and regional levels to ensure a greater access to energy and natural resources. At the same time, it wants to assure its neighbors that its rise does not constitute a threat to regional peace and stability.

Notably, China's economic miracle instilled confidence in the ruling class. Its model of economic development, based on its state-led capitalism, helped build its economic and military sinews. Undoubtedly, its "staggering economic success" catapulted China to a position from which it can convert its economic might into global assertiveness. Viewed through a realistic prism, China's engagement in a charm offensive is part of its strategy to not only polish its image around the world but also counterbalance US power and influence in the Asia-Pacific region. Wrapped up in its military and economic prowess, China's soft power projection is also directed at the United States. The intention is to malign the States in the eyes of the world community, exposing how the world's sole superpower has had to pay a heavy price in terms of blood and treasure in a series of escapable wars and conflicts in Afghanistan and Iraq without tangible gains. In other words, the flawed US model of promoting unilateral global and regional security order led to its decline as an invulnerable power.

China's growing military and economic power further motivated its leadership to promote its cultural soft power abroad to project itself as a benign and responsible international actor. In this context, William A. Callahan comments on China's "three global spectacles—Beijing's Olympic Games in 2008, the PRC's sixtieth anniversary celebrations in 2009, and Shanghai's World Expo in 2010," with which he says, "China is presenting itself to the world as the source of ancient wisdom and high technology, which together form an alternative model of progress and development. China's challenge to the Euro-American dominance of international politics became even sharper just after the Olympic Games ended when the global financial crisis erupted in the United States in September 2008."[2]

Before we discuss China's notion of soft power, it will be a useful exercise to elaborate in brief the term "soft power," coined by Joseph S. Nye. The overriding idea behind soft power was to sensitize US public-policy makers to the notion that America was no longer invulnerable or an unchallengeable power that could dictate its terms to its foes and allies alike. In effect, the US could ill-afford to go alone in an anarchical world order, especially after the tragic events of 9/11 and subsequent US invasion of Iraq in 2003. Nye's inclination was to let the administration realize the limits of American power in pursuing its agenda of maintaining US global supremacy. In other words, if alternative means of dialogue and persuasion could achieve the preferred outcomes, then the United States ought to avoid exercising hard power.

DEFINING SOFT POWER

As mentioned before, Joseph Nye made an effort through his writings to prod the administration on the imperative of redefining US foreign policy and revising its old instruments of promoting national interests within the framework of diffusion of power in the age of information and communication technology. Nye defines soft power as the "ability to shape preference of others." He explains, "One of the notable trends of the past century that is likely to continue to strongly influence global politics in this century is the current information revolution. And with it comes an increase in the role of soft power—the ability to obtain preferred outcomes by attraction and persuasion rather than coercion and payment."[3]

Illuminating the underlying logic behind soft power, he writes, "I first coined the term 'soft power,' in my 1990 book *Bound to Lead* that challenged the then conventional view of the decline of American power. After looking at American military and economic power resources, I felt that something was still missing—the ability to affect others by attraction and persuasion rather than just coercion and payment. I thought of soft power as an analytic concept to fill a deficiency in the way analysts thought about power."[4]

What he underlines is the importance of noncoercive means to achieve the desired goals. Nye endeavors to bring home the point that reliance on "persuasion, attraction and co-optation," rather than military means, constitutes "sustainable means" of maintaining the US hegemony.[5] The crux of his argument is that major powers ought to first exhaust the instruments of soft power to win over their adversaries by engaging them in a bilateral or multilateral dialogue. He further refined it in another book, *Soft Power: The Means to Success in World Politics.*[6] The most recent example of the efficacy of employing soft power diplomacy is the conclusion of the much-awaited multilateral P5+1 agreement on Iran's nuclear program in 2015, under which the Tehran regime agreed to accept restrictions on its nuclear program.

Before we examine China's soft power as a tool of foreign policy and diplomacy to advance its national interests overseas, it is important to understand the perceptual prism of Chinese leadership in order to uncover the contextual underpinnings of China's notion of soft power. This will help identify how China's peaceful transition to power in the post-Mao era led to Deng Xiaoping's embrace of economic reforms, which in effect meant an abandonment of the socialist model of economic development. While retaining a repressive and monolithic political system, China disallowed plural political liberalism and tolerance from taking root in the country. Alternatively, China embarked on a path of proactive diplomacy to project its image as a responsible and peaceful international actor. In this context, David Shambaugh observes, "Beijing has mounted a major public relations offensive in recent years, investing billions of dollars around the world in a variety of efforts."[7]

PERCEPTUAL PRISM

China's perceptions of foreign relations have undergone myriad phases from the early twentieth century to the dawn of the twenty-first century. The revolutionary phase, which lasted from 1921 to 1949 under the mesmerizing impact of Mao Tse-tung, left an indelible mark on the party's ideology regarding dealing with the outside world. Mao, as a philosopher, thinker, and strategist, had systematically instilled the revolutionary ideology of his peculiar mix of Marxism, Stalinism, and his own Maoism brand into the minds of Chinese people, as implicit in his famous doctrine the three worlds theory, which states that power comes out of "the barrel of gun."[8] Samuel S. Kim, a noted Sinologist, offers a plausible explanation about Mao's military thinking. He writes, "The historical experience of Western and Japanese imperialism during the century of national humiliation, far from being forgotten, seems to have endowed the Chinese with the nineteenth-century conception of absolute sovereignty and taught the lesson of the importance of power politics in international relations and its corollary—that China could not be respected without power."[9] Alastair J. Johnston, another scholar of Chinese affairs, takes the past-as-prologue approach to identify the impact of China's strategic culture on the issues of war and peace in the study of contemporary Chinese foreign policy and relations.[10]

A set of other approaches might help us to understand the nature and pattern of China's foreign policy behavior. Of them, the psychocultural approach is important since it focuses on the psyche, cultural norms, and traditions of a country. It will not be out of place to quote Indian prime minister Jawaharlal Nehru's perception of the Chinese psyche. He once stated:

> In regard to China, I feel that we have to deal with, what might be called, a one track mind, very much so. . . . What is more, I am not saying this as criticism but as some kind of appraisal, right or wrong-this is all a national trait which has existed for considerable time past because China was a great, advanced and powerful country at various stages of history. . . . Anyhow, from fairly early in history they had a sensation of greatness of the Middle Kingdom as they called themselves, all the fringes belonging to lesser developed countries and human beings who paid tribute to them.[11]

Writings of well-known scholars of Chinese affairs, such as Peter Hays Gries, Gilbert Rozman, and Allen S. Whiting, are useful guides in a better understanding of the role of Chinese nationalism in articulating its perceptions and images of the outside world. Peter Hays Gries advanced the concept of "face nationalism" to explain the emotional and instrumental motivations of China's nationalists and the elite-mass legitimacy dynamic, which is central to Chinese national politics. Rozman and Whiting adjudge China's foreign policy behavior within a "cognitive mapping framework" to demonstrate that the underlying nuances of policy behavior of Chinese leaders can scarcely be grasped without understanding their self-images and national and international images rooted in China's local traditions and cultural values, including in the political ideology inherited from Mao's personality cult.

If viewed in the historical context, the Mao-in-command model dominated China's foreign policy and its external relations until his death in 1976. During a long spell under Mao's authoritarian regime, China's foreign policy remained iconcentric amid unprecedented upheavals in international politics, ranging from Cold War politics to the era of détente. No doubt, Mao remained an uncrowned monarch both in domestic and foreign policies. In effect, China's foreign policy responses to the international system primarily emanated from Mao's personal idiosyncrasies and preferences, from his strong whims and fancies. Perhaps it is not an exaggeration to say that Mao was totally dominant in making big decisions in foreign policy and international affairs. Corroborating this, Nehru states that Chairman Mao was a "symbol to them [the Chinese people] of everything, and that anybody should insult Chairman Mao's picture made them livid with rage."[12]

Mao's cultural revolution (1966–1976) is an example par excellence of one-man's-super command-in-hand to purge capitalist roaders. His cultural revolution not only alienated China from the world community but also contributed to China's economic stagnation and social backwardness.

After Mao's demise in 1976, Chinese foreign policy shifted from ideological determinism to pragmatism based on the interest-driven policy under the "paramount leadership" of Deng Xiaoping. Though Deng was not a political heavyweight in comparison to Mao, he did command high respect from the rank-and-file of the Communist Party apparatus. Deng's vision, based on the hard-boiled realities of the international system, impelled him to revise China's foreign policy; unless China opened up to the outside world, it would remain not only isolated from the mainstream of international politics but also economically poor and socially backward in the eyes of the world community. Joshua Kurlantzick writes, "Following Chinese leader Deng Xiaoping's advice, an insecure Beijing still pursued a defensive foreign policy and focused on rebuilding China's domestic economy from the ravages of the Cultural Revolution."[13]

In his drive for economic modernization, Deng launched a four-point program in the fields of agriculture, industry, defense, science, and technology in order to transform China into an economically strong and militarily self-reliant nation-state. Time and again, Deng impressed on the world community that China did not believe in a policy of confrontation with any country. Instead, he stressed that peaceful relations with other countries were indispensable for China's economic development and prosperity at home. As an architect of modern China, Deng had a vision to transform China into an advanced economy while reinforcing his commitment to the classical concept of realism. Mel Gurtov and Byong-Moo Hwang testified that the salience of the PRC foreign policy under Deng was based on a realistic assessment of the country's national interest, power politics and geopolitics.[14]

This apart, a strategic culture forms one of the key components of China's worldview. This is based on China's past experiences in terms of rebellions, wars fought with foreign powers, and humiliation suffered at the hands of imperialists. Naturally, China was prodded into thinking that peace and stability at home demanded a constant vigil and war preparedness. Samuel S. Kim observes, "If Chinese analyses of their own concepts of military strategy and operations are any indication, Chinese military planners are deeply wedded to the para bellum doctrine that preparing for war is still the only way to keep peace."[15] This view is broadly shared by realists. William T. Tow writes, "Realists argue that China is a dissatisfied power that will try to project decisive force further afield as its military strength grows—that as a result China will threaten the security of other regional states to an extent that they will be forced to form a countercoalition, or if they do not they will have no choice but to submit to China's will and ambitions."[16]

The post-Deng leadership witnessed intraparty contradictions and got hemmed in by a perpetual tension between nationalism and internationalism. Some Western Sinologists believe that China is obsessed with its great history, heritage, and culture. This is why the Chinese take pride in the repository of their country's great civilizational values, for which they expect the world community to respect them. It could be said that the nationalistic fervor among Chinese people is far deeper and stronger compared to people of other nationalities. The logic behind this assertion is that the Chinese suffered more at the hands of foreign powers than others. Also, China has fought full wars rather than civil wars throughout its history.[17]

The Chinese psyche is fundamentally derived from China's sociopsychic structure rooted in its social beliefs, values, and practices. From a historical perspective, their peculiar national psyche is a culmination of their bitter experiences at the hands of imperialists as well as suppressed national ego and pride. Edgar Snow writes, "If, after a nation has been exploited, robbed, opium soaked, plundered, occupied and partitioned by foreign invaders for a century, the people turns upon its persecutors and drives them from the house, along with the society whose weakness permitted the abuses, is it suffering from paranoia?"[18] Not astonishingly, China saw Western powers as exploiters divorced from moral scruples.

CHINA'S NOTION OF SOFT POWER: NORMATIVE APPROACH

As mentioned earlier, the post-Mao leadership realized that China's cultural revolution not only besmirched its image abroad but also isolated it internationally. Deng Xiaoping, the father of economic reforms, attempted to reverse China's negative image by adopting an open-door policy. Furthermore, with its membership in the WTO in December 2001, China got integrated into global economy, resulting in a phenomenal increase in its economic power capabilities, which richly contributed to its aspiration as a global power. Gradually, China took to the path of soft-powerism.

What has attracted China to embrace and institutionalize soft power in its foreign policy and diplomacy? In this regard, it must be remembered that the biggest focus of the Beijing leadership is to make the best use of the research findings and recommendations of top Western scholars on Chinese studies, especially from the United States. This methodology, a strategic tactic on the part of Chinese leaders, has paid off in terms of saving the country's valuable resources. As noted by Jason Lang, "Surging investment by Chinese companies in U.S. research labs is yielding a fast-growing trove of patents, part of a push to mine America for ideas to help China shift from being the world's factory floor to a driver of innovation."[19] Lang further observes that "Chinese firms including Huawei Technologies and ZTE [Zhongxing Telecommunication Equipment] Corp are now using U.S. researchers to create patents ranging from new software to internet infrastructure, according to an analysis of Thomson Reuters' global intellectual property database."[20]

It is no secret that world-class American universities and think tanks such as the Carnegie Endowment for International Peace, Brookings Institution, Rand Corporation, and Heritage Foundation spend much of their resources on research on China. Findings and recommendations of these institutions—including those of established scholars such as Henry Kissinger, David Shambaugh, and Edgar Snow—are closely studied, followed, and implemented by Chinese leaders. It is in this context that we need to understand the reason behind China's embrace of the soft power concept based on Chinese characteristics. According to Joshua Kurlantzick, "For the Chinese, soft power means anything outside of the military and security realm, including not only popular culture and public diplomacy but also more coercive economic and diplomatic levers like aid and investment and participation in multilateral organizations."[21]

Saul Gomez, reviewing Joshua's book, writes:

> China has taken advantage of its soft power capabilities to become a leader for the developing world. It has strengthened its attraction through the expansion of cultural centers, student-scholar exchanges, development aid, state-directed foreign investment, and its influence at multilateral organizations. These initiatives are helping China to achieve its goals of, while quoting Joshua, "maintaining peace and stability on its borders, portraying itself to other nations as a benign and constructive actor, possibly becoming a model of development to other nations, obtaining resources needed to power the Chinese economy, isolating Taiwan, and demonstrating the possibility that it can eventually become a great power."[22]

Emboldened by their country's global political influence, China's ruling leaders are seriously engaged in evolving a new world order based on Chinese characteristics that are opposed to the Westphalian system, to demonstrate that the Western model of the international system is outdated and ill-suited. This is why the fifth-generation leadership in China is talking about a "harmonious world" based on its old civilizational values. Callahan in this regard observes that China is promoting the idea of a harmonious world order as its "contribution to world civilization and global order. The soft power in IR theory is thus seen as an outgrowth of hard power. China needs to cash in its new economic power for enduring political, cultural, and normative power."[23]

How was the idea of soft power conceived, developed, and popularized by the Chinese ruling class ? Bonnie S. Glaser and Melissa E. Murphy credit Chinese scholar Wang Huning with publishing China's first article on soft power. Jiang Zemin drafted Huning into the Policy Research Office of the Chinese Communist Party, and later Hu Jintao promoted Huning to head the office. Glaser and Murphy explain, "Wang evaluated Nye's theory regarding the resources of soft power: culture, political values and ideas, and foreign policies. It is noteworthy—given the central role subsequently accorded to culture in the exercise of China's soft power—that back in 1993 Wang focused on culture as the main source of a state's soft power: 'if a country has an admirable culture and ideological system, other countries will tend to follow it. . . . It does not have to use its hard power which is expensive and less efficient.'"[24]

At the party level, President Hu Jintao first conceived the concept of soft power in the early twenty-first century, based on Chinese civilization, culture, social norms, and thoughts of Confucianism, Daoism, and Buddhism. The intent behind launching a charm offensive was to project China's image as a benign, reasonable, and responsible power within the comity of nations rather than that of a menacing power. Hu began a publicity blitz when he officially announced the imperative of soft power in China's foreign policy and diplomacy in his speech at the Seventeenth Party Conference in 2007. He emphasised the need for Chinese culture to "go global." For this, he gave a clarion call to his countrymen to reverse China's negative international image as an "expansionist and aggressive power" by building on its soft power assets in cultural and educational terms through a vast network like CCTV news channels.[25]

Hu Jintao envisioned that the entire governmental machinery would need to be geared toward the task of spreading the message of peace, prosperity, and stability across the world. He called upon Chinese academia, diaspora, and diplomats to propagate China's cultural power. Hu further appealed to Western powers to not make concerted efforts to divide China by infiltrating into the country's "ideological and cultural fields." He urged his party men and indigenous think tanks to employ the soft power strategy to "fight back" against those who were besmirching China's image. David Shambaugh, a well-known expert on Chinese affairs, does not share the thesis that a continual propagation of Chinese language, culture, and traditional values will produce China's desired global image. As he stresses, culture alone is unable to erase China's deeply entrenched image of an expansionist and aggressive power. It may be partially true, yet, according to one study, China ranked seventh in both culture and education in 2011, and in 2012 China ranked sixth in culture and fifth in education—indicators of soft power.[26]

CONFUCIUS INSTITUTES AS A VALUABLE RESOURCE

As a core component of its soft power, Chinese foreign policy focused on establishing Confucius Institutes to promote Chinese language and culture. As a "responsible stakeholder" in the current international system, the primary objective of setting up Confucius Institutes is to familiarize the world with the glory of Chinese culture and language. As reported, the Chinese Ministry of Education has "established 500 Confucius institutes and 1,000 Confucius Classrooms in 134 countries and regions, with a total of 1.9 million students to promote 'cross-cultural exchanges.'"[27]

Revivalism of Confucian studies, promoted by Chinese diaspora, became easier when the Chinese government provided huge financial support under a five-year-plan. The "New Confucianism" project fit the political goal of Beijing leadership to legitimize the state-led authoritarian regime. As Kelvin C. K. Cheung writes, "Hu Jintao and Wen Jiabao recognized the benefits of using Confucianism to justify the one-party rule, the government appropriated certain Confucian teachings to construct the discourses of harmonious society, the peaceful rise, and minben (people-based or people-as-root) rule."[28]

Chinese leaders perceived that Confucian capitalism could be an alternative to Western capitalism. Under Confucian capitalism, socioeconomic resources can be better mobilized and used for efficient development. The reason they cite is that authoritarian rule can boost growth and guarantee economic prosperity in the country. Says Cheung, "Seen from this perspective the Chinese leaders acknowledge that Confucianism does more than justifying an alternative model of state-led capitalism; it can counter the West and reframe the normative order of international System."[29] This is a simple case of politicization of Confucianism with intent to maintain the Communist regime's control over society and governance under the garb of the Chinese model of soft power. Communist leaders are using Confucianism as a valuable resource, as a psychological tool to not only consolidate their grip on society but also convince the world of China's peaceful rise and role as a stabilizing force in world politics. In realistic terms, first, Chinese leaders are using Confucianism as a political instrument to advance the country's interests in an inevitably interdependent world order. Second, Communist leaders want to use Confucianism, which is rooted in hierarchical order, individual sacrifices, and social harmony to legitimize their authoritarian regime.[30]

Chinese leaders got a further boost to project an alternative model of soft power, different from that of the West, when overseas Confucian scholars invoked the spiritual aspects of Confucian thought, which they emphasize should be revived and imbibed by the Chinese people. Writes Sébastien Billioud, "Confucian culture is a cultural resource which we cannot distance ourselves from in the construction of a harmonious socialist society. . . . As cadres and leaders, we must nourish ourselves with Confucian culture. . . . Every Communist Party cadre must contribute to the radiance of the spiritual specificities of Confucian culture by aspiring to the highest moral qualities and behaviour."[31]

The Chinese leadership has attempted to synchronize China's model of soft power with its image of an economic powerhouse based on state-led capitalism without political liberalism. Cheung notes that, seen from this perspective, "Chinese leaders acknowledge that Confucianism does more than justifying a superpower alternative model of state-led capitalism; it can counter the West and reframe the normative order of international system."[32]

Furthermore, to silence critics of the Confucius Institutes (CIs), on which the Chinese government is spending billions of dollars, President Xi remarked that CIs "belong to China and the world" and called for "joint efforts to promote civilization among mankind, enhance people's heart-to-heart communication and create a brighter future for mankind together."[33]

David Shambaugh has elaborated on China's three schools of soft power: (1) culture, (2) politics, and (3) economic development. These three schools of thought are interconnected. What does China intend to achieve by propagating its culture abroad as a source of soft power? Hu Jintao, in his keynote speech at the Seventeenth Party Congress, stated, "The great rejuvenation of the Chinese nation will definitely be accompanied by the thriving of Chinese culture. . . . We must enhance culture as the part of the soft power of our country. . . . We will further publicize the fine traditions of Chinese culture and strengthen international cultural exchanges to enhance the influence of Chinese culture worldwide."[34]

Hu's call for propagation of Chinese culture evoked an overwhelming response from academia and the strategic community by way of organizing seminars and conferences on soft power at Chinese universities and research institutes. While projecting China's image as an unaggressive, peaceful, and responsible international actor, the pro-administration academia is engaged in propagating the idea that China has no intention to come into a direct conflict or war with its neighbors. In this propaganda warfare, China is reported to have spent $2–7 billion. On this, Nye comments that investment in government propaganda is not a "successful strategy" to increase a country's soft power.[35]

President Xi Jinping intensified the momentum of propagating soft power diplomacy. While speaking to top leaders of the politburo of the ruling Communist Party of China Central Committee in Beijing, he underlined the need for building China's national image. According to the *Times of India*, he stated that "China should be portrayed as a civilized country featuring rich history, ethnic unity and cultural diversity, and as an oriental power with good government, developed economy, cultural prosperity, national unity and beautiful mountains and rivers."[36] He further laid emphasis on more publicity for modern Chinese values, or socialist values with Chinese characteristics. He said, "To strengthen China's soft power, the country needs to build its capacity in international communication, construct a communication system, better use the new media and increase the creativity, appeal and credibility of China's publicity."[37]

In addition, the Chinese government has introduced a state policy of offering scholarships to foreign students. Also, it has stressed the need for promoting Chinese culture through sports, fine arts, films, music, and such other activities. Since then, Chinese scholars have been proactively engaged in spreading the Chinese version of soft power, based on Confucian thought, with an intent to advance the Chinese-based normative order of the international system. Besides developing the "institutional soft power of the Confucian Institutes that teach Chinese language and culture around the world," writes Callahan, "it also needs to develop normative soft power in order to create and export its understandings of the world—such as 'harmonious world'—that conceptualize globalization in new and different ways."[38]

Needless to stress, the soft power concept is much confused, much misunderstood, and often misapplied by scholars and public-policy makers. Primarily, its use and interpretation depends on who defines it and who interprets it in what ways. There is no clear-cut or concise definition of soft power. Nor is there any solid criterion for measuring it. In the case of China, for instance, it is not yet clear whether its notion of soft power originated from its societal beliefs and values. On the one hand, some scholars of Chinese studies subscribe to the view that the Chinese brand of soft power is rooted in its indigenous characteristics in terms of culture, history, language, and social norms.[39] On the other hand, some critics argue that, in terms of doctrine, China's soft power is weak when compared to that of the United States because China's political system does not permit political pluralism, political liberalism, or political autonomy.[40]

Some Chinese scholars and intellectuals like Yu Xintian lament and lambast soft power for being circulated as a "pure culture" in terms of Confucian thought. Yu advocates that soft power be located in the socialism of Chinese characteristics, though she has not replied to critics who question how socialism can be as appealing to the world as political democracy. Socialism has already been rejected in the market-led globalizing world. Further, she does not expatiate on how China's monolithic political system can generate soft power as a tool to improve and enhance its international image.

Chinese intelligentsia and the political leadership will need to redefine the meaning of soft power in the globalized world, where there is a liberal political order and the role of state is minimal. It is a paradox that the Chinese leadership is, on the one hand, not prepared to introduce a model of liberal democratic values to enhance its image abroad while, on the other hand, propagating that its political model generates soft power. In fact, Chinese scholars need to refine the concept of soft power in tune with the prevailing realities of the interdependent world order.

The Chinese version of soft power is not very attractive globally, except in Africa, where China has made huge investments to exploit abundant natural resources and to win the sympathy of Africa's poor. Its trade with African countries has touched $222 billion. Elsewhere, in the United States, Europe, India, Japan, and South Korea, China's soft power tactics, like setting up Confucius Institutes, has not been very attractive. The reasons are crystal clear. First, China's political system is a one-party showpiece that does not allow freedom of opinion, as evidenced by its attempts to gag the press and prevent Internet freedom. Second, China has seen a rise in human rights abuses, reflected in its nearly five thousand annual death penalties compared to India's average of fewer than two. Moreover, China's international image has been tarnished with the imprisonments of Nobel Peace laureate Liu Xiaobo and artist Ai Weiwei.[41] Third, the Chinese government's constant surveillance of students in CIs abroad has irked the US government. That is why, as reported by Lotus Ruan in 2014, CIs are being viewed as a "threat to academic freedom." The University of Chicago has "refused to renew its five-year contract with its CI, making it the first major U.S. research institution to cut ties with the program."[42] One might recall that the Chinese government invested over $278 million into the CI program, but its net result has been disappointing, even to the Chinese leadership.

President Xi announced in 2014, "We should increase China's soft power, give a good Chinese narrative, and better communicate China's messages to the world."[43] In this regard, Shambaugh observes, "Under Xi, China has bombarded the world with a welter of new initiatives: 'the Chinese dream,' 'the Asia-Pacific dream,' 'the Silk Road Economic Belt,' 'the Twenty-First-Century Maritime Silk Road,' 'a new type of major-country relations,' and many others. It is easy to dismiss such talk as slogan diplomacy, but Beijing nonetheless attaches great importance to it."[44]

Under the dispensation of Xi, as reported by Jamil Anderlini in 2015, Western values have been forbidden in Chinese universities. The education minister has "vowed that 'western values' will never be allowed into the country's classrooms as the Communist party steps up efforts to consolidate autocratic rule and stave off demands for democracy and universal human rights." "Never let textbooks promoting western values enter into our classes," Minister Yuan Guiren said. according to China's official Xinhua news agency. "Never let textbooks promoting western values appear in our classes." The article goes on to say, "China has tightened controls over all aspects of public life and clamped down hard on freedom of expression since President Xi Jinping took over as leader in 2012."[45]

According to Human Rights Watch, "Under President Xi Jinping, the Chinese government and Communist party have unleashed the harshest campaign of politically motivated investigations, detentions and sentencing in the past decade, marking a sharp turn towards intolerance of criticism."[46]

The Chinese model of governance will be unable to sustain itself for too long in the face of the growing strident voices for democracy and political liberalism, as is evident from recent student demonstration on the streets of Hong Kong, where students were pleading for the institutionalization of democracy. In order to crush the democratic movement, the monolithic state-sponsored leadership has been encouraging courts, academia, and the diaspora to reinvent traditional, cultural, and social values to revive historical memories in order to deal with any unprecedented situation in the future stemming from structural problems, rampant corruption, and internal crises. How can China's much-propagated soft power notion be attractive in the face of its Internet censorship regime, which harshly deals with dissenters, as well as political challenges posed by a borderless technological system?

There are more than 450 million web users in China and many are active on social media. In order to meet the growing popularity of social media, the government has tightened its control over cyberspaces by eliminating news, deleting antigovernment speeches, and tightly monitoring the flow of information between China and the outside world.[47] The only source of legitimacy that the government claims to have and uses to silence its political critics is its "sound" economic performance. But how long will it survive? Indeed, China's economic growth rate has slumped to 6.6 percent, down from double digits. This may be attributed to the global economic meltdown, which affected not only China but also many countries across the world.

It is a myth circulated by Chinese leadership that China's peaceful rise will help maintain and contribute to world peace and will also dispel the misplaced fear that China's growing military and economic power signal serious threats to global peace and economic development. Only time will tell. This may, however, happen if the United States clings to false stories circulated by overenthusiastic pro-China scholars and public policy makers. For example, some claim that American power is almost depleted or is in a steep decline, citing examples that China has surpassed the United States as the largest trading partner of South Korea and Japan.[48]

By logical implications, China will replace the United States as a sole superpower soon. This is a superficial analysis without palpable evidence. However, the writings of Western Sinologists have a demoralizing impact on American society. Hence, this sort of lame-duck analysis must be cautiously evaluated by the administration. In this context, one must remember that the 2008 global financial crisis is generally attributed to intellectual arrogance of American economists. Their one section was of the opinion that roots of American economy were so strong that America did not need to worry about an economic meltdown that might shake up its foundation. Without appreciating the real-world complexity, they offered methodological explanations based on statistics to justify their assessment. Another section of American economists painted a dismal scenario of American economy, arguing that there was lack of accountability and effective governance of financial institutions in the country. Thus, the debate surrounding the nature of American economy confused American public policy makers in taking the impending financial crisis seriously. Pitiably, the United States, which houses some of the world's top economists, could not extricate itself from the cobweb of the financial crisis. Then what is the benefit of the expertise of many Nobel laureates in economics?

The point I am trying to hammer in is that America needs to take seriously the Chinese challenge of its soft power brand based on Chinese characteristics. At the same time, the United States need not feel that it has lost the battle or is bound to exit from the scene of the current international system. This is not going to happen in the near future, given that China's own house is not in order; its citizens do not have access to health care facilities, employment, or job security. Nor is the monolithic state sensitive enough to the rights and legitimate demands of minorities—for instance, Tibet's demand for cultural autonomy, which is being crushed by the Chinese government with an iron-handed policy. Moreover, there is a lack of interethnic tolerance as well as gender equality. With these conditions, the question arises as to how China's model of soft power will be acceptable globally.

In a seeming contradiction, the state-led market can bring about the social harmony, a process Hu Jintao optimistically, perhaps enthusiastically, promoted in order to show that the Chinese model of soft power is capable of generating and sustaining the values of tolerance and harmony espoused by Confucius. The persistence of the coercive and repressive regime that we find in China today reveals the "internal cracks" and "fundamental fissures" in the state structure. [49]

China is not a plural society with a decentralized structure that permits diverse voices and divergent beliefs or respects composite cultural values. Its monolithic, centralized system mauls autonomy and the dignity of people, severely undermining the cohesion and harmony of the nation. Therefore, China can no longer be an exemplar of a nation that takes care of its common people and its minority sections of society. One might recall that the prodemocracy movement on Tiananmen Square in June 1989 was crushed with an iron hand.

CHINESE NATIONALISM AND SOFT POWER

The contemporary debate over Chinese nationalism raises many fundamental questions at a time when China is poised to apply its soft power diplomacy to win more allies and consolidate its power and influence in the current international system. It should not be forgotten that Chinese nationalism is strongly embedded in the psyche of the people since the country's history, civilization, and culture span millennia. In this context it should be recalled that China suffered a great humiliation at the hands of foreign powers in the nineteenth century—for example, the Opium War of 1844; the European war with China in 1858–1860; and unequal treaties with France, Russia, and Great Britain.

Given this, there is an apparent contradiction between China's aggressive nationalism and its soft power approach to international politics. The leadership in Beijing is troubled by having to manage this contradiction and reverse its image as that of an aggressive nation through blogs and social media. Discourse on Chinese nationalism, often bracketed by patriotism, will continue to inform the thought process and decision making of the state apparatus controlled by the monolithic Communist Party of China (CPC). It leaves little room for accommodating minority ethnicities, causing the Muslim Uighurs community in the Xinxiang province and the Tibetan Buddhist community to clamor for separate state and cultural autonomy, respectively. The festering wound of unrest in these regions is not dealt with by peaceable means by the local governments, which employ the People's Liberation Army (PLA) forces to crush the opposition movements.

Similarly, recent prodemocracy demonstrations led by students in the heart of Hong Kong in September 2014 were brutally suppressed by the police force. Demonstrators had blocked traffic on multilane roads, resulting in the suspension of school classes. As reported by CNN, "Demonstrations began in response to China's decision to allow only Beijing-vetted candidates to stand in the city's 2017 election for the top civil position of chief executive. Protesters say Beijing has gone back on its pledge to allow universal suffrage in Hong Kong, which was promised 'a high degree of autonomy' when it was handed back to China by Britain in 1997."[50] It was further reported that "images of heavy-handed treatment of protesters by police shocked many residents of Hong Kong, where large-scale, peaceful protests are common, but police crackdowns are not."[51]

Naturally, a moot question arises as to whether Chinese nationalism fits in the global system, of which China is an influential player. Its answer lies in the fact that political expediency has prodded Chinese central leadership to strike a balance between strong nationalism and its imperative of projecting an image of a peaceful nation—a crucial element of its pragmatic foreign policy and diplomacy.

HARMONIOUS SOCIETY: RHETORIC OR REALITY?

What is the harmonious society expounded by Hu Jintao? In Hu's perception, a harmonious society could be a building block for a new global architecture for a peaceful resolution of conflicts. The underlying idea is to project China as a responsible international actor that acquiesces to a consensus-building approach to conflict resolution. It sounds good in theory, but in practice it has been observed that China is resorting to muscle flexing in its neighborhood. The Association of Southeast Asian Nations (ASEAN) member states are wary of Chinese strategic designs in the region, with special reference to China's sovereignty claims in the South China Sea, over the Spratly and Paracel Islands, which are considered rich in oil and natural resources. China is energy hungry, pooling its diplomatic and military resources to gain unhindered access to oil and natural resources in the region. Indeed, the looming fear of China's threat to Southeast Asia's peace, security, and stability is one of the prime motivations behind the recent ten-year pact (January 2015) between Manila and Washington, as the pact allows the United States to have military bases in the Philippines. It is interesting that the United States has floated the idea of a plan similar to the Marshall Plan for Vietnam, against whom it fought a long, bloody war during the Cold War period. It must be remembered that Vietnam has serious security and strategic clashes with China over the sovereignty of the Spritely Islands. At the ASEAN foreign ministers meeting in Kuala Lumpur in August 2015, the Joint Communique was issued that stated that "land reclamations in the South China Sea . . . may undermine peace, security and stability" in the region. [52] At the meeting US secretary of state John Kerry issued a warning to China that, as paraphrased by the *Guardian*, "Washington would not tolerate any restrictions on freedom of navigation in the strategically important waters."[53]

CHINA'S SOFT POWER INITIATIVES IN SOUTH ASIA: SCOPE AND LIMITATIONS

China's stranglehold over South Asia for the past five decades has not only been an irritant between China and India but also a conspicuous challenge to India's preeminent role in the region. The stranglehold has been further consolidated by China's rising economic might and its burgeoning trade with major Asian nations, superseding India and the United States. Undeniably, the economic rivalry between the two Asian giants is being cautiously watched by small South Asian states who see China as a major source of economic aid, indispensable for their infrastructure development and trade promotion.

If seen from a holistic perspective, China's soft power strategy in South Asia is composed of three principal components: (1) cultural diplomacy, (2) economic assistance, and (3) trade and investment. Cultural diplomacy is not a new instrument of promoting national interests. But ever since discourse on soft power became popular, it has been incorporated into the lexicon of cultural diplomacy. South Asia is no an exception. China, for instance, set up CIs at Kathmandu University, Nepal (2006); at the University of Kelaniya, Sri Lanka (2007); in Islamabad (2005); at North South University, Bangladesh (2006). These institutes' primary focus is on promoting Chinese language and culture, but it differs from country to country. For instance, the CI in Pakistan has a strategic element.

"It is the first Confucius Institute based on the all-weather strategic partnership between China and Pakistan, and also it is the first Confucius Institute in Islamic world," says one source.[54] To cater to needs of the business community in Pakistan, the institute conducts business Chinese language courses and offers a PhD program of advanced courses on science on Chinese characters. The CI at Kathmandu University organizes Chinese language orientation programs especially for the students in the Department of Language and Mass Communication. Also, cultural picnics are organized, during which lessons on Chinese food culture are imparted to students. At the University of Kelaniya, the institute has introduced language skill courses, and Chinese movies are shown to make students appreciate the Chinese way of life, its societal and cultural structures, and processes of nation-building initiatives. In its Bangladesh institute, more than six hundred students are enrolled to learn courses in Chinese language and culture as a three-credit-hour course. As reported by the *China Daily*, "In Bangladesh, thousands of people are now studying Chinese language in a number of varsities including Dhaka University, North South University, BRAC University and also in some middle schools like BIT in Dhaka."[55]

Also, a large number of scholarships are offered to Bangladeshis to study Chinese language and culture and return home as teachers. Md. Jahidul Islam, a lawyer, said, "Learning Chinese is now a demand of time. It's not only important to minimize the gap of relations between the two countries but also to enhance cooperation in various areas."[56] The Chinese ambassador to Bangladesh, Zhang Xianyi, stated, "It [the institute] makes positive contributions to promote mutual understanding and appreciation of each other's culture, tradition between our two peoples and strengthen the friendly relationship between China and Bangladesh."[57]

In brief, CIs have helped promote bilateral relations between China and South Asian states in the field of education and culture by expanding and intensifying cultural exchange programs. Under the cultural exchange program, the Chinese government offers scholarships to South Asian students below the age of thirty-five to learn Chinese, mainly Mandarin, for business and other purposes. No doubt, China's clientele in smaller, poor countries has expanded, which is a long-term investment. Young students completing courses in Chinese languages or completing a PhD program are useful assets to China in cementing ties with South Asian countries inasmuch as they are the potential carriers of China's positive image both in their respective countries and regionally.

FOREIGN AID AS A RESOURCE

With its increasingly robust economy, China has began using foreign aid as an instrument of diplomacy to promote its economic, trade, and investment interests globally and regionally as well as enhance its influence in the aid-recipient countries. As reported in the *Wall Street Journal*, "Between 2001 and 2011, China's pledged foreign aid was $671 billion, divided among 93 emerging-market countries. In 2010, annual aid pledged by China was $169 billion and in 2011, $189 billion—equivalent to about 3% of its reported GDP and more than twice the size of the officially reported budget of the ministry of defence."[58] China provides development aid with the intention to capture markets and gain access to the natural resources of aid-recipient countries.[59]

Given the geostrategic primacy of South Asia, China's principal instrument of expanding its strategic space in the region is to channel huge economic aid into smaller countries like the Maldives, Sri Lanka, and Nepal to propel their economic growth. In addition, China has been providing emergency food and relief aid to South Asian states—notably in Nepal, Bangladesh, and Pakistan—in which China's image in the public perception has elevated considerably. Of late, China has embarked on investment and development aid. In this context, David Shambaugh writes:

> It is backing up its soft-power ventures with serious money: $50 billion for the Asian Infrastructure Investment Bank, $41 billion for the New Development Bank, $40 billion for the Silk Road Economic Belt, and $25 billion for the Maritime Silk Road. Beijing has also pledged to invest $1.25 trillion worldwide by 2025. This scale of investment is unprecedented: even during the Cold War, the United States and the Soviet Union did not spend anywhere near as much as China is spending today. Together, these recent pledges by Beijing add up to $1.41 trillion; in contrast, the Marshall Plan cost the equivalent of $103 billion in today's dollars.[60]

In realistic terms, China's economic intrusion into South Asia is fundamentally driven by its intention to curtail India's role and influence in the region. China's ulterior design behind channeling massive aid to medium and smaller South Asian nations is to expand and stabilize its strategic and security roles in South Asian affairs, which implies limiting India's diplomatic and economic options in the region. The impact of Chinese aid to smaller countries of the region is perceptible in the domains of trade, commerce, and investment, benefitting China more since the balance of trade is hugely in its favor. India's exports to Bangladesh have declined while China's exports to Bangladesh have multiplied; China has dominated the Bangladeshi markets in textiles, engineering, and mechanical appliances.

MYTHS

The Chinese model of soft power, anchored on its culture, past traditions, and Confucian thought, is not acceptable to a majority of nations, including authoritarian regimes in several parts of the Middle East and Central Asia. There is a clear-cut contradiction between the underlying values of soft power and China's authoritarian governance. More important, China suffers from a credibility syndrome in the realm of public diplomacy, which has a negative effect on its image. The only source of information is the state-controlled print and electronic media. Therefore, foreign audiences rarely rely on information filtered through the state media.

Moreover, civil society organizations and autonomous institutions are denied open access to sensitive information pertaining to China's record on human rights violations and jail conditions. Everything is censured by the state-controlled media. That is why there is a widely held perception that the Chinese media is not credible. It is futile to expect that the media would ever attain the credibility generally enjoyed by international media such as CNN (Cable News Network) and the BBC (British Broadcasting Corporation). On the contrary, the Chinese accusation is that Western media projects China's negative image. Keeping this in mind, China will need to relaunch a new movement for projecting its positive image through structural reforms in its media by giving full access to the foreign press and electronic media via the Internet. If this is so, then China's version of Nye's soft power concept is a myth. By this yardstick, there is a blurred distinction between hard and soft power, based on Chinese characteristics. "Coercion" and "attraction" in the Chinese lexicon have an identical meaning that best serves its national interests. Therefore, Chinese ideas and values are not appealing to developed countries, only in poor, developing, and underdeveloped Third World countries, especially in Central Africa and the Horn of Africa.

Furthermore, there is a myth that China will be able to transform its traditional culture into one of universally desirable values. But how can the West or the rest of the world be attracted to, accept, or imbibe Chinese culture when China refuses to embrace political liberalism or cultivate tolerance for others' belief systems, faiths, and values? Moreover, traditional culture alone cannot be a criterion for making the world realize that China has abandoned using hard power against its neighbors. It is a wild dream entertained by China that by opening CIs and setting up public diplomacy, associations worldwide would create a large constituency across the world. Since CIs are being controlled by the government, some top universities in America have decided not to continue with the institutes. In September 2014 the University of Chicago decided not to renew its five-year contract. In October 2014 Pennsylvania State University declared closure of the CI on its campus. Nye has said that China has spent billions of dollars on establishing CIs but has not gained anything substantial. Rather, Nye considers this a sheer waste of money. He argues that China not only lacks civil society organizations but also "squashes" them. Moreover, there is no room for civil society organizations that take up the causes of human rights, refugees, women's empowerment, and many more humanitarian tasks. During his visit to a CI in Germany in 2014, President Xi argued that "some people are biased against China, and that is mainly out of unfamiliarity, estrangement and misunderstanding."[61]

It is a sheer myth that by circulating its brand of soft power along the trajectory of language, culture, and Confucian thought China will be able to attract, if not the West, some developing countries, yet China does not trust soft power as a means to spread its influence or win allies. It is also a myth that hybrids of old Confucian Leninism and market socialism are universally appealing, as Leninism and socialism have lost their appeal and are buried in the pages of history. So far as the Chinese school of international relations theory is concerned, nothing substantial has come out of its conception except the rhetoric of opposing power politics and hegemony. These clichés are often employed by political leaders in official statements.

Political analysts are of the view that Xi may face tough challenges when dealing with the outside world on issues of democracy, human rights, and transparency. Besides, challenges on domestic fronts are no less formidable. Upbeat voices among the Chinese youth for political freedom, the democratization of society, and a real participation of the people in the decision-making process cannot be muzzled easily by the Xi leadership. Modernization, Westernization, and consumerism conspicuously impact the lifestyle of Chinese youths.

One should not gloss over the reality that there may be some international fascination with tangible sources of China's soft power, like Chinese food, movies, crafts, and paintings, but it does not mean that its domestic policy, based on repression and authoritarianism, and its aggressive postures, for instance in the South China Sea, will be appealing internationally. In other words, China's soft power does not hold charm for the international audience on the questions of democracy, refugees' concerns, human rights, freedom of the media, and academic freedom.

China's notion of soft power with Chinese characteristics is myopic, based on its narrow national interests rather than global acceptability and being liked by others. A glaring example can be seen when China asked India not to include any student from Arunachal Pradesh in a delegation to the annual India-China youth exchange since China considered Arunachal Pradesh a Chinese territory. This example shows that China is intolerant to minor issues like this in order to justify and reassert its territorial claim. Rather, this is an inherent tactic of the Chinese diplomatic game plan. China raised a protest in another case, when Taiwanese vice president Wu Den-yih was at the Delhi airport on his way to Rome to prove that China believed in a one-China theory.

In an attempt to influence and dominate global politics, China has been following in the footsteps of US hegemonism, which very well suits the Chinese psyche and its monolithic power structure. The Chinese desire the Western world to respect their theoretical innovations, for instance, the idea of a harmonious world society, socialist market economy with Chinese characteristics, and scientific outlook on development. In reality, however, China is bent on replicating the sources of American soft power, which are largely accepted internationally. By implication, China's leaders want their notions of soft power and cultural values as part of a spiritual civilization to be respected and admired by the West. In order to gain legitimacy, China has been trying to ape, adopt, and apply all those elements and sources of American power that helped sustain its status as a superpower in all realms. Interestingly, China is extremely circumspect about not committing or repeating escapable flawed policy decisions or any strategic follies committed by the United States.

CONCLUSION

The main idea behind China's soft power projection is to build and promote its positive image in the world community by invoking its glorious past, its great culture and civilization, which in Chinese perception contributed a great deal to world peace and harmony. In this context, China's hierarchical order during the Ming dynasty is reflective of China's view of world order, based on the doctrine of peaceful coexistence, which their leaders claim was, according to Callahan, more peaceful than "Europe's egalitarian Westphalian world order."[62] By propagating a Confucian philosophy of peace, love, and harmony that fits in a world order of any brand, China's ruling party has been endeavoring hard to showcase China's "ancient wisdom." By interlinking Chinese traditional culture and the current world order, Chinese leaders and intellectuals want to give an unambiguous message to the international community that the unipolar world led by the United States is violence ridden and has produced chaos and anarchy in volatile regions like the Middle East.

Accordingly, the current Beijing leadership emphasizes the imperative need to replace the anarchical international system by a Sino-centric world order based on the leadership's normative vision and values and informed by the country's pristine civilization and cultural ethos. But such laudatory claims, whether by the Chinese leadership, intellectual community, or diaspora, have not stood the test of the time. A fundamental question arises as to who will trust China's repeated claims that it is opposed to the notion of world hegemony when its peripheries in Southeast Asia, India, and Northeast Asia fear the roar of the PLA along their borders. Who will believe that China subscribes to a policy of peaceful resolution of territorial disputes when it is issuing overt threats to its neighbors? Who will trust that China's foreign policy is anchored to welding its normative vision of the world order into an integrationist approach of establishing a harmonious world? These concerns need to be addressed dispassionately to plumb the depths of China's soft power policy as it fits in a competitive and rivalry-prone world order.

Though China's normative soft power has sparked a great interest among international relations theorists, they debunk the potency and relevance of the Chinese version of soft power as being inconsistent with Nye's soft power notion, which is based on liberal and tolerant values. Some Sinologists believe that the Chinese model of a harmonious world order is far from being an exceptional model of a perfect world, of one world and one dream.

One should bear in mind two important things when attempting to find out China's real intentions and objectives behind projecting its normative soft power. The first is its universal appeal for a broad-based acceptability by the world community of the legitimacy of a Sino-centric world order. The second is how far China's regional peripheries are convinced that China would observe its supposed cultural norms of treating its neighbors as "womb brothers" or all-weather friends. China's policy of pitting one neighbor against another can scarcely be bracketed by its notion of a harmonious world order based on traditional Chinese culture and Confucian thought. In other words, there is an inherent contradiction in China's soft power approach and its actions on the ground. So the argument runs that there is a contradiction between China's pronouncements and its practices (*kathani* versus *karni*). Hence, it is yet to be seen how China will deal with the challenge of implementing its soft power strategy.

China's purpose behind launching its soft power diplomacy is to convince South Asian states that it does not constitute a threat to their national security or regional peace and stability. Concomitantly, it intends to send a loud message to them that it is seriously concerned about their well-being and economic prosperity. Nevertheless, the unresolved territorial dispute with

India has produced a deep mutual mistrust between the two countries. This will remain a major obstacle to lending legitimacy to China's soft power diplomacy. Even then, other South Asian countries are fascinated by China's soft power engagement with them. Their attraction can be attributed to China's massive foreign aid to their infrastructure and economic development. But India does not subscribe to the view that China's increasing economic and trade engagement with South Asian nations is a win-win situation, since the South Asian nations suffer a heavy trade imbalance.

China faces enormous challenges in South Asia on multiple fronts. First, India remains a potential rival in every domain of foreign policy and diplomacy, particularly in economic, trade, and investment realms. The Narendra Modi government, unlike its preceding United Progressive Alliance government, has been pursuing proactive diplomacy in South Asia. Modi has assigned top priority to India's South Asian neighbors in order to reverse India's image as a hegemon in the region. To counter China's overwhelming influence over Sri Lanka, for instance, Modi pledged financial aid amounting to $1.81 billion to Sri Lanka during his official visit to Colombo in March 2015. President Maithripala Sirisena assured him that Sri Lanka accorded a high priority to its relationship with India. In addition, Modi offered India's help in making Trincomalee "a petroleum hub" and announced $318 million as a line of credit for Sri Lanka's railways sector.[63]

Second, China's megaproject of building an economic corridor worth $46 billion in Pakistan is punctuated with uncertainty because of threats from terrorists and jihadists. Many times Chinese engineers and workers have been targeted by radical and jihadists in Baluchistan, in the North-West Frontier region.

Third, South Asian countries face a heavy trade deficit with China. It is not clear how China will resolve this issue. Moreover, economies of countries like Sri Lanka have been crippled due to mounting debts. There is an increasing realization among smaller countries of the region that Indian economic aid, though it may be marginal, was better than China's much larger credits.

The study suggests that though China's soft power influence in the region is likely to grow and India's influence diminished, the future in South Asia is still indistinct. Strategic rivalry and economic competition between India and China will make it harder for China to sell its soft power and promote its benign face in South Asia. However, there is a strong possibility that China will be able to persuade countries such as the Maldives, Bhutan, and Nepal to downgrade their relationship with India. With this game plan, China enjoys a diplomatic edge over India. The Modi government may make tall claims of winning the trust of a majority of India's neighbors, but the fact remains that Indian diplomacy lacks foresightedness as well as a long-term, well-calibrated, and a well-integrated policy approach to deal with its immediate neighbors. Another challenge before the Modi government will be to counter China's benign image among South Asian states.

However, if perceived in a larger context, China's soft power resources have not proved impressive because of the inherent contradiction in China's theory of soft power and its practice. For instance, China's record on compliance with international laws and treaties is scarcely impressive. On issues of global significance, China deviates from the practice of supporting democratic forces and antiterrorism causes. China twice blocked India's move at the UN to designate Masood Azhar as a terrorist, even though he was directly involved in terror attacks on Mumbai in 2008. China's doublespeak on counterterrorism does not evoke respect for it as a responsible and peaceful international actor. Similarly, China has not displayed an image of a restrained and peaceful nation when it comes to prodemocracy demonstrations in Hong Kong, or the cultural autonomy issue in Tibet, or the simmering unrest in its Xinxiang province. These instances at least partially reinforce China's degraded image at home.

Also, China supports authoritarian regimes, whether in Myanmar or Sudan, Pakistan or Zimbabwe. China's aggressive foreign policy behavior is manifest from its deployment of surface-to-air missiles in the South China Sea to assert its exclusive territorial claims over the Spratly and Parcel Islands. Its noncoercive strategy in African countries paid off, allowing it to develop markets and access their many natural resources. Similarly, China's soft power policy succeeded in wooing poor, small countries of South Asia into its strategic fold. This enabled China, for instance, to surpass India as the largest trading partner of Bangladesh.[64] In the case of India, China's objective will be focused on offsetting India's influence in South Asia. In brief, China's soft power diplomacy toward smaller countries will continue to be guided by persuasion and attraction rather than force and coercion. Yet China has no inhibitions about exercising hard power when dealing with intransigent major powers like India to achieve its desired goal, such as resolution of a territorial or water dispute. Therefore, India must learn from the Chinese strategy of soft power engagement in South Asia to win back the trust, confidence, and goodwill of its neighbors. But when it comes to defending its national interests, India cannot succeed by persuading and impressing China with its soft power resources, such as tolerance, nonaggression, empathy, and yoga. To deal with China's strategic challenges, India will need to develop appropriate strategic tools.

NOTES

1. Steve Chan, *China, the U.S., and the Power-Transition Theory: A Critique* (London: Routledge, 2008; Sujian Guo, ed., *China's "Peaceful Rise" in the 21st Century: Domestic and*

International Conditions (Surrey, UK: Ashgate, 2006); Zhiqun Zhu, *China's New Diplomacy: Rationale, Strategies and Significance*, 2nd ed. (Surrey, UK: Ashgate, 2013).

2. William A. Callahan, "Introduction: Tradition, Modernity and Foreign Policy in China," in *China Orders the World: Normative Soft Power and Foreign Policy*, eds. William A. Callahan and Elena Barabantseva (Washington, DC: Woodrow Wilson Center Press, 2001), 3. See also Joseph Tse-Hei Lee, Lida V. Nedilsky, and Siu-Keung Cheung, *China's Rise to Power: Conception of State Governance* (New York: Palgrave Macmillan, 2012).

3. Joseph S. Nye, "The Information Revolution and Soft Power," *Current History* 113, no. 759 (January 2014): 19–22, http://dash.harvard.edu/bitstream/handle/1/11738398/Nye-InformationRevolution.pdf?se.

4. Ibid.

5. Richard Javad Heydarian, "Is China's Soft-Power Bubble about to Burst?," *National Interest*, August 25, 2015, http://nationalinterest.org/feature/china%E2%80%99s-soft-power-bubble-about-burst-13683.

6. Published in 2004 (New York: Public Affairs).

7. David Shambaugh, "China's Soft-Power Push: The Search for Respect," *Foreign Affairs* (July/August 2015), https://www.foreignaffairs.com/articles/china/2015-06-16/china-s-soft-power-push.

8. Samuel S. Kim, "China and the World in Theory and Practice," in *China and the World: Chinese Foreign Relations in the Post-Cold War Era*, ed. Samuel S. Kim (Boulder, CO: Westview, 1994), 13.

9. Ibid., 13–14.

10. Ibid., 15.

11. Jawaharlal Nehru, "In the Lok Sabha: White Paper on India and China," Motion on India-China Relations, November 25, 1959, Lok Sabha Debates, 2nd series, 35, cols 1680–1708, *Selected Works of Jawaharlal Nehru* 54 (November 1–30, 1959), http://www.claudearpi.net/wp-content/uploads/2016/12/SW-Vol-54.pdf

12. Nehru, "In the Lok Sabha."

13. Joshua Kurlantzick, "China's Charm Offensive in Southeast Asia," *Current History* (September 2006): 270–76, http://carnegieendowment.org/files/Kurlantzick_SoutheastAsia_China.pdf.

14. For a comprehensive discussion of realism and pragmatism in China's foreign policy, see Weixing Hu, Gerald Chan, and Daojiong Zha, eds., *China's International Relations in the 21st Century: Dynamics of Paradigm Shifts* (Lanham, MD: University Press of America, 2000).

15. Kim, "China and the World," 15.

16. William T. Tow, *Asia-Pacific Relations: Seeking Convergent Security* (New York: Cambridge University Press, 2001), 13.

17. For a perceptive analysis of this part, see Jean-Pierre Cabestan, "The Many Facets of Chinese Nationalism," *China Perspectives* 59 (May–June 2005): 26–40.

18. B. M. Jain, *India in the New South Asia: Strategic, Military and Economic Concerns in the Age of Nuclear Diplomacy* (London: I.B. Tauris, 2010), 141.

19. Jason Lang, "Chinese Firms Are Spending Billions to Mine America's Research Labs for Ideas," *Business Insider*, June 21, 2015, http://www.businessinsider.com/r-chinese-firms-pour-money-into-us-rd-in-shift-to-innovation-2015–6#ixzz3i7nI6SHm.

20. Ibid.

21. Joshua Kurlantzick, *Charm Offensive: How China's Soft Power Is Transforming the World* (New Haven, CT: Yale University Press, 2008), 6.

22. Ibid., 130.

23. William A. Callahan, "Conclusion: World Harmony or Harmonizing the World?" in *China Orders the World*, Callahan and Barabantseva, 252.

24. Bonnie S. Glaser and Melissa E. Murphy, "Soft Power with Chinese Characteristics: The Ongoing Debate," in *Chinese Soft Power and Its Implications for the United States: Competition and Cooperation in the Developing World*, ed. Carola McGiffert (Washington, DC: Center for Strategic and International Studies, 2009), 10–26, http://csis.org/files/media/csis/pubs/090310_chinesesoftpower__chap2.pdf.

25. For a perceptive and critical analysis, see Qingxin Wang, "Cultural Norms and the Conduct of Chinese Foreign Policy," in *China's International Relations in the 21st Century: Dynamics of Paradigm Shifts*, eds. Weixing Hu, Gerald Chan, and Daojiong Zhopp (Lanham, MD: University Press of America, 2000), 143–69.

26. Siqi Gao, "China's Soft Power in the Arab World through Higher Educational Exchange," Wellesley College, April 2015, http://repository.wellesley.edu/cgi/viewcontent.cgi?article=1334&context=thesiscollection.

27. "China Has Established 500 Confucius Institutes Globally," *People's Daily Online*, December 14, 2015, http://english.hanban.org/article/2015–12/14/content_626902.htm.

28. Kelvin C. K. Cheung, "Appropriating Confucianism: Soft Power, Primordial Sentiment, and Authoritarianism," in *China's Rise to Power*, Lee, Nedilsky, and Cheung, 35.

29. Ibid., 37.

30. Ibid., 32–33.

31. Sébastien Billioud, "Confucianism, 'Cultural Tradition' and Official Discourse in China at the Start of the New Century," in *China Orders the World*, Callahan and Barabantseva, 231.

32. Cheung, "Appropriating Confucianism," 37.

33. Lotus Ruan, "Chinese Doubt Their Own Soft Power Venture," *Tea Leaf Nation*, October 17, 2014, http://foreignpolicy.com/2014/10/17/chinese-doubt-their-own-soft-power-venture/.

34. "Hu Jintao Calls for Enhancing 'Soft Power' of Chinese Culture," *Xinhua*, October 15, 2007, http://news.xinhuanet.com/english/2007–10/15/content_6883748.htm.

35. Nye, "Information Revolution," 21.

36. "Concerned over Negative Image, China to Project Itself as Cultural Soft Power," *Times of India*, January 1, 2014, http://timesofindia.indiatimes.com/world/china/Concerned-over-negative-image-China-to-project-itself-as-cultural-soft-power/articleshow/28245874.cms.

37. Ibid.

38. Callahan, "Introduction," 6.

39. For a perceptive analysis of this part, see Lee, Nedilsky, and Cheung, *China's Rise to Power*.

40. See Joseph Nye, "Why China Is Weak on Soft Power," *New York Times*, January 17, 2012, http://www.nytimes.com/2012/01/18/opinion/why-china-is-weak-on-soft-power.html?_r=0.

41. See Nye, "Why China Is Weak."

42. Ruan, "Chinese Doubt."

43. "Xi Eyes More Enabling Int'l Environment for China's Peaceful Development," *Xinhuanet*, November 30, 2014, http://news.xinhuanet.com/english/china/2014-11/30/c_133822694_4.htm.

44. Shambaugh "China's Soft-Power Push."

45. Jamil Anderlini, "No Room for 'Western Values' in University Education," *China Digital Times,* January 30, 2015, http://chinadigitaltimes.net/2015/01/no-room-western-values-university-education/.

46. Cao Shunli, "China: Political Repression at a High Mark," Human Rights Watch, January 29, 2015, https://www.hrw.org/news/2015/01/29/china-political-repression-high-mark.

47. Sidney Y. Liu, "Harmonious Online Society: The China Model in the Information Age," in *China's Rise to Power*, eds. Lee, Nedilsky, and Cheung, 94.

48. For a comprehensive analysis, see Esther Pan, "The Promise and Pitfalls of China's Peaceful Rise," Council on Foreign Relations, April 14, 2006, http://www.cfr.org/china/promise-pitfalls-chinas-peaceful-rise/p10446.

49. Joseph Tse-Hei Lee and Lida Nedilsky, "Appeal and Discontent: The Yin and Yang of China's Rise to Power," in *China's Rise to Power*, Lee, Nedilsky, and Cheung, 6.

50. Jethro Mullen and Catherine E. Shoichet, "Hong Kong's Leaders to Protesters: China Won't Back Down," CNN, September 30, 2014, http://edition.cnn.com/2014/09/29/world/asia/china-hong-kong-protests/.

51. Ibid.

52. Joint Communiqué, "Our People, Our Community, Our Vision," 48th ASEAN Foreign Ministers Meeting, Kuala Lumpur, Malaysia, August 4, 2015, p. 25, http://www.asean.org/

storage/images/2015/August/48th_amm/
JOINT%20COMMUNIQUE%20OF%20THE%2048TH%20AMM-FINAL.pdfp.25.

53. "Asean Talks: Beijing's South China Sea Island-Building 'Increasing Tensions," *Guardian*, August 7, 2015, http://www.theguardian.com/world/2015/aug/07/asean-talks-beijing-south-china-sea-increasing-tensions.

54. "The Confucius Institute in Islamabad," http://english.hanban.org/confuciousinstitutes/node_10868.htm.

55. "Confucius Institute in Bangladesh Cements Ties," *China Daily*, August 21, 2009, http://www.chinadaily.com.cn/china/2009–08/21/content_8599027.htm.

56. Ibid.

57. Ibid.

58. Charles Wolf Jr., "The Strategy Behind China's Aid Expansion," *Wall Street Journal*, October 8, 2013, http://www.wsj.com/articles/SB10001424052702303796404579099843923882238.

59. For a historical background of China's foreign aid, beginning from 1950, see the Chinese government's white paper *China's Foreign Aid* (Beijing: Information Office of the State Council, 2011), http://www.unicef.org/eapro/China_White_Paper_on_Foreign_Aid.full_text.pdf.

60. Shambaugh, "China's Soft-Power Push."

61. "Xi Jinping Holds Discussion with German Sinologists, Faculty Representatives of Confucius Institutes and Student Representatives of Chinese Language Learning," Consulate-General of the People's Republic of China in Gothenburg, March 29, 2014, http://gothenburg.chineseconsulate.org/eng/xwdt/t1164906.htm.

62. Callahan, "Introduction," 6.

63. "India, Sri Lanka Sign Four Agreements," *DNA*, March 13, 2015, http://www.dnaindia.com/india/report-india-sri-lanka-sign-four-agreements-during-pm-modi-s-visit-2068450.

64. See Daniel Twinning, "A Chinese Charm Offensive Will Work Better Than a Military One," *Foreign Policy*, February 23, 2016, http://foreignpolicy.com/2016/02/23/a-chinese-charm-offensive-would-work-better-than-a-military-one/.

Chapter Two

China-India Relations

Sources of Conflict and Cooperation

The fulcrum of world power in the twenty-first century is rapidly shifting to Asia, of which India and China are the two most influential global players. Emerging as major global powers, they are poised to reshape the contours of the international system inasmuch as they not only represent the conjunction of growth poles in Asia but also deeply impact the course and direction of international politics. At the same time, Beijing and New Delhi have proven to be strategic rivals in Asia, with divergent perceptions and interests on myriad issues that range from the bilateral border dispute to the Sino-Pakistan strategic nexus in South Asia.

However, the altered economic and strategic milieu at global and regional levels is marked by an inevitable interdependence in key areas such as trade, investment, environmental protection, and counterterrorism. In effect, there are enormous opportunities before China and India to forge a meaningful and productive relationship. They also must call upon each other to dispel the deeply entrenched prejudices, rooted in the legacy of the British Empire, toward each other in order to closely work together to promote security and stability in the Asian region and ensure economic prosperity at home. In fact, both countries are at a crossroads of human history. Confronted with gigantic domestic problems and issues, they are struggling hard to attain the status of developed nations by the middle of this century or maybe even before. Though China is the second-largest economy in the world in terms of GDP, it ranks ninety-first on the human development index, with a poor population of two hundred million (according to the World Bank). Similarly, the delivery component of India's economic development has been trenchantly disappointing. The Indian government has failed to fulfill the basic needs of the poor and marginalized sections of society in terms of water, sanitation, health, and education, even though the Indian ruling class may make tall claims to have accomplished extraordinary feats in military, nuclear, missile, and space sectors.

Given this backdrop, this chapter examines and evaluates the sources of conflict as well as cooperation between China and India within the framework of each country's perception of the other, resulting from the influences of intermeshing variables such as history, geography, culture, nationalism, and geopolitics. An attempt has been made in this chapter to look at the extent to which China's soft power strategy is applicable in the case of India. To this end, the chapter will delve deeply into the historicity of their connections in order to prove or reject possible conjunction or disjunction of the inherent potential of soft-powerism. The chapter argues that core irritants such as the unresolved boundary dispute, which began in 1962, and the Sino-Pakistan strategic nexus vis-à-vis India are by-products of the cognitive dissonance of the ruling class in both countries. These lingering problems make it extremely difficult for China to attract India using its soft power initiatives and approaches while dealing with South Asian nations.

CHINA'S PERCEPTION OF INDIA

At the outset, it is important to understand how interactive factors such as geography, history, culture, and nationalism have cumulatively shaped China's perception of its neighbors. Japan is case in point. China lost fifteen million people, soldiers and civilians, during World War II. For the first time in Chinese history, President Xi Jinping made the momentous decision to commemorate their bravery at a gala held on the Beijing parade ground in September 2015. The other purpose was to display Chinese military might and to revive the bitter memories of the Japanese occupation of China from 1937–1945, with an underlying intent to remind China's countrymen about the supreme sacrifices made by millions of Chinese soldiers for the pride and honor of the nation.

The historical narrative has a deep meaning. Xi wanted to demonstrate to the domestic audience that Japan was still dangerous, posed a serious threat to Chinese ascendancy, and was downgrading its soft power resources. Demonizing Japan clearly reveals that China's old war wounds have not yet healed. The *Economist* writes that Chinese schools, museums, and TV programs constantly warn that the spirit of aggression still lurks across the water. A Chinese diplomat has implied that Japanese prime minister Shinzo Abe is a new Voldemort, the epitome of evil in the Harry Potter series. "At any moment Japan could menace Asia once more, party newspapers intone. China, again, is standing up to the threat."[1] The *Economist* further elaborates that the "parade is not just about remembrance; it is about the future too. This is the first time that China is commemorating the war with a military show, rather than with solemn ceremony. The symbolism will not be lost on its neighbors. And it will unsettle them, for in East Asia today the rising, disruptive, undemocratic power is no longer a string of islands presided over by a god-emperor."[2]

From this historical narrative, the point I'd like to illuminate is how China's perception of India is diametrically contrary to its perception of Japan. For this, there are a host of reasons. First, China does not consider India a military threat. Most Chinese scholars and strategic analysts are of the view that India is not even a distant security threat to China. By this logical implication, they subscribe to the view that India is not in a priority of Chinese foreign policy. On the contrary, China's relationship with the United States regarding Taiwan as well as its security and strategic concerns in East Asia, ASEAN, and the South China Sea do figure prominently in Beijing's foreign policy and diplomacy. Some Indian strategic analysts hold the view that India's recent reach-out to Vietnam for oil exploration is a source of tension between China and India. But quite interestingly, China does not take India seriously as a challenge in Southeast Asia.

Second, to China, India has neither the political will nor the matching military capabilities to launch an offensive against China to avenge its humiliating defeat in the 1962 Sino-Indian War.

Third, China perceives India as a peaceful neighbor without strategic or expansionist designs. Rather, China considers India a victim of the British Empire.

Fourth, history and geography bind the two countries, at least in theoretical terms, to remain as peaceful and friendly neighbors. Without the history of a direct territorial conflict, Chinese hold the British colonial legacy responsible for the persisting hostility between the two countries over the boundary dispute. From China's perception, border incursions stem from the absence of well-defined and properly demarcated borders. China both questions the validity of the 1914 Simla Convention and rejects the legality of the McMahon Line (named after Sir Arthur Henry McMahon, chief delegate of the British government and chairman of the Tripartite Conference at the Simla Convention) as the international border between two countries.

It may be pointed out that even though China walked out of the Simla Convention, the British and Tibetan delegates initialed the agreement. India, being a natural heir to the British Empire, is obligated to abide by the provisions of the 1914 Simla Accord. As such, China has no ground to challenge the legality of the McMahon Line as an international boundary between China and India.[3] China may, however, contest it on the ground that the McMahon Line was a brainchild of the British Empire meant to perpetuate their imperial interests. But intriguingly, China did not question the legality of the McMahon Line until the late 1950s. Rather, it capitalized on India's defense unpreparedness by unleashing an unprovoked aggression against the country in the winter of 1962.

Wei Wei, Chinese ambassador to India, remarked in a speech on February 18, 2013, "Our geographical location binds us—so let us be good neighbors, good friends and good partners."[4] He reiterated that both the countries should view each other as "partners," not as "rivals."

While describing China's impression about the Modi government, Zhinge Zhu says, "China is now putting most of its attention in the South China Sea and East China Sea and wants to maintain peace and good relations with its neighbors in the west. Therefore, generating nationalist pressure against India within its domestic public is not seen as a good option for its current foreign policy. . . . Therefore, sensitive issues such as the border disputes and Japan-India relations do not receive salient coverage. The public has thus not been primed for tense relations with India."[5] He further writes, "Most articles in the Chinese press argue that economic and social development in India will be an opportunity for China."[6]

Above all, the scholarly community in China perceives that problems of bureaucracy and low efficiency in Indian politics cannot be solved easily. Ma Jiali, research professor at China Institutes of Contemporary International Relations, thinks that "the economic ties between China and India would be closer after Modi came into power."[7] Hu Zhiyong, at the Shanghai Academy of Social Sciences, told the *Global Times* in an interview, "The BJP has long held a hard-line position toward China. Modi will no doubt inherit the party stance. He will be tougher against Beijing and use border disputes, the Tibet question and the Dalai Lama to bargain with China."[8]

These are sketchy viewpoints and opinions reflecting the perception of Chinese media and scholars. It is yet to be seen whether the Modi government will adopt a hard-line approach when dealing with China. It is too early to predict. It should be remembered that when Prime Minister Atal Bihari Vajpayee accepted Tibet as part of China, his top party leaders dubbed him a moderate leader with a liberal approach to domestic and external policies.

INDIA'S EARLY INTERACTION WITH CHINA

India and China have traversed through a complex web of historicocultural trajectory spanning millennia. The common key to contacts between them is Buddhism, which brought them closer to each other. These contacts were further expanded and enriched through trade and scholarly interaction between them:

> Chinese pilgrims and scholars traveled to India across the Gobi Desert and the plains and mountains of Central Asia and over the Himalayas; the sea route

was via Indochina, Java and Sumatra, Malaysia, and the Nicobar Islands. This is how Buddhism and Indian culture spread all over Central Asia and into parts of Indonesia, and there were large number of monasteries and study centers dotted all over the vast area.[9]

Among the best-known scholars visiting India were Fa Hien, Sung Yun, Hsuan Tsang, and I-Tsung. Fa Hien and Hsuan Tsang evinced special interest in Indian literature and went back with a heavy load of Sanskrit manuscripts that described the Indian education system, administration, and culture. Notable among Indians who visited China were Kumarajiva, Jinagupta, Jinbhadra, and Bodhidharma. These scholars made significant contributions to Chinese literature. Nehru observed, "During these thousand years and more of intercourse between India and China, each country learned something from the other, not only in regions of thought and philosophy, but also in the arts and science of life. . . . China took much from India but she was always strong and self-confident enough to take it in her own way and fit it in somewhere in her own texture of life."[10] From Nehru's observations, one can glean some important Chinese characteristics that contributed to forming India's perception of China: sound common sense, strong self-confidence, and a capacity to absorb good qualities of others.

NEHRU'S PERCEPTION OF CHINA

Nehru had a profound knowledge and understanding of world history and an incisive grasp of contemporary international politics. His intellectual acumen and idealistic orientation coupled with his Fabian Socialistic leanings made him a popular and well-known statesman. Nehru's Socialist ideas grew much stronger in the early phase of his political life after he and his father visited the Soviet Union in 1927. He was greatly influenced by the Soviet Union's rapid economic development through its planning system. Hence, soon after India's independence, as India's first prime minister Nehru introduced a new planning system with the establishment of the Planning Commission in the early 1950s. To him, planning economic development was the surest means to overcoming hunger and poverty. Also, he felt that the country's territorial integrity, security, and economic prosperity lay in cultivating friendly relationships with neighbors and great powers of the Cold War period. Peace, he stressed, was an essential condition for the political stability and economic development of India. No doubt Nehru was a diehard opponent of Cold War politics. In order to keep India disinterested in the buffets of the Cold war, he charted a course toward the nonalignment policy in international relations. In brief, Nehru's Socialistic leanings and nonaligned policy convinced him that there were no obvious reasons for any direct conflict or confrontation between Socialist India and Communist China.

Nehru greeted the birth of Communist China in October 1949. From then on, he fervently advocated for China's membership in the UN, arguing that the "legitimate interests" of the most populous nation in the world could not be ignored by the international community. The recent evidence reveals that the United States wanted to assist India in assuming a permanent seat at the UN Security Council. Anton Harder writes:

> Nehru's rejection of the US offer underlined the consistency of his conviction that the PRC's legitimate interests must be acknowledged in order to reduce international tensions. Integrating the PRC into the international community by conceding its right to the Chinese seat at the Security Council was in fact a central pillar of Nehru's foreign policy. Nehru's skepticism about accepting this offer, and thereby disrupting the dynamics of the UN, revealed the reverence he had for the international organization, despite its flaws. Furthermore, his principled rejection of the US's suggestion indicates Indian agency in its difficult relations with the US at this time. [11]

India was the first among non-Communist countries to recognize the PRC, much to US chagrin. As a rare gesture, India exhibited an "excessive zeal" in supporting the PRC's membership to the UN. To the disappointment of the US administration, Nehru did not subscribe to the view that Communism was a threat to world peace or stability. On the contrary, he held a firm view that the Western hatred of Communism might become a boomerang. To Nehru, nationalism in China was stronger than Communism. "For the present the Indian Prime Minister was convinced that Chinese nationalism played a far more important part than communism and that Chinese civilization was too old to succumb completely to Marxist dogma." [12]

Nehru correctly gauged that the current of patriotism was running so high in the blood of the Chinese people that no nation could stop it from becoming a great power. It would perhaps be unfair to blame Nehru for his lack of proper understanding of the Chinese psyche. In a mild warning, Nehru often used to reiterate that to deal with China, one would need to understand its peculiar mental makeup. At times, he did not mince words when he described China as have a one-track-mind. This he attributed to China's lack of diplomatic experience and interaction with the outside world. [13]

PANCHSHEEL: THE FOUNDATION

The Panchsheel was the brainchild of Prime Minister Nehru as a part of his strategy to conduct relations with China to dissuade it from undertaking offensive measures against India. Contrary to the common perception about Nehru's soaring idealism, he was guided by pragmatism. It would be in India's national interests, he thought, to deal with the resurgent China, with the background of its revolutionary history, in a prudent and restrained way. He felt that India's social and economic development demanded tranquil, peaceful, and stable borders. Nehru, though quite often charged with an idealistic approach to contemporary international politics, was endowed with the ability to blend idealism with a subtle and artful sophistication in diplomacy in dealing with an aggressive and unpredictable China. This was conspicuous from his extension of diplomatic succor to China and continual advocacy for China's admission in the UN, based on his assessment that it would cement long-term friendly ties with China. In his estimation, a peaceful and restrained China would be in the interest of India's nation-building process and economic development.

At the height of the Cold War era in 1950s, the United States was awed by Nehru's superficiality for making fervent appeals to the world community to recognize to China. By supporting China, Nehru believed that Communist China could be restrained from any moves against India. As mentioned before, his assessment of China's one-track-mind approach was reinforced when China attacked Tibet in 1950 soon after its establishment in October 1949. To deal with an unpredictable China, Nehru worked hard on evolving the Panchsheel. Steadily and surely, Nehru's approach produced a propitious political climate, resulting in the conclusion of the historic Panchsheel agreement between the two countries in April 1954. The agreement contains five principles, which are as follows:

1. Mutual respect for each other's territorial integrity and sovereignty
2. Mutual nonaggression
3. Mutual noninterference
4. Equality and mutual benefit
5. Peaceful coexistence

The agreement formed the bedrock for bilateral and multilateral relations. The Bandung Conference of April 1955 gave further momentum to the existing friendly bonds between the two countries.[14]

But the agreement's barrenness was soon proved and its relevance exposed when China launched an unprovoked attack against India in 1962. Since then it has been buried in the dustbin of history. It must also be noted that, in theory, China-India relations ought to be guided and conducted on the basis of the Panchsheel, both in letter and spirit. Likewise, Chinese leaders have occasionally reiterated that China favors conducting its relations with the outside world on the basis of peaceful coexistence. But practically speaking, the Panchsheel has remained moribund.

Today the Sino-centric world is in the offing. Kissinger, in a 2015 interview for *National Interest* Magazine, said, "The challenge of China is a much subtler problem than that of the Soviet Union. The Soviet problem was largely strategic. This is a cultural issue: Can two civilizations that do not, at least as yet, think alike come to a coexistence formula that produces world order?"[15]

BOUNDARY QUESTION

The Sino-India border dispute is traceable to the legacy of British rule in the Indian subcontinent. The British legacy has left the scars.[16] When Communist China came onto the chessboard of world politics in October 1949, India's first prime minister, Jawaharlal Nehru, made it crystal clear that the emergence of China constituted no security threat to India. This assessment was rooted in his thinking that India and China did not inherit a territorial dispute like that of India and Pakistan over the Kashmir issue.

In the late 1950s, mutual bickering began to surface following China-led border skirmishes. Exchange of official letters continued between New Delhi and Beijing. Each side continued harping on the other's respective position while justifying the territorial claim both historically and legally. Nehru, in his letter of December 14, 1958, to Chinese premier Chou En-lai wrote, "You will remember that when the Sino-Indian Agreement in regard to the Tibet region of China was concluded, various outstanding problems including some related to our border trade, were considered. No border questions were raised at that time and we were under the impression that there were no border disputes between our respective countries. In fact we thought that the Sino-India agreement, which had happily concluded in 1954, had settled all outstanding problems between our two countries."[17] In reply to Nehru's letter, Chou wrote on January 23, 1959, "First of all I wish to point out that the Sino-Indian border has never been formally delimited. Historically no treaty or agreement on the Sino-Indian boundary has ever been concluded between the Chinese central government and the Indian government."[18]

To India's utter astonishment, China launched an unprovoked act of aggression against it in October 1962. During a three-week war, China occupied thirty-eight thousand square kilometers of Indian territory. At that critical juncture, Nehru appealed to US president John F. Kennedy for immediate military aid to bail India out. President Kennedy reassured him of prompt military assistance to save Indian democracy from the onslaught of Chinese Communism. The US administration ordered the immediate dispatch of military equipment and transportation aircraft, including essential items for Indian soldiers. Undoubtedly, the emergency military aid acted as psychological deterrence, forcing China to announce the ceasefire unilaterally in November 1962. China's original plan was to strike India again in December 1962 to seize more Indian territory.[19]

Without going into a detailed history of the Sino-Indian War, it should be pointed out that the political stalemate on the boundary issue lingered until India took a political initiative to normalize relations with China. Toward that end, the Janata-led government overseen by Prime Minister Morarji Desai sent his external affairs minister, Atal Bihari Vajpayee, to China in February 1979 to plumb the mood of Chinese leaders on the boundary issue. In order to test the nerves and morale of the Indian ruling class, China attacked Vietnam—India's friend—when Vajpayee was on Chinese soil as its guest. Bruised by the deliberate insult China heaped on India, Vajpayee had to cut short his visit and returned to India empty-handed. Despite the diplomatic setback suffered by India, the its government kept the bilateral dialogue alive, resulting in eight rounds of talks between 1980 and 1988. Border skirmishes once again surfaced when Chinese troops invaded the Chu Valley in Arunachal Pradesh (earlier known as the North East Frontier Agency [NEFA]) in 1987.

A thaw in Sino-India relations began with Prime Minister Rajiv Gandhi's state visit to China in December 1988. This was the first visit of an Indian prime minister to China in thirty-four years, since Gandhi's grandfather Nehru's visit in 1954. During Gandhi's visit, a major breakthrough was achieved with the signing of a historic agreement setting up a Joint Working Group (JWG) tasked with maintaining peace and tranquility on the borders. The JWG meetings are held annually at the foreign secretary's level in Beijing and New Delhi alternatively.

Rajiv Gandhi's visit to China paved the way for several confidence-building measures (CBMs) undertaken by the governments of New Delhi and Beijing. Continuing the process of high-level political visits, Chinese premier Li Peng paid a return visit to New Delhi in 1991 to further improve both countries' understanding on myriad issues of mutual interest at bilateral and regional levels. In September 1993 Indian prime minister P. V. Narasimha Rao's visit to China broke new ground when both sides signed off on the Agreement on the Maintenance of Peace and Tranquility along the Line of Actual Control (LAC) in the India-China Border Areas, "providing for both sides to respect the status quo on the border."[20]

Under the LAC Agreement, both countries agreed to withdraw their respective forces, currently interlocked in an eyeball-to-eyeball position at the borders, to help avoid a direct confrontation between the troops. Also, Prime Minister Rao expatiated upon India's soft power diplomacy by highlighting the virtue and values of Indian culture and its civilizational underpinnings in a speech delivered at the Chinese Academy of Social Sciences in Beijing. These steps produced positive momentum in the countries' bilateral ties. Furthermore, President Jiang Zemin's first visit to India as a Chinese head of state in November 1996 helped firm up a comprehensive relationship between the two countries. Four agreements were signed, including, according the Indian government, "CBMs in the Military Field along the LAC covering adoption of concrete measures between the two militaries to enhance exchanges and to promote cooperation and trust."[21]

SUDDEN SETBACK

The process of warming up Sino-Indian relations received a sudden setback following India's multiple thermonuclear tests in May 1998. Though China's initial reaction was mild, its acerbic rebuff came when the Indian government justified the tests by citing China as a potential threat to Indian security in Prime Minister Vajpayee's official letter to US president Bill Clinton. The letter was leaked to the *New York Times*, which published it on May 13, 1998. The Chinese government brushed aside the Indian accusation as utterly groundless. As immediate fallout, the Beijing government canceled its decision to participate in the prescheduled 1998 meeting of the Joint Working Group (JWG), who'd been entrusted with the task of boosting CBMs.

As regards China's reaction to Pakistani tests, the Beijing leadership dubbed them reactive to India's hegemonic designs in South Asia. President Zemin expressed his consternation that these weapon tests would not only escalate the arms race in the region but also exacerbate the persisting tensions between New Delhi and Islamabad. This further widened a chasm in Sino-Indian relations. Nevertheless, to bring their relationship back on right track, the Vajpayee government embarked on a strategy of proactive diplomacy. Towards diluting the persisting mutual mistrust, Indian external affairs minister Jaswant Singh visited China in June 1999, and he reiterated that "neither country is a threat to the other."[22] This facilitated the Security Dialogue meeting between two countries, held in Beijing in March 2000, and also the resumption of the JWG meeting in April 2004.

During Prime Minister Vajpayee's visit to China in 2003, an agreement was signed on the India-China boundary question at the level of special representatives (SRs) to expedite political settlement of the boundary dispute.[23] Since then, regular meetings are being held at the SR level. Until April 2016, nineteen rounds of border talks had been held between special representatives of the two countries. During the nineteenth round of border talks held in April 2016, officials said that "the two sides are currently in the second stage which focuses on working out a framework of settlement to be followed by final step drawing the boundary line based on framework agreement."[24]

In order to maintain tranquility along the LAC, Prime Minister Singh and Chinese premier Li Keqiang agreed to the Border Defense Cooperation Agreement (BDCA) in Beijing in October 2013. Under the agreement, several mechanisms have been incorporated to remove the communication gap and create mutual misunderstanding with an objective that troops on both sides would exercise "maximum self-restraint" so as not to foment tension along the LAC. Under the agreement, both sides will supervise the "contested territory" through a constant vigil and their military presence. The BDCA is not a guarantee to prevent skirmishes along the borders, but at least it provides a mechanism to diffuse further escalation. It ought to be noted that at the end of their meeting Singh and Keqiang expressed the hope and confidence that if they remained united, they could change the geopolitical map of Asia, in particular, and the global reordering, in general. But this kind of soothing expression is mostly symbolic rhetoric with little value, given their irreconcilable competing and rival interests.

It is important to mention that at the seventeenth border talk, the Indian government notes, both SRs "discussed the continued maintenance of peace and tranquility in the India-China border areas, the cornerstone of an expanding India-China relationship. The Special Representatives elaborated on possible additional confidence building measures, including the early implementation of the Border Defence Cooperation Agreement. . . . These measures augur well for building the habit of regular discussions between the two sides which will enhance trust and understanding."[25]

Be that as it may, the net outcome of CBMs has been that both sides have shown flexibility in their attitudes and approaches by conceding that borders would be demarcated afresh. This task has been assigned to engineers, technocrats, geographers, and cartographers. On receiving their comprehensive report and recommendation, next steps will be taken at the political level to proceed further on this issue.

Much to India's chagrin, despite the structured arrangement to defuse tension on the borders, Chinese incursions have not let up. It merits a special mention that PLA troops entered twenty-five to thirty kilometers into Indian territory in Ladakh, Jammu and Kashmir, when President Xi was on Indian soil confabulating with Prime Minister Modi on a swing at Ahmedabad, Gujarat, in September 2014. In 2013 alone, 411 border violations took place from the Chinese side. Xi took these violations lightly. Indeed, he obliquely defended them, arguing that such violations take place because there were no well-defined borders between the two countries. Chinese troops withdrew from Indian territory after more than three weeks at the personal intervention of President Xi.

Easing tension on the borders was the goal of the eighteenth round of border talks between Indian national security adviser Ajit Doval and Chinese state councilor Yang Jiechi in New Delhi on March 23, 2015. According to a statement from the Indian Ministry of External affairs, "They expressed satisfaction on the progress made in the negotiations and emphasized commitment to the three-step process to seek a fair, reasonable and mutually acceptable resolution of the border question at an early date."[26] They added,

"The Special Representatives continued the discussions to reach a mutually acceptable Framework for resolution of the Boundary Question on the basis of the Agreement on the Political Parameters and Guiding Principles."[27] Though no breakthrough was achieved, the SRs discussed a wide range of international and regional issues, including maritime security, threat of terrorism, and the alleged move of China to establish a naval base in the Indian Ocean.

During his three-day state visit to China in May 2015, Prime Minister Modi and his Chinese counterpart Keqiang agreed to maintain "peace and tranquility" in the border region. Modi insisted on exploring the possibility of a "fair, mutually acceptable resolution" of the border dispute.[28] It seems ridiculous how long India has explored the possibility. This issue has been hanging fire since the 2003 Agreement on Political Parameters and Guiding Principles on the Boundary Question. It appears that the boundary issue is likely to remain tortuous and complicated in the face of contesting claims and contrary perceptions of each side over the territory. For instance, "China says the border dispute is confined only to 2,000 kms. mostly in Arunachal Pradesh whereas India asserts that the dispute covered the western side of the border spanning to about 4,000 kms, especially the Aksai Chin area annexed by China in 1962 war."[29] The road is still bumpy. Both sides have yet to go a long way. Without them thinking outside the box, it will be an excruciating task to resolve the boundary issue in a fair, reasonable, and mutually acceptable manner. Chinese premier Keqiang, in an interview to *India Today* on May 8, 2015, elaborated on the modus operandi of resolving the boundary dispute. He said, "The two sides have formulated a roadmap for the settlement of the boundary question, signed an agreement on political parameters and guiding principles and reached the important agreement on a package settlement through making meaningful and mutually acceptable adjustments. . . . This is an important accomplishment for both sides."[30]

TIBETAN ISSUE

The Tibetan issue has been a major irritant in the Sino-Indian relationship ever since China occupied Tibet by invading it in 1950. India could not do anything to prevent Chinese troops from military onslaught to take over Tibet. On the contrary, Chinese leaders and their scholarly community formed a fractured perception of Nehru, charging him with a mindset of British imperialism. In their perception, he wanted to seize Tibet and make South Asia an Indian empire. This kind of perception about Nehru was patently false. In fact, Nehru's socialization, culture, and political upbringing were antithetical to imperialism and colonialism. He fought against British imperialism and colonial forces not only for India but also for the entire

Afro-Asian world. In order to keep the newly independent countries of Asia and Africa away from Cold War politics, he came up with the idea of the nonaligned movement, which emerged as a major international force in fighting against political, economic, and cultural imperialism, of which Third World countries were the worst victims.

Chinese leaders either misunderstood Nehru or wanted to teach him a lesson by unleashing an unprovoked military invasion over India, given Nehru's growing international stature in the nonaligned world. In other words, it was China's flawed assessment that Nehru was in favor of keeping Tibet as India's protectorate. John W. Garver is also of the view that "Chinese perceptions of Indian policies toward Tibet were fundamentally erroneous, and that, moreover, these misperceptions contributed substantially to the 1962 war."[31]

If viewed from a geostrategic point of view, Nehru, of course, wanted to keep Tibet as a buffer zone to ensure Indian security against the potential threat of China, to promote India's border trade and energy interests (water as a source of energy), and also to ensure cultural autonomy for Tibetans. But the presence of the Dalia Lama, the exiled spiritual leader, and the presence of over 100,000 Tibetan refugees on Indian soil at Dharamsala, Himachal Pradesh, have always been irksome to China. India, being a democratic, liberal, and tolerant society in its outlook and having a composite culture, has been a vocal advocate of victims of repression and persecution, although India is extremely cautious in granting political asylum, by judging the merit of a case.

The problem with China is that it is hyperallergic to the Dalai Lama, whom Chinese leaders think is directly involved in maligning its image abroad by projecting China as an incorrigible violator of human rights in Tibet. His lobbying in the West throughout the 1980s and his hard-hitting speech to the US Congress over the plight of Tibetans on many occasions infuriated Chinese leaders. As a counteroffensive, China has been delivering the message to the world community that it must take the country's specific social conditions, norms, and cultural values into account before accusing it of human rights violations. China has also been apprising the world community that it has taken sufficient steps in developing Tibetan art, culture, and literature.[32]

India's soft approach to the Tibetan issue emboldened China to encourage settlement of a large number of Chinese people belonging to the Han dynasty. They are alleged to be responsible for denigrating the religious, cultural, and spiritual values of the Tibetan community. An egregious blunder was committed by Prime Minister Vajpayee when he officially recognized Tibet as a part of the PRC during his state visit to Beijing in 2003. The Indian legitimacy emboldened China to not only embark on a vast network of building strategic infrastructure in Tibet but also lay its exclusive claim over

Arunachal Pradesh as an integral part of South Tibet. Thus, Chinese leaders tricked India into recognizing Tibet as a part of China, which indirectly meant that Arunachal Pradesh constituted a part of South Tibet. Is this China's soft power approach? The answer is no.

India's biggest loss is that it has lost Tibet as a buffer zone between the two countries. Brahma Chellaney writes, "In this light, the reference to China's Tibet region in the Modi-Xi joint statement (September 2014) granted Beijing via the backdoor what India has refused to grant upfront since 2010. This sleight of hand implicitly endorsed Tibet as being part of China without Xi committing to a 'one India' policy."[33] He further elaborates on this point, saying:

"The more important reason is that China is seeking to advance its strategic interests in the Sikkim-Bhutan-Tibet tri-junction, which overlooks the narrow neck of land that connects India's northeast with the rest of the country. Should the chicken's neck ever be blocked, the northeast would be cut off from the Indian mainland. In the event of a war, China could seek to do just that."[34]

India has virtually lost its leverage over Tibet, giving China a free hand to carry on its repressive policies against Tibetans by way of denigrating their cultural values, symbols, and salience. The Modi government should not trust China's soft power approach; rather, it will need to sensitize Chinese leaders to understand the psyche of Indian and Tibetan people in order to maintain friendly and harmonious relations between Beijing and New Delhi. The Dalai Lama's core concern is the preservation of the cultural freedom and autonomy of Tibetans. For that India owns the moral and political responsibility to work out proactive diplomacy to ensure Beijing leadership respects Tibetans' cultural freedom and autonomy.

Apart from this, India needs to be extremely circumspect about China's strategic move to project its political choice as the heir of the Dalai Lama, while Dalai Lama thinks, according to Evan Osnos, that "Tibetans might vote on whether the institution of the Dalai Lama should continue at all. Or, he says, he might select his own reincarnation while he is still alive—a theological twist known as madhey tulku—which would give him the chance to train a successor and avoid the gap in leadership that has always been a time of instability for Tibetans. Only one thing is certain, he says: his successor will be found outside Tibet."[35] Given the gravity of the Tibetan issue, especially in view of the aging Dalai Lama, Xi needs to rethink the importance of resolving the Tibetan issue through political reconciliation, essential for regional peace and stability and to avoid exacerbating tensions in Arunachal Pradesh, Sikkim, Tibet, and Nepal.

THE CHINA-PAKISTAN STRATEGIC NEXUS

Another source of irritation between China and India is the solidity of the Sino-Pakistan strategic nexus, traceable to the 1963 border agreement. Under the agreement, Pakistan ceded more than five thousand square kilometers of land of Pakistan-occupied Kashmir to China. That was a premeditated and well-orchestrated diplomatic move on the part of Pakistan to forge an inalienable partnership with China to counter India. For China also, strategic partnership with Pakistan would serve its national interest in weakening Indian influence in South Asia, though China maintained a noncommittal stance in the India-Pakistan Wars of 1965 and 1971. Except for providing Pakistan with conventional military hardware, China preferred to remain aloof from the Cold War politics of superpowers. This is obvious from China's flat refusal to jump into the December 1971 India-Pakistan War despite Kissinger's repeated appeals to China to enter into the fray in favor of Pakistan. Also, Chinese leaders were aware of the Soviet Union's commitment to safeguarding Indian territorial integrity under the 1971 Indo-Soviet Treaty of Peace, Friendship, and Cooperation. The treaty acted as a psychological deterrence that restrained China to directly enter the 1971 war to oblige Pakistan.

However, China's nuclear- and missile-building assistance to Pakistan is well known. The US intelligence community disclosed in 1990 that it had "detected the transfer to Pakistan of a training M-11 ballistic missile and associated transporter-erector launcher including that operational missiles were not far behind."[36] On the contrary, Toby Dalton maintains that there was no evidence that China was involved in supplying uranium or transferring missiles to Pakistan. One reader commented on August 8, 2013, on Toby Dalton's paper, "The writer is unfamiliar with the book *Nuclear Express* written by Danny Stillman and Thomas C. Reed who have cited Chinese experts telling them that they had supplied not just a bomb design, but also fissile material for a weapon and, to top it all, tested a Pakistani weapon of Chinese design in 1990."[37]

China is also reported to have given assistance to Pakistan in building drones. China has developed its indigenous Drone CH-5. It is feared by the Indian strategic community that China and Pakistan, with their drone technologies, are capable of creating serious security problems for India. India is also reported to be trying to procure the US Avenger Drone, which proved very effective in tracking down and killing dreaded militants in Afghanistan and Pakistan. China's all-weather friendship with Pakistan is also manifest from its unconditional political and diplomatic succor to Pakistan on sponsoring terrorism, delivering diplomatic punches against India on several occasions at the United Nations. A few prominent instances may be cited. China twice blocked India's bid in 2016 at the UN Security Council to designate JeM chief Masood Azhar as a terrorist. China opposed granting a waiver to India by the Nuclear Suppliers Group (NSG) in its meeting in 2008. China also opposed India's membership to the NSG cartel at the behest of Pakistan. Pakistani foreign secretary Aizaz Ahmad Chaudhry reacted by saying that "China acted upon its 'principled stance' in opposing Indian membership of the Nuclear Suppliers Group (NSG)" and added that "the truth has won."[38]

Also, China is poised to abort any diplomatic move aimed at granting India a permanent membership in the UN Security Council. These instances clearly reveal that the China-Pakistan strategy is to clip Indian wings to dilute its influence and weaken its security and strategic role in regional and global affairs.

SOURCES OF COOPERATION

India and China are the fastest-growing economies in the world, with abundant human and material resources. Both countries face common challenges stemming from poverty, social backwardness, and income disparities between the rich and poor, and social and ethnic unrest. At the same time, their economies are complementary. They began the process of economic and trade interaction in the 1980s. With the signing of a protocol on economic cooperation in 1984, they granted a most favored nation status to each other. This gave a new lease on the life of their trade relationship, which had remained suspended in the aftermath of the 1962 Sino-Indian War.[39]

The Modi government's priority is strengthening India's economic ties with China. He has been a great admirer of China for its fast economic growth and its innovative approach to modernizing the Chinese economy. As a chief minister of Gujarat, Modi had visited China four times, inviting Chinese investors to his home state. When Modi became prime minister, he invited President Xi to visit India. In his first stopover in Ahmedabad in September 2014, Xi announced to make Gujarat an "economic power house," and announced putting in billions of dollars into the development of an industrial park in Gujarat. Modi was profusely impressed by Xi's so-called soft diplomacy and praised him.

His political critics, however, say that Modi is not likely to be tough on China even though he vehemently criticized the United Progressive Alliance government during his election rallies for being soft on China's frequent transgression of Indian borders. Apparently Modi is more malleable, more pliable, and softer toward China when he talks of doing business with China on trade and investment issues. He seems to have put aside the territorial dispute in order to strengthen India's economic partnership with China. Moreover, Modi is trying to base his content and style on the Gujarat model rather than thinking touside the box when India's territorial interests are being jeopardized by Chinese incursions into Indian territory.

Though Sino-Indian trade has phenomenally increased, it is not said to be as satisfactory as it was expected from the two Asian giants, with a combined population of 2.5 billion people, and more significantly the fastest-growing economies in the world, with their GDP growth between 6.7 percent for China and 7.6 percent for India's in the third quarter of 2016.[40] Even then, bilateral trade volume increased in the first decade of the twenty-first century, standing at $70.25 billion in 2014 according to the Indian Embassy in Beijing.[41] But India's exports to China have gravely suffered. The trade deficit between India and China increased to $48.43 billion in 2014–2015, according to commerce and industry minister Nirmala Sitharaman in her written reply to the Rajya Sabha on May 13, 2015. According to provisional figures, in 2014–2015 India's exports to China stood at $11.95 billion, while imports were $60.39 billion.

India's decline in exports is attributed to a fall in Chinese purchases of iron ore—the biggest Indian export to China. India has also reduced purchases of power and telecom equipment as part of its security concerns. Economic affairs analysts are of the view that India's trade deficit with China might further increase to $60 billion, as the trade deficit touched $48.3 billion in 2013–2014. As reported by the *Economic Times*, based on the report of the Ministry of Commerce and Industry, just prior to Modi's visit to China in May 2015, "India's trade deficit with China could nearly double to $60 billion in the next two years if the two partners do not address market access constraints and nontariff barriers faced by Indian goods in the neighbouring country."[42]

This alarming situation warrants India to take corrective measures immediately. Several economists are of the view that India might be in a serious predicament in coming years since India's trade deficit vis-à-vis China has become unbearable. "If the current situation persists, by 2016–17, merchandise imports from China will exceed $80 billion while India's exports will be around $20 billion, leaving an unsustainable trade deficit of $60 billion," the commerce department said.[43] There are several reasons for this. For example, a series of nontariff barriers have blocked India's exports in pharmaceutical, information technology, and agricultural commodity sectors. India has not been able to make a breakthrough in the information technology sector, because China's strategic sector in telecom is completely state regulated.[44] Yet consumer imports from China, like cheap mobile phones, have crossed over $12 billion. In order to slash its trade deficit and discourage the import of nonessential goods from China, India needs to revise its policy. To address India's concerns, President Xi, during his maiden visit to India in September 2014, announced an investment of $20 billion in India over the next five years.

Despite the Indian media hype, Prime Minister Modi's visit to China in May 2015, mainly aimed at augmenting Chinese investments into India, especially in infrastructure, power, and tourism, did not make a difference on India's trade deficit vis-à-vis China. President Xi did not make any commitment to make concessions or offer incentives to Indian entrepreneurs who enter Chinese markets. In his meeting at Shanghai with a group of Chinese entrepreneurs, he tried to convince them to invest in India, citing that the business climate was congenial and free from bureaucratic hassles.[45]

Chinese ambassador to India Le Yucheng sounds an optimistic note, that "in terms of business cooperation, the two big markets of China and India have much to offer each other. Chinese accumulative investment in India almost tripled to 2.7 billion this year [i.e., 2015]. There is huge demand and desire on both parts to join hands, especially in such key areas as manufacturing and infrastructure."[46]

STRATEGIC AND ECONOMIC DIALOGUE

Dialogue between nations is the essence of bringing about a positive transformation in misperceptions and misunderstandings toward each other. It spurns ruling leaders into propping up bilateral cooperation for socioeconomic welfare of their people by creating congenial conditions, essential for improving their lifestyles by promoting openness, inclusiveness, entrepreneurship, and innovation.

Moreover, political discourse around the development process is needed to guarantee the fulfillment of the basic needs of the people. Toward that end, Asia's two largest countries, which have the fastest-growing economies in the world, are making strenuous efforts. This has been inevitable in view of the changing nature of power and national interest in an increasingly interdependent world, shaped and articulated by economic, energy, and resources considerations. Still struggling hard for attaining the status as developed nations, Beijing and Delhi have expanded the scope of economic dialogue at the regional and global level.

The idea of strategic economic dialogue (SED) germinated in the collective thinking of the leadership on both sides when Chinese premier Wen Jiabao visited India in December 2010. Indeed, buoyed by crossing the mark of the set bilateral trade target from $60 billion to $61.7 billion by 2010, as laid out during Wen's visit to India in 2005, further prompted Premier Wen and his Indian counterpart, Manmohan Singh, to establish a regular bilateral SED mechanism. In their discussions, they arrived at a broad consensus that being the fastest-growing economies in the world, with convergence on many and varied global and regional issues—including on the question of restructuring the International Monetary Fund (IMF), World Bank, and

World Trade Organization (WTO)—they ought to move forward to help create a just, fair, and equitable economic global order for a larger neglected strata of Third World societies through cooperation and coordination of collective efforts.

This idea seems to have crystallized with the establishment of the New Development Bank of BRICS nations (Brazil, Russia, India, China, and South Africa). At the seventh BRICS summit, in Ufa, Russia, in July 2015, the leaders of the five countries were in a broad agreement that BRICS, which provides an important multilateral forum, will become "new growth poles for the world economy."[47] They are capable of playing a leading role in international organizations such as the UN and G20.

How is SED different from bilateral trade and commerce? What is the rationale behind it? How can SED resolve core issues facing the global economic community in areas such as infrastructure, energy, and communication? The answer lies, first, in the fact that India and China are actively participating in institutions such as BRICS, G20, and the East Asia Summit. These provide them with unique opportunities to interact on global and regional issues that have long-term implications for developing economies in Asia, Africa, and Latin America. Second, both countries share identical concerns over the imperative of bringing reforms to the old-fashioned global financial institutions of the World Bank and IMF, which have long been dominated by the Western world, especially the United States, while ignoring the development priorities of developing and underdeveloped nations in terms of eradicating poverty, ensuring health services, and improving educational conditions. At the seventh BRICS Summit, the leaders agreed that, "with the bank's [New Development Bank of BRICS] funding, developing countries, especially the African states, can improve their infrastructure, rather than struggling with the limited funds the current international agencies provide them."[48] In other words, as the world's major emerging economies, the BRICS has a potential to help reshape the global governance of international institutions and organizations.

Third, China and India recognize that the fulcrum of power from the East-West axis has clearly shifted to the Asia axis. In effect, an integrated global political and economic architecture cannot be conceived without China and India. At the same time, the current Chinese leadership has clearly recognized that the Asia axis is more complicated and problematic than the erstwhile East-West axis of power that operated throughout the Cold War period.[49] Also, ruling sections in both countries have accepted the stark reality of competition and rivalry among nations for power and influence.

While keeping this backdrop in mind, China and India decided to move forward to translate the concept of SED into a reality. Their first meeting was held in Beijing on September 26, 2011. The Indian delegation was headed by Montek Singh Ahluwalia, then deputy chairman of the Planning Commission, and his counterpart, Xu Shaoshi, chairman of the National Development and Reform Commission. The second and third meetings of the SED were held in November 2012 and March 2014 (Beijing) respectively. According to the Indian Ministry of External Affairs, "Both delegations had extensive and in-depth discussions on bilateral trade, investment, and economic cooperation and on the regional and global economic situation with a view to enhancing macro-economic policy coordination and to join hands to address issues and challenges. Bilateral cooperation in sectors like railways infrastructure, information technology, energy, and finance was emphasized. The two sides agreed to continue deepening bilateral coordination and engagement in multilateral frameworks like the United Nations, Group-20 and BRICS."[50]

According to one report, "The working groups covered areas like infrastructure, mainly the railways and operationalize the agreement for service centres to be set up in India for Chinese power equipment, environment and resources protection, water management and policy coordination, collaboration on planning and urbanisation, cooperation in high technology including the IT sector."[51]

The fourth India-China SED was held in Delhi on October 7, 2016, under the theme "Development, Innovation, and Cooperation for Mutual Benefit." The Indian side was led by Arvind Panagariya, vice chairman of the National Institution for Transforming India, and the Chinese side was again led by Xu. Panagariya emphasized that India would like to benefit from China's expertise in "redevelopment: of railway stations in India, development of coastal economic zones, smart cities, and waste management."[52]

The Modi government is all set to push China for greater investments into the Make in India program. But in recent years tensions between Beijing and New Delhi have been heightened after China's complete tilt toward Pakistan on any controversial issue in which India has been involved. Hence, Pakistan would remain a negative factor in Sino-Indian relations. Moreover, India's stance on the South China Sea, in sync with the United States, has produced consternation in China that India is moving much closer to America strategically. But at the same time, both countries have realized that being the largest emerging economies in the world, they are bound to engage with each other. What is most important is that through expanding economic cooperation in areas of mutual interest, Beijing and New Delhi must undertake concrete measures so that ultimate benefits should trickle down to their people. This is yet to be seen how they would move forward given the persisting trust deficit between them.

STRATEGIC COOPERATIVE PARTNERSHIP

The pace and speed in the strengthening of bilateral ties can be easily gauged from the fact that both countries agreed to establish a strategic cooperative partnership, an agreement signed during Premier Wen's official visit to India April 9–12, 2005. This was unthinkable in the Cold War period. Surely the establishment of the strategic partnership demonstrates, as the Chinese Embassy in India puts it, that "China-India relations have now acquired a 'global and strategic character.'"[53]

Moreover, strategic partnership has entered a "new stage of comprehensive development" that would lend further momentum and add strength to their existing ties with a fresh opportunity to explore and expand unexplored areas of mutual cooperation.[54] There are two parts of the agreement. Under the strategic partnership, India and China hold joint military exercises and consult each other on strategic issues that impinge directly on their relationship. Since 2007 they have been conducting joint military exercises, though interrupted at times due their relationship bedeviling for one reason or another. The 2008 Exercise Hand in Hand injected new blood into military and security cooperation bilaterally. As the *Hindu* reported, "The joint Hand-in-Hand counterterrorism exercises between India and China started on Monday (October 12, 2015), following the arrival of 175 personnel from the Naga Regiment of the Eastern Command in Kunming. An equal number of Chinese personnel from the Chengdu-based 14 Corps are participating in the manoeuvres whose aim is 'to develop joint operating capability, share useful experience in counter-terrorism operations and to promote friendly exchanges between the armies of India and China.'"[55] It is important to note that simultaneously India was holding the nineteenth Malabar naval exercises in the Bay of Bengal with the United States and Japan (now a permanent participant in the nineteenth, 2015, edition) to give an unequivocal message to Beijing that India's military and security ties were not exclusively focused on China. More important, these naval exercises with the United States and Japan are an indicator that the trio have a convergence on the freedom of navigation in the South China Sea, India's Act East Policy, and the Obama administration's Asia-Pacific Rebalance.[56]

Cooperative partnership involves clear-cut understanding between India and China to cooperate on regional and international issues of common concern and interest. At the international level, both countries are cooperating, for instance, on climate change. They have displayed identical approaches and similar official positions at international conventions, whether in Copenhagen in December 2009 or in Paris in November 2015. Their delegates speak with one voice. Both countries are in favor of cuts in carbon emissions but oppose developed countries', for instance the United States and European Union member nations, insistence that they are responsible for the environmental degradation as they are still developing countries and will need to boost industrialization for economic growth and economic prosperity of their people. Their cooperative approach has yielded positive results. The United States and European Union have appreciated the viewpoints of New Delhi and Beijing and are urging them to cooperate so that the logjam could be cleared by arriving at a win-win consensus. Apart from this, India and China have displayed their convergent perceptions and approaches on many other issues like human rights, Iran's nuclear program, counterterrorism, and the Palestinian cause, despite India's strong and deep defense, security, and strategic and nuclear relationships.

CONCLUSION

As regards the China-India soft power equation, there are enormous challenges as well as opportunities. The singular biggest challenge to their relationship is the long unresolved boundary dispute between the two countries. Frequent encroachments of Indian territory by Chinese forces across the LAC have created a warlike situation. It is not yet certain how long this process will continue, despite nineteen rounds of border talks held so far (until 2016) between SRs of the two governments. The Chinese government keeping the boundary issue on hold for so long has resulted in a huge trust deficit between Beijing and New Delhi. Rather, it is a litmus test of China's soft power policy to win India's goodwill and trust. Even then both the countries have enormous opportunities to work together closely on the shared challenges posed by terrorism, insurgency, drug trafficking, maritime piracy, and cyber crimes.

The new center-right government led by Prime Minister Modi is trying to ride two horses at a time. One the one hand, Modi is keen to develop sturdy ties with China to learn from its experience in infrastructure development. On the other hand, he has been paying extraordinary attention to building strategic ties with Japan—the main adversary of China. It will be a tough task for Modi to strike a fine balance in India's relationship with China and Japan, and also with China and the United States. Besides this, the gargantuan challenge before the Modi government will be how to tame Pakistan as a permanent troubleshooter for India. At the same time, how will India address the fallout of the enduring strategic partnership between China and Pakistan on multilateral global and regional issues in which Indian interests are at stake? For instance, India's permanent membership in the UN Security Council will remain hostage to the Sino-Pakistan friendship. Also, China several times blocked India's bid at the UN to designate Masood Azhar and Zakiur Rehman Lakhvi as terrorists—both Pakistani citizens overtly involved in terror attacks on India—simply to defend its longtime ally Pakistan.

So far as China's soft power initiatives in South Asia are concerned, they are not appealing to India. As explained earlier, the historic baggage of mutual mistrust stemming from intermeshing variables such as the unresolved boundary dispute, transfer of nuclear and missile technology, and diplomatic succor to Pakistan, and its recent announcement of the $46 billion China-Pakistan Economic Corridor project are, cumulatively speaking, a pointer that China will further calcify its strategic grasp over South Asia at the cost of India. Yet it is important to underline that smaller countries of the region will welcome China's presence in the region as a counterweight to India. Undoubtedly, they will remain under the spell of China's soft power influences, mainly driven by China's massive economic and infrastructure aid to them. However, it is difficult to predict precisely whether China's soft power resources will continue to allure new partners, especially smaller countries in the Indian subcontinent. But it is a sad commentary on Indian diplomacy that because of its neglect of their geopsychological impulses to be treated on equal footing, they have been forced to move out of the orbit of Indian influence and to embrace China as their real friend and well-wisher.

NOTES

1. "Xi's History Lessons: The Communist Party Is Plundering History to Justify Its Present-Day Ambitions," *Economist*, August 15, 2015, http://www.economist.com/news/leaders/21660977-communist-party-plundering-history-justify-its-present-day-ambitions-xis-history.

2. Ibid.

3. For a comprehensive and logical discussion of this part, see Nirmal Sinha, "The Simla Convention 1914: A Chinese Puzzle," *Presidency College Magazine: Diamond Jubilee Number* (1974): 35–39, http://himalaya.socanth.cam.ac.uk/collections/journals/bot/pdf/bot_1977_01_05.pdf.

4. "A Promising Future—China and India Must View Each Other as Partners, Not Rival," *News from China*, February 18, 2013, http://in.china-embassy.org/chn/xwfw/zgxw/P020130401828336299980.pdf.

5. Zhinghe Zhu, "China's Perception of India's New Government," 1–12, Academia, https://www.academia.edu/8621880/China_s_perception_of_India_s_new_government.

6. Ibid.

7. Ibid.

8. Ibid.

9. Jawaharlal Nehru, *The Discovery of India*, 4th ed. (New Delhi: Jawaharlal Nehru Memorial Fund, 1985), 192–93.

10. Ibid., 99.

11. Anton Harder, "Not at the Cost of China: New Evidence Regarding US Proposals to Nehru for Joining the United Nations Security Council," Cold War International Project (Washington DC: Woodrow Wilson Centre, 2015), 2, https://www.wilsoncenter.org/sites/default/files/cwihp_working_paper_76_not_at_the_cost_of_china.pdf.

12. W. F. Van Eekelen, *Indian Foreign Policy and the Border Dispute with China* (The Hague: Martinus Nihoff, 1967), 55. For the psychological consequences of the Sino-Indian War of 1962, see Jaswant Singh, *Defending India* (New York: Macmillan, 1999).

13. Henry Kissinger also shares his analysis. See his article "As China Modernizes: Obstacles on the Way," *Times of India*, January 25, 1986.

14. B. M. Jain, "India-China Relations : Issues and Trends," Occasional Paper No. 1, Centre for Asian Studies, University of Hong Kong, 2004, 5.

15. Jacob Heilbrunn, "The Interview: Henry Kissinger," *National Interest*, August 19, 2015, http://nationalinterest.org/feature/the-interview-henry-kissinger-13615?page=2.

16. For a perceptive and detailed analysis pertaining to this part, see A. G. Noorani, *India-China Boundary Problem, 1846–1947: History and Diplomacy* (New Delhi: Oxford University Press, 2011).

17. G. V. Ambekar and V. D. Divekar, eds., *Documents on China's Relations with South and Southeast Asia, 1949–1962* (New Delhi: Oxford University Press, 1964), 113.

18. Ibid.

19. For details, see B. M. Jain, *India-US Relations, 1961–1963* (London: Sangam, 1987).

20. Indian Embassy in Beijing, http://www.indianembassy.org.cn/Chinese/PoliticalRelations.aspx; see also Maharajakrishna Rasgotra, ed., *The New Asian Power Dynamic* (New Delhi: Sage, 2007), p. 171.

21. "India-China Bilateral Relations," Ministry of External Affairs, Government of India, January 2012, http://mea.gov.in/Portal/ForeignRelation/China-January-2012.pdf.

22. Ibid.

23. The document is called the Agreement between the Government of the Republic of India and the Government of the People's Republic of China on the Political Parameters and Guiding Principles for the Settlement of the India-China Boundary Question.

24. "India, China Hold 19th Round of Border Talks," *Arunachal Times*, April 21, 2016, http://www.arunachaltimes.in/india-china-hold-19th-round-of-border-talks/.

25. "17th Round of Talks between the Special Representatives of India and China on the Boundary Question," Ministry of External Affairs, Government of India, February 11, 2014, http://mea.gov.in/press-releases.htm?dtl/22861/
17th+Round+of+Talks+between+the+Special+Representatives+of+India+and+China+on+the
+Boundary+Question%27.

26. "18th Round of Talks between the Special Representatives of India and China on the Boundary Question," Ministry of External Affairs, Government of India, March 25, 2015, http://mea.gov.in/press-releases.htm?dtl/25002/
18th+Round+of+Talks+between+the+Special+Representatives+of+India+and+China+on+the
+Boundary+Question.

27. Ibid.

28. Abdul Ruff, "India and China Ink Economic Agreements, UN Veto and Border Dispute in Cold Storage!," *Asian Tribune*, May 17, 2015, http://www.asiantribune.com/node/86993.

29. Press Trust of India, "Ahead of Modi's Visit, China Says 'Huge Dispute' with India over Arunachal Pradesh an 'Undeniable Fact,'" *Indian Express*, April 9, 2015, http://indianexpress.com/article/india/india-others/dispute-with-india-over-arunachal-an-undeniable-fact-china.

30. PRC Embassy, *News from China* 27, no. 5 (May 2015): 31.

31. John W. Garver, "China's Decision for War with India in 1962," Indian Strategic Knowledge Online, http://www.chinacenter.net/wp-content/uploads/2016/04/china-decision-for-war-with-india-1962.pdf.

32. See B. M. Jain, "India-China Relations."

33. Brahma Chellaney, "Why Tibet Remains the Core Issue in China-India Relations," *Forbes,* November 27, 2014, http://www.forbes.com/sites/brahmachellaney/2014/11/27/why-tibet-remains-the-core-issue-in-china-india-relations.

34. Ibid.

35. Evan Osnos, "The Next Reincarnation," *New Yorker*, October 4, 2010, http://www.newyorker.com/magazine/2010/10/04/the-next-incarnation.

36. "China's Missile Exports and Assistance to Pakistan—Statements and Developments," Center for Nonproliferation Studies, http://cns.miis.edu/archive/country_india/china/mpakchr.htm.

37. Toby Dalton, "Strategic Triangle," Carnegie Endowment for International Peace, August 5, 2013, http://carnegieendowment.org/2013/08/05/strategic-triangle-pub-52584.

38. "China Opposed India's NSG Bid on Principle: Aizaz," *Dawn*, June 26, 2016, http://www.dawn.com/news/1267180.

39. Jain," India-China Relations."

40. For China's GDP growth estimate, see *Fortune*, October 19, 2016, http://fortune.com/2016/10/19/china-gdp-growth/.

41. For information on the India-China bilateral trade, see " India-China Economic Relations," Embassy of India—Beijing, China, http://www.indianembassy.org.cn/DynamicContent.aspx?MenuId=97&SubMenuId=0.

42. Dilasha Seth, "India's Trade Deficit with China to Double in the Next Two Years," *Economic Times*, April 6, 2015, http://economictimes.indiatimes.com/news/economy/foreign-trade/indias-trade-deficit-with-china-to-double-in-the-next-two-years/articleshow/46818672.cms.

43. Ibid.

44. Roselyn Hsueh, *China's Regulatory States: A New Strategy For Globalization* (Ithaca, NY: Cornell University Press, 2011).

45. See "Text of the Keynote Address by Prime Minister Narendra Modi at India-China Business Forum," *Hindu*, June 6, 2015, http://www.thehindu.com/news/resources/text-of-the-keynote-address-by-modi-at-indiachina-business-forum/article7213391.ece?ref=relatedNews.

46. Le Yucheng, "China-India Relations, Soaring to New Heights," *News from China* 27, no. 10 (October 2015): 34.

47. "President Xi Jinping Attends the BRICS and SCO Summit," *News from China* 27, no. 7 (July 2015): 13.

48. Ibid., 12.

49. For a perceptive analysis of this, see Rajni Kothari, *Transformation and Survival: In Search of a Humane Order*, 2nd ed. (New Delhi: Ajanta, 1990).

50. "Third India-China Strategic Economic Dialogue Meeting in Beijing," Ministry of External Affairs, Government of India, March 18, 2014, http://mea.gov.in/press-releases.htm?dtl/23124/Third+IndiaChina+Strategic+Economic+Dialogue+Meeting+in+Beijing.

51. K. J. M. Varma, "India-China Strategic Economic Talks to Focus on High Speed Rail Tracks," *Live Mint*, March 16, 2014, http://www.livemint.com/Politics/vgP15aBacOdBWriUOX3U5M/IndiaChina-strategic-economic-talks-to-focus-on-high-speed.html.

52. "NITI Aayog Seeks to Shift Focus of India-China Economic Dialogue," *Economic Times*, September 24, 2016, http://epaperbeta.timesofindia.com/Article.aspx?eid=31816&articlexml=NITI-Aayog-Seeks-to-Shift-Focus-of-India-24092016011039.

53. "China, India Agree on 'Strategic Partnership'," Embassy of the People's Republic of China in the Republic of India, April 12, 2005, http://in.chineseembassy.org/eng/ssygd/zygx/t191496.htm.

54. Ibid.

55. Atul Aneja, "India, China Begin Counter-Terrorism Drills," *Hindu*, October 13, 2015, http://www.thehindu.com/news/exercises-in-kunming-and-bay-of-bengal-underscore-indias-balancing-act/article7752793.ece.

56. See Pranav Kulkarni, "Significance of the India-US-Japan Malabar Naval Exercise," *Indian Express*, October 21, 2015, http://indianexpress.com/article/explained/significance-of-the-india-us-japan-malabar-naval-exercise/#sthash.Sull12YW.dpuf.

Chapter Three

China-Pakistan Relations

Closeness without Commonality

Over the last six decades, China and Pakistan have continued to maintain close and stable relations without hiccups, even though they lack commonality in terms of ethnicity, religion, culture, language, and societal values. This unique relationship warrants an objective and dispassionate analysis of what has bound them together. The most plausible explanation quite often offered in this regard is their shared perception of an imperative necessity to keep India's rise in check, though with divergent goals and interests. For Pakistan, China is not only a reliable source of military hardware but also a security assurance against India's potential threat. For China, as revealed by Pakistan's former ambassador to the United States Husain Haqqani in 2006, "Pakistan is a low-cost secondary deterrent to India."[1] What is the core background behind it? Surely its roots can be traced to the 1962 Sino-India War, when India suffered a humiliating defeat at Chinese hands. In the Indian defeat Pakistan perceived a rare opportunity to forge inerasable ties with China to ensure its national security against the potential Indian threat. In March 1963 Pakistan concluded a border agreement with China under which it ceded to China an area of 5,010 square kilometers of PoK, an area that remains under Chinese control. The agreement laid a solid foundation for their bilateral relationship. Since then their strategic alliance has played a central role in shaping the geopolitical and geostrategic landscape of South Asia and beyond. India remains at the center of their geopolitical calculations.

However, there is a myopic view among most of scholars that China is the most trusted military partner of Pakistan. It is not fully true. It must be remembered that in international politics there is no such thing as trust between nations. What really matters is how to secure and promote one's national interests. If viewed through a realist prism, China has been using Pakistan as a convenient tool to fulfill its geopolitical and geostrategic interests, for instance, to access natural resources and markets in Afghanistan and Central Asian states, ensure an uninterrupted oil supplies from the Middle Eastern and Gulf regions, and build naval bases in the Gulf region. Jonah Blank writes in this regard, "Leaders of each nation routinely describe the other as its closest partner on earth, as its 'all-weather friend.' But does the substance match the rhetoric? The two nations have virtually no shared culture, history, or economic ties. The glue sticking them together would appear to be military ties and an interest in keeping their common rival, India, off balance."[2]

Initially, China was recalcitrant to intervene in South Asian affairs. But with the changing geopolitical dynamics in South Asia, the Beijing leadership embarked on working out a well-orchestrated game plan to bring Islamabad within its strategic fold by offering incentives in the form of military hardware and nuclear and missile technology assistance to Pakistan. China has been able to exploit the psychology of Pakistani military elites, who look upon China as a more reliable strategic ally than the United States. As regards China, it finds Pakistan to be an indispensable strategic post for the expansion of its strategic space in the Gulf, Arabian Sea, and Indian Ocean region. This is manifest from Pakistan's acquiescence in handing over the Gwadar port to China on a forty-year lease. The emerging scenario looked to be replicating Cold War history when Pakistan allowed the United States to build military bases in its territory in return for American military and economic aid. Indeed, the all-weather partnership between Beijing and Islamabad may not be as stable and as tension-free as it used to be in the past couple of decades. It is a well-known fact that China faces serious internal threats from Uighur separatists in its Xinxiang region who receive open support from extremist groups operating near Pakistan's western border with Afghanistan. China has been issuing mild warnings to Pakistan to keep its jihadi elements under control since they pose a grievous threat to physical security of Chinese workers and engineers on Pakistani soil. But it is intriguing that Pakistani military elites describe their alliance with China as "deeper than the ocean and taller than the Himalayas."[3] President Xi's maiden visit to Pakistan in April 2015 also drew unprecedented attention from the media and political community in South Asia, especially in Pakistan. He exuded rhetorical love for Pakistan on the eve of his visit to Islamabad. He wrote, "I feel as if I am going to visit the home of my own brother."[4] The China-Pakistan friendship was described as "higher than mountains, deeper than oceans, sweeter than honey, and stronger than steel."[5] The *Washington Post* termed Xi's political rhetoric as a "sort of romantic sloganeering." Pakistani military elites were more than happy with Xi's announcement of the "eye-popping" gift worth $46 billion for Pakistan's energy and infrastructure development.[6] This reflects a strong and stable strategic bonding between the two countries without political gyrations. This chapter discusses how the Sino-Pakistan all-weather friendship has flourished over the last five plus decades. The chapter also examines the wide-ranging bilateral and regional issues between the two countries and their implications for South Asia and beyond.

Since the establishment of diplomatic relations in 1951, China-Pakistan ties have steadily strengthened and deepened. Their relations took an unprecedented turn following the 1962 Sino-Indian War. India's abysmal defeat at the hands of China was a huge political comfort to Pakistan, from which it tried to derive maximum political mileage. First, Pakistani military junta mounted pressure on the Kennedy administration to make India agree to hold talks to resolve the Kashmir issue to Pakistani satisfaction, though the administration did it reluctantly. At the persuasion of the US administration, an India-Pakistan dialogue was held on the Kashmir dispute in December 1962 and March 1963, albeit without any tangible outcome. Second, Pakistani military elites sought to pamper China into concluding a border deal in March 1963, under which it gave away a large chunk of PoK territory to China. Intriguingly, Pakistan orchestrated the plan to kill two birds with one stone. First, in the Pakistani perception, the territorial gift to China will create sturdy ties between Beijing and Islamabad—a sure guarantee against India's potential threat to its national security. Second, the Islamabad-Beijing strategic nexus will act as a reliable strategic hedge against India's expanding role and influence in South Asia at a low cost. However, it is interesting to note that there is no commonality between China and Pakistan in terms of social, cultural, and political outlook. Nor is there any ethnic or religious affinity between them, except that China's Xinjiang province is dominated by the Uighur Muslims.

PAKISTAN'S GEOSTRATEGIC IMPORTANCE

Pakistan's strategic location—as the gate to Afghanistan and Iran—has always proved to be a boon for Islamabad in times of crises, whether it was the Soviet military invasion of Afghanistan in December 1979 or the US military offensive against Afghanistan in October 2001 in pursuit of its global war on terror. During these wars, the United States assigned Pakistan the status of a frontline state. Naturally, Pakistan became eligible to be a top recipient of US military assistance on a massive scale. During the Soviet military presence in Afghanistan until February 1989, Pakistan managed to divert a large chunk of US financial aid toward building its nuclear program. This is a classic case of Pakistan's geostrategic importance. It is a patent fact that Pakistan might not have ever emerged as a nuclear weapon state without the massive US military and economic aid that Islamabad had received as a reward for providing training to Afghan mujahideen to fight against Soviet forces in Afghanistan. Undoubtedly, the Reagan administration had full knowledge that Pakistan was diverting a large chunk of American aid to building its nuclear program—an overt violation of US nonproliferation laws. But the administration would not slap sanctions—under the Symington Amendment (1976), Glenn Amendment (1977), or Pressler Amendment (1985)—on Pakistan so long as Soviet forces were stationed in Afghanistan. The administration placed embargo on aid transfer to Pakistan in October 1990 when the Soviet Union withdrew its forces in 1989.

Another classic example of Pakistan's primacy in US strategic policy was manifest when the Bush administration made the momentous decision to attack Afghanistan in October 2001 after the 9/11 terror attacks on the World Trade Center in New York and the Pentagon in Washington, DC. Without Pakistani logistical and intelligence support, the United States could not effectively deal with Al-Qaeda and Taliban forces in Afghanistan. Since then, Pakistan has received American aid worth nearly $14 billion. This massive aid helped not only revive the gasping economy of Pakistan but also resuscitate the Taliban by diverting US funding to terrorist outfits like the Haqqani network, which was actively involved in fostering terror across the borders of Afghanistan and Pakistan. It is in this context that the Pentagon blocked $300 million in military aid to Pakistan after defense secretary Ashton Carter "declined to give a certification to the Congress that Pakistan is taking sufficient action against the dreaded Haqqani network."[7] Withholding of American military assistance to Pakistan is perceived as a potential blow to Washington-Islamabad ties. This has prodded China to derive maximum political mileage once US forces finally leave Afghanistan, by filling the strategic vacuum through its well-known tactical network of investment in infrastructure development in Afghanistan.

Pakistan and China are already feverishly engaged in holding rehearsals on how to provide a new face to Afghanistan in the postwithdrawal of US forces from there. For Pakistan, Chinese economic aid is indispensable for rebuilding Afghanistan's infrastructure and fulfilling its energy requirements. At the same time, it is a propitious opportunity for China to exploit Pakistan's economic plight and the brewing domestic unrest stemming from over sixty thousand killings by its homegrown terrorists. Apart from this, the current leadership under Xi Jinping is all set to widen the already rocky relations between Washington and Islamabad in light of the Pentagon's blocking $300 million in military aid. Starved by the trimming of American aid, an alternative source of aid to Pakistan is no other country than China. Understandably, China has already embarked on establishing a network of railways, ports, and pipelines by announcing an investment of $46 billion in the China-Pakistan Economic Corridor project, estimated to be completed in three years. The corridor, connecting Kashgar in Xinxiang to Gwadar on the Arabian Sea, will shorten the transportation route by 1,200 kilometers, for transporting oil from the Middle East and Gulf region to China.[8] Prime Minister Modi protested the Economic Corridor project, passing through the disputed territory in PoK during his visit to China in May 2015. But China did not take notice of his protest.[9]

POLITICAL EQUATIONS

China and Pakistan enjoy an exceptionally cozy political equation based on mutually beneficial interests. There are only rare examples of China and Pakistan openly clashing or diverging on sensitive political issues, like Kashmir, Tibet, and Xinjiang. Unsurprisingly, China has been an open supporter of Pakistan on the Kashmir dispute, caring little about Indian sensitivity. In fact, China has displayed a gesture of unalloyed friendship by introducing stapled visas for the people of Jammu and Kashmir (J&K) to display its political solidarity with Pakistan. India lodged protests with China on numerous occasions, but China adroitly neglected Indian objections.

Similarly, Pakistan has been supporting China on Tibet, Xinjiang (regarding Uighur Muslim separatists), and Taiwan. While separatist elements in Xinjiang are demanding an independent state, Pakistan has been helpful in fighting those militants.[10] During Pakistan Prime Minister Nawaz Sharif's visit to China in 2014, China "urged Islamabad to weed out what it says are militants from Xinjiang, who are holed up in a lawless tribal belt, home to a lethal mix of militant groups which include the Taliban and Al-Qaeda."[11] Sharif reassured President Xi that his country would "continue to resolutely fight the East Turkestan Islamic Movement terrorist forces . . . increase its coordination with China on Afghanistan as well, so as to jointly maintain regional peace and stability."[12] China reciprocated Pakistani support by continuing since 2014 to block India's bid at the UN on declaring "Pakistan-based terrorists." In May 2015 India's permanent mission at the UN raised the question about releasing Zakiur Rehman Lakhvi, a commander in Lashkar-e-Taiba, responsible for the November 2008 Mumbai terror attacks, by the Pakistani court, which was a violation of the 1267 UN resolution dealing with "designated entities and individuals."[13] Also, China twice blocked India's move at the UN Security Council to designate Masood Azhar a global terrorist. In the case of listing Hizbul Mujahideen chief Syed Salahuddin, China put a technical hold on India's request. This evidence exposes China's double standards on terrorism.

The real motivation behind Sino-Pakistan's shared priority is to constrict India's expanding role in South Asia and beyond its shores. But given unbridgeable asymmetries in terms of power and capabilities, Pakistan's teaming with China may prove dangerously counterproductive in the long term. Their common alliance against India is not likely to endure, as China is skeptical about its potential to survive as a viable and stable nation-state when its civilian ruling leaders have failed to defeat their homegrown terrorist outfits and jihadi elements.

It is incorrect to say, as some Western scholars believe, that China has been projecting Pakistan as a classic case of maintaining the balance of power between India and Pakistan. But China clearly understands that Pakistan neither is a superior military power compared to India nor can attain parity vis-à-vis India in economic, industrial, scientific, and technological fields to challenge Indian preponderance in the region. At best, Pakistan can be a troubleshooter for India. China will, however, continue to use India-Pakistan tensions to advance and fulfill its own strategic agenda by engaging Pakistan with India on the J&K border to prevent the advancement of Indian troops beyond the territory of Arunachal Pradesh. Lisa Curtis of the Heritage Foundation in her testimony before the US-China Economic and Security Review Commission, on May 20, 2009, stated, "Chinese officials also view a certain degree of India-Pakistan tension as advancing their own strategic interests as such friction bogs India down in South Asia and interferes with New Delhi's ability to assert its global ambitions and compete with China at the international level.[14]

CHINA'S STRATEGIC PRESENCE IN PAKISTAN-OCCUPIED KASHMIR

PoK possesses geopolitical and geostrategic significance for China. It may be recalled that Pakistan transferred over five thousand square kilometers of PoK to China under an agreement signed in March 1963. Since then Beijing-Islamabad relations have grown deeper, stronger, and more stable, without any ripples. PoK is a direct link between China and Pakistan, which not only makes the former geographically proximate to India's J&K but also facilitates its strategic surveillance over the sensitive region of J&K. Undoubtedly, Chinese strategic presence in PoK serves its manifold purposes. First, it offers the strategic maneuverability to stabilize its permanent physical presence in the region. Second, Brigadier Manjit Singh raises a valid apprehension that China has a long-term strategy to transform the Gilgit-Baltistan area into a buffer state to stem the spread of Islamic fundamentalism into its restive Xinxiang province, demanding a separate Muslim state.[15] Third, the presence of PLA forces in PoK will enable China to effectively deal with the radical extremist across Pakistan's tribal areas.

China does not want a permanent resolution of the Kashmir dispute, due to its own security, political, and strategic interests. China's Kashmir problem has evolved since the early 1950s. In the initial period, China was neutral on the issue, but after the conclusion of the 1963 agreement, Beijing supported Islamabad. With the warming up of ties between Beijing and New Delhi, the Chinese leadership has adopted the policy of treating the Kashmir problem as a bilateral issue that ought to be resolved peacefully by India and Pakistan in the interest of regional peace and stability. In practice, China is ill-prepared to dilute its strategic ties with Pakistan, with whom it enjoys an excellent traditional relationship. [16]

This is evident from China's introduction of stapled visas for the people of J&K, to display its geopolitical proximity with Pakistan. The Indian government contested and lodged a strong protest with China, arguing that such a practice did not exist anywhere in the world. But China's underlying intention is to project itself as a party to the Kashmir dispute so that it can perpetuate its strategic activities in PoK. It has been reported that China has been carrying out hundreds of projects there, which include infrastructure development, construction of roads, and setting up of hydropower projects worth billions of dollars.

Pakistan needs Chinese investments. Its economy is already on the verge of collapse. More important, China will remain the only dependable source of foreign aid to Pakistan, with US aid to the country shrinking. China understands Pakistani compulsions very well. This has prodded China to use Pakistan as a ploy for its myriad national interests in Afghanistan and Central Asia, including eliciting Pakistani support to control Uighur separatists. In this context, Ishaan Tharoor writes in the *Washington Post*, "China views Pakistan also through the lens of counter-terrorism: number of extremist outfits allegedly linked to ethnic Uighur separatists within Xinjiang have training camps in Pakistan's rugged borderlands with Afghanistan. Curiously, in a country where there are frequent displays of solidarity with Muslims suffering elsewhere in the world, the Uighurs, a Turkic Muslim minority chafing under Chinese rule, rarely galvanize much Pakistani support." [17]

Andrew Small, an expert on China-Pakistan affairs at the German Marshall Fund in Washington, does not agree with this view that China is maintaining a friendship with Pakistan simply for realizing its strategic ambitions in South Asia, or that Afghanistan will ignore China's relations with Washington and New Delhi. He writes that "it would be an oversimplification to see China's expanding role in Pakistan as just a challenge to a U.S.-India consensus that's emerged in recent years. China, after all, likely values its bilateral relations with the U.S. and India as much—and likely more—than its ties with Pakistan." [18]

CHINA-PAKISTAN MILITARY AND SECURITY TIES

China is the largest exporter of conventional military weapons to Pakistan, despite the US military aid to Pakistan, which is now the top recipient of Chinese arms. Military cooperation between Beijing and Islamabad goes back to the 1963 boundary agreement. In the 1980s and 1990s China not only transferred conventional military equipment such as T-85 tanks, F-7 fighter crafts, M-11 ballistic missiles, jet trainers, and frigates of multiple variants but also helped build Pakistan nuclear arsenals and missile systems such as 750-kilometer-range solid-fueled Shaheen-1 missiles. Michael Beckley writes, "Between 1978 and 2008, China sold roughly $7 billion in military equipment to Pakistan, typically accounting for 40 percent of Pakistan's total arms purchases in any given year. China also helped build two nuclear power plants in Pakistan in the 1990s and signed a deal in 2009 to build two more."[19]

It is no secret that China relentlessly engaged in modernizing Pakistan's defense industry when the Bush administration slapped sanctions on Pakistan under the 1985 Pressler Amendment in October 1990. Meanwhile, China played a key role in assisting Pakistan's nuclear weapon program. In 2013 China announced it would set up two civilian nuclear reactors to help meet Pakistan's soaring energy needs. Also, China and Pakistan are collaborating in projects to coproduce armaments "ranging from fighter jets to guided missile frigates."[20]

China assisted Pakistan in building a nuclear bomb. Based on the public revelation of Pakistani nuclear scientist A. Q. Khan, known as the father of Pakistan's nuclear program, China provided Pakistan 50 kilograms of weapons-grade uranium, enough to make two nuclear bombs, as part of a "broad-ranging, secret nuclear deal" between Mao Zedong and Bhutto.[21] The following year, China reportedly provided Pakistan the complete design for a 25 kt nuclear bomb. As reported in the *Washington Post*, "The uranium transfer in five stainless-steel boxes was part of a broad-ranging, secret nuclear deal approved years earlier by Mao Zedong and Prime Minister Zulfiqar Ali Bhutto that culminated in an exceptional, deliberate act of proliferation by a nuclear power."[22] A US State Department memo at the time concluded that "China has provided assistance to Pakistan's program to develop a nuclear weapons capability. Over the past several years, China and Pakistan have maintained contacts in the nuclear field. . . . We now believe cooperation has taken place in the area of fissile material production and possibly also nuclear weapons design."[23]

According to the *Diplomat*, "The first signs of Sino-Pakistani nuclear cooperation emerged in 1977. U.S. government officials noted China's commitment to Pakistan to provide 'fuel services' and that Chinese technicians visited at Karachi Nuclear Power Plant (KANUPP) to familiarize themselves with the operation of the reactor. By 1978, Khan was able to produce small quantities of enriched reactor-grade uranium at Kahuta."[24]

It was alleged in 1995 that China sold Pakistan five thousand ring magnets needed for high-speed gas centrifuges, and a US intelligence report in 1997 holds that "China was the single most important supplier of equipment and technology for weapons of mass destruction"[25] in the world. The report further elaborates:

China's civil nuclear trade commitments with Pakistan have gained considerable momentum since Pakistan's nuclear tests in May 1998. The China-Pakistan Power Plant Corporation's Chashma-1 and Chashma-2 power reactors, which were under item-specific IAEA safeguards, were held not to be in violation of NSG guidelines as they were pre-existing commitments and thus "grandfathered" in at the time of China's induction into the NSG in 2004. However, China then entered into agreements in 2009 for the construction of two new 340 MW power plants (Chashma-3 and Chashma-4). There have since been reports of undertakings for the construction of additional plants in Chashma and Karachi.[26]

China is now building two sizeable civilian nuclear reactors to help mitigate Pakistan's huge energy shortage. According to the *Economist*, "As China expands its reach throughout Asia, Pakistan has become central to its plans for a network of ports, pipelines, roads and railways that will bring oil and gas from the Middle East. The Chinese government is offering tens of billions of dollars for Pakistani projects. . . . As America's influence recedes, China is stepping in, though officials will doubtless keep a wary eye on Pakistan's nuclear weapons."[27]

In this context Lisa Curtis observes, "China has helped Pakistan build two nuclear reactors at the Chashma site in the Punjab Province and continues to support Pakistan's nuclear program, although it has been sensitive to international condemnation of the A. Q. Khan affair and has calibrated its nuclear assistance to Pakistan accordingly . . . but did not propose or agree to a major China-Pakistan nuclear deal akin to the U.S.-India civil nuclear agreement. U.S. congressional members have expressed concern about China's failure to apply Nuclear Suppliers Group (NSG) 'full-scope safeguards' to its nuclear projects in Pakistan."[28]

It was reported that Pakistan claimed to have concluded a deal to export a JF-17 to Myanmar. If this is true, then Pakistan is fast emerging as a supplier of weapons to Third World countries. In this regard, Jonah Blank writes, "China has not merely contributed technology to the effort but has also reportedly sought to open doors to friendly states in Africa, Asia, and Latin America. In 2009, Pakistan signed a deal to purchase 36 of China's more advanced fourth-generation fighter, the J-10. Observers have noted that Pakistan's two unmanned aerial vehicles, the purportedly indigenous Burraq and Shahpar models, bear an uncanny resemblance to China's Rainbow CH-3."[29]

In brief, China has been instrumental in beefing up Pakistan's nuclear and missile capability, without which it would have been a Herculean task for Pakistan to develop nuclear and missile capabilities at a faster speed. In this context Jonah Blank observes:

> What Pakistan gets out of its engagement with China is relatively easy to see. China has provided Pakistan with much of its nuclear weapons program, an even greater portion of its ballistic missile program, a steady stream of conventional arms, and steadfast diplomatic support that has spanned over half a century. This support justifies a lot of Pakistan's flowery rhetoric. In the nuclear realm, the substance of China's involvement has lived up to the hype: without China's assistance, Pakistan's nuclear capability would certainly have been developed much later (if ever), and its missile delivery system for nuclear weapons might not have been developed at all.[30]

Whatever military and nuclear aid China may provide to Pakistan, certainly it cannot help maintain military balance between India and Pakistan, as some Indian defense and security analysts maintain. In effect, China's fostering of a military parity doctrine in South Asia is very much likely to meet the same fate as one comes across in the case of the United States during the Cold War period. And, moreover, it is a fatuous estimate, as shared by the Indian strategic community, that South Asia will emerge successful as the power struggle between China and the United States continues.

INDIA-US NUCLEAR AGREEMENT

Pakistan became deeply frustrated over the US-India nuclear deal in 2006. Pakistani military elites also urged the United States to accord the same treatment and status to Pakistan as India, an idea spurned by the Bush administration. The administration argued that Islamabad's nuclear record in the past had not been above board in comparison to India's impeccable nuclear record. Even then Islamabad continued harping on that India neither was eligible for concluding a nuclear deal with the United States nor qualified for receiving a waiver by the NSG since India was not a party to the Nonproliferation Treaty and Comprehensive Test Ban Treaty. But that argument did not cut ice with the Bush administration. On the contrary, the administration reminded Pakistan again that its nuclear scientist A. Q. Khan was directly involved in secretly supplying sensitive information, technical know-how, and nuclear technology–related material and equipment to "rogue states"— North Korea and Iran. Later, A. Q. Khan himself publicly acknowledged his direct involvement in shady nuclear deals.

China lost no time in exploiting Pakistani anger, frustration, and woes. It sent out a loud message to Islamabad-based military and civilian elites that the United States was not a reliable partner and had left friends and allies in the lurch. The Beijing leadership came forward to assist, announcing its commitment in April 2010 to help build two nuclear power reactors in Pakistan. But China received a rebuff when its diplomatic efforts failed to scuttle the waiver granted by the NSG in September 2008. To the last moment, China endeavored to prevent a consensus on granting a waiver to India. Thus, China's anti-India posture confirmed that it could not stomach India's rise as an emerging global power. In this context, P. Chidambaram, the then home minister, while describing China as India's "rival" and "unpredictable" neighbor, said, "From time to time, China takes unpredictable positions that raise a number of questions about its attitude towards the rise of India. The most recent example is the negative stance adopted by China in the meeting of NSG."[31]

A moot question arises as to whether China will be able to dissuade Pakistan from maintaining close strategic links with the United States. It is also important to rethink whether the "robust" strategic partnership between China and Pakistan will be able to insulate Islamabad from Washington. In this regard, there are contrary opinions and interpretations among strategic analysts. For instance, Beckley does not subscribe to the view that China and Pakistan share a robust all-weather friendship. He firmly opines that "they engage in limited cooperation on a narrow set of interests, and these interests have been diminishing over time. Second, China will not militarily intervene to defend Pakistan if threatened by the United States. One might recall, China had maintained a stoic silence over the US surgical raid on Pakistani soil on which Al Qaeda chief Bin Laden was killed in 2011. It means that the United States can impose punitive measures on Pakistan without the fear of catalyzing an anti-American Sino-Pakistani alliance."[32]

This assessment may be partially true. There are three palpable reasons behind their rocklike friendship. First, if seen through a realistic prism, China needs Pakistan as a troubleshooter for India in order to keep its hegemony in South Asia. Second, Pakistani cooperation and support is essential for preventing Islamic militants across the tribal areas to fan the bloody separatist movement in China's Xinxiang province. For Pakistan, China's diplomatic succor on critically important issues is indispensable at multilateral forums, including the United Nations, apart from China's military hardware against India's potential threat to its national security. Pakistan also requires Chinese investments in developing its ports and infrastructure facilities. This is manifest from China's proposed economic corridor project worth $46 billion, announced during President Xi's maiden visit to Islamabad in April 2015. Third, both the countries have a single-minded goal of joining hands to weaken and internally destabilize India to fulfill their respective myopic national interests. In other words, the shared geopolitical interests have brought them closer to serve as a credible deterrent against India's rise in every realm. Chinese general Xiong Guangkai went to the extent of saying that "Pakistan is 'China's Israel.'"[33]

CHINA: FILLING UP THE VACUUM

The retreat of US forces from Afghanistan will create a strategic vacuum in the region. Toward that end, China has already offered its good offices to Pakistan to mediate with the Afghan Taliban. This is a major shift in China's diplomacy to expand and deepen its role in the region, as Beijing has much to offer to the devastated Afghanistan, with a lucrative economic package for infrastructure development. It is theorized that Chinese eyes are cast on playing a much bigger strategic role in the emerging new Afghanistan, with Pakistan as its surrogate or its strategic corridor. It is through Pakistan that China has prioritized the projection of its regional influence with the instruments of aid and grants. Scholars and policy analysts dealing with South Asian affairs may see this policy as a component of China's soft power diplomacy. But in reality, China's overriding concern and interest in a new Afghanistan is to use it as a gateway to the oil- and natural gas–rich Central Asia, Iran, and Persian Gulf.

As pointed out earlier, China's primary focus is on oil and strategic resources of the region, especially Afghanistan's mineral reserves. According to a US geological study, "Afghanistan has nearly $1 trillion (Rs 52.5 trillion) of untapped mineral deposits—iron, copper, cobalt, gold and lithium. Afghan authorities say the country aims to generate revenue of $2 billion annually by 2017–18 from the mining and exploration business, including oil and gas, from about $100 million now."[34]

This implies that China' game plan is to deny India a strategic space in the region and to dilute its strategic role in this part of the world. It is unlikely that New Delhi will offer a calibrated and coherent response to China's perceived diplomatic maneuvers in the Af-Pak region. Since the traditionally strong alliance between Islamabad and Washington is cooling down, China will spare no effort to expand its strategic footprint in Afghanistan. In this context Louis Ritzinger comments, "Close relations between China and Pakistan are certainly nothing new and are generally framed in terms of the two countries' mutual rivalry with India. Indeed, this strategic triangle has been the greatest impetus for Beijing and Islamabad's "all-weather friendship," which extends to the diplomatic, economic, and military realms. China has proved to be a reliable alternative for Pakistan to the United States in providing military assistance, including support for its nuclear program."[35]

A NEW TWIST TO ALLIANCE

Pakistan's importance to China can be gauged from Prime Minister Nawaz Sharif's first foreign visit to China in July 2013, after assuming the office of prime minister. His visit broke new ground in several fields. Eight agreements were signed, the most important of which concerning the economic corridor—a two-hundred-kilometer tunnel that will connect Pakistan's Gwadar port and Kashgar in China. Both sides also signed an agreement on laying fiber-optic cable from the Chinese border to Rawalpindi, facilitating Pakistan's access to international communication networks. At the end of his visit, Nawaz Sharif and his Chinese counterpart, Li Keqiang, issued a joint communiqué under which China pledged its "unwavering support" to Pakistan's sovereignty and territorial integrity, with wider implications. It may commit China to come to Pakistan's rescue if its national security is threatened by another country. In addition, an agreement on economic and trade cooperation between the two countries will boost Pakistan's fledging economy. To implement these agreements, Sharif made a momentous decision to establish an exclusive China Cell at his office. As reported by *Dawn*, the cell will "coordinate and oversee timely implementation of all the projects to be developed with Chinese assistance. . . . None can deny the fact that partnership for progress with a dependable and time-tested friend like China has all the potential to change the destiny of this nation."[36] So far Pakistan has "received Chinese financing worth $135 billion between 2001 and 2014."[37] It ought to be remembered that President Xi's announcement in 2015 of the $46 billion economic corridor project even surpasses the total military and economic aid that Pakistan has received from the United States between 2002 and 2015. While compared to China's one-time huge infrastructure investment aid commitment to Islamabad, the US aid is a paltry sum. This has naturally shifted the pendulum towards Beijing.

Apparently there are four major strategic objectives behind the China-Pakistan Economic Corridor (CPEC) project. First, China, in its quest for finding alternative oil supply routes, wants to reduce its current dependence on oil imports through the Indian Ocean, where it perceives a combined challenge of the United States and India. Second, the proposed project will facilitate China's access to the oil-rich Central Asia, whose oil resources might contribute to boosting China's economic growth. Third, given the shared understanding between Beijing and Islamabad, the proposed project might act as a strong strategic hedge against India's role and influence in Afghanistan and Central Asia. Fourth, it will not only promote China's trade and investment in the region but also help improve Pakistan's fledgling economy.

Some analysts of Chinese affairs hold the view that China's massive investment in the project has global geopolitical objectives under the One

Belt, One Road (OBOR) initiative. While China perceives Pakistan as being an indispensable partner in realizing its larger economic and strategic goals, Pakistani civil and military leadership, including the media, see the project as a game changer and fate changer. But for China the project has a huge potential to fulfill its grand strategic interests, globally and regionally. In this context, Louis Ritzinger observes that the OBOR initiative "seeks to link China's economic partners in Southeast Asia to Europe by means of overland and maritime trade routes, including key Middle East energy resources and emerging African markets. Pakistan, by virtue of its status as a long-term ally and its geographic position linking western China to sea routes through the Middle East, Africa, and, perhaps most importantly, Europe, could serve as a central crossroads for Beijing's expanding global ambitions."[38]

Be that as it may, the CPEC project might face gargantuan challenges on myriad fronts. First, the political environment in Pakistan is murky and inhospitable. Political leaders hailing from backward and poor provinces like Baluchistan have questioned the feasibility and utility of the project. Regional and ethnic affinities in Pakistan are involved in the success or failure of the project. A common criticism flung at the relevance of the project is that it will mainly bring jobs and prosperity to an already rich and prosperous Punjab province, bypassing the interests of the poor Baluchis. Political leaders in Baluchistan have been protesting that they will not allow their country's resources to be exploited by China or by Pakistan to benefit the Punjab province by changing the route of the corridor project. Second, the Modi government questioned the legality of the project, arguing that over three thousand kilometers of the CPEC passes through the contested territory of PoK that India claims as an integral part of a unified Kashmir. Given this, Pakistan's top military brass is also skeptical about the feasibility of the project and are accusing India's Research and Analysis Wing intelligence agency of attempts to sabotage the project. Third, Prime Minister Modi's raising the issue of human rights violation in Baluchistan and PoK from the rampart of the Red Fort on India's Independence Day on August 15, 2016, produced a strong anti-Pakistan wave in Baluchistan and PoK. Its fallout is negative, unnerving China as to whether the project would be an encumbrance-free enterprise. Last, extremist and jihadi elements are not under the control of Pakistan's civilian administration and pose a serious security threat to the project. To address the seriousness of this challenge, Pakistan has committed to establishing "a 12,000-man security force to protect Chinese workers. . . . An attack on Chinese civilians by militants with links to Pakistan could throw a wrench in diplomatic relations, as it has in the past."[39]

CONCLUSION

From the foregoing discussion, it becomes unambiguously clear that the Sino-Pakistan strategic alliance is fundamentally rooted in their shared objective of weakening and destabilizing India. But interestingly, China has not offered a blanket security guarantee to Pakistan under a treaty obligation to defend Pakistan's territorial sovereignty and integrity against an external threat stemming from India. Rather, China feels embarrassed over Pakistan's overt or covert hand in sponsoring terror attacks on India. Moreover, China is conscious about its image and reputation in India and the United States so far as its nuclear and missile assistance to Pakistan is concerned. On numerous occasions China encountered an unpalatable situation when it had to defend itself against the American onslaught of its violation of Missile Technology Control Regime guidelines. China had to pay a price when America slapped sanctions on it for its alleged transfer of M-11 missiles to Pakistan, an act denied by Chinese leaders.

It needs to be underlined that China's public rhetoric describing its relationship with Pakistan as "sweeter than honey" and higher than "the Himalayan heights" has no substance. China has specific and focused objectives, which include eliciting Pakistani support on dealing with Uighur separatists in the Xinxiang province, on engaging Indian troops to its northwestern borders, and on encircling India through a series of strategic projects, ranging from Gwadar naval base to strategic roads in the PoK region. In addition, Pakistan should no longer expect that China would support it in the UN Security Council on the question of holding plebiscite in the Kashmir valley.

Studies suggests that on numerous occasions in the past China did not intervene on behalf of Pakistan. The Beijing leadership under Mao outright rejected the pleas of US president Richard Nixon and his national security adviser Henry Kissinger to attack India to save Pakistan in the 1971 War. Also, China did not give military aid or diplomatic succor to Pakistan during the Kargil conflict in 1999. Much to Pakistan's chagrin, Chinese leaders outright rejected Pakistan's request for military intervention. Moreover, one cannot brush aside the geopolitical reality that China and India are not only cooperating on regional and global issues but also conducting joint military exercises. But the fulcrum of the Sino-Pakistan relationship is offsetting India's role and influence in South Asia and Afghanistan. Also, China may oblige Pakistan on less important issues such as torpedoing India's membership to the Asia-Pacific Economic Cooperation and the NSG. But China is not likely to support costly proposals of Pakistan to placate it.

There is palpable evidence that there is a paradox in China's foreign policy. Though China is supportive of the UN action against global terror, it observes stoic silence over the Pakistan-sponsored terrorism against India. Thus, China's double standards on terrorism have besmirched its image as a responsible stakeholder. Similarly, China's threat of blocking the waters of the Brahmaputra River has caused ripples in Sino-Indian relations. This Chinese move coincides with the Modi government's attempt to review the Indus Waters Treaty with Pakistan as a retaliatory measure following the killing of eighteen Indian soldiers by Pakistani terrorists at the Uri sector in J&K in September 2016. The aforementioned instances provide tangible evidence that China's retributive actions against India are carried out on behalf of Pakistan, driven by its myopic strategic motivation to offset India's influence in the region in tandem with Pakistan.

However, as a hard-core pragmatist, President Xi will not risk putting Sino-Indian relations on the back burner. Given the current security and strategic environment at global and regional levels, China is not interested in forging a tacit military alliance with Pakistan in the American pattern. Yet India needs to be wary of Chinese designs in South Asia, primarily focused on its strategic containment, whether directly or through a network of China's friendship with Pakistan, Bangladesh, Nepal, and Sri Lanka. But China's soft power approach to Pakistan has no meaning since their friendship is already firm and stable. More important, China's core concerns will be to save Pakistan from becoming a failed state, which will not be in China's interest, and to foster and fulfill its strategic ambitions and goals in the region.

NOTES

1. Jamal Afridi and Jayshree Bajoria, "China-Pakistan Relations," Council on Foreign Relations, July 6, 2010, http://www.cfr.org/china/china-pakistan-relations/p10070.

2. Jonah Blank, "Thank You for Being a Friend: Pakistan and China's Almost Alliance," *Foreign Affairs*, October 15, 2015,https://www.foreignaffairs.com/articles/china/2015-10-15/thank-you-being-friend.

3. Bruce Riedel, "One Year of Modi Government: Us versus Them," Brookings Institution, May 25, 2015, https://www.brookings.edu/opinions/one-year-of-modi-government-us-versus-them/.

4. "Pakistan Trip Like Visiting Home of Own Brother: Xi Jinping," *India Today*, April 19, 2015, http://indiatoday.intoday.in/story/xi-jinping-says-pakistan-trip-like-visiting-home-of-own-brother/1/431023.html.

5. Ishaan Tharoor, "What China's and Pakistan's Special Friendship Means," *Washington Post*, April 21, 2015, https://www.washingtonpost.com/news/worldviews/wp/2015/04/21/what-china-and-pakistans-special-friendship-means/.

6. Ibid.

7. Press Trust of India, "Pentagon Blocks $300 Mn Military Aid to Pakistan," *Business Standard*, August 4, 2016, http://www.business-standard.com/article/international/pentagon-blocks-300-mn-military-aid-to-pakistan-116080400227_1.html.

8. "China and Pakistan: Geopolitical Friends," *Economist*, January 24, 2015, http://www.economist.com/news/books-and-arts/21640297-casting-light-little-known-friendship-geopolitical-friends.

9. "China Rejects India's Objections over $46 Billion Economic Corridor: Nawaz Sharif," *Economic Times*, June 2, 2015, http://economictimes.indiatimes.com/articleshow/47514772.cms?utm_source=contentofinterest&utm_medium=text&utm_campaign=cppst.

10. See "Karakorum Conundrum," *Week in China*, February 6, 2015, http://www.weekinchina.com/2015/02/the-karakoram-conundrum/.

11. Associated Press of Pakistan, "Pakistan Says Will Help China Fight Xinjiang Militants," *Dawn*, November 8, 2014, http://www.dawn.com/news/1143134.

12. Ibid.

13. Smriti Kak Ramachandran, "China Blocks Bid for U.N. Action on Pak. over Lakhvi," *Hindu*, June 24, 2015, http://www.thehindu.com/news/national/china-blocks-bid-for-un-action-on-pak-over-lakhvi/article7347637.ece.

14. Lisa Curtis, "China's Military and Security Relationship with Pakistan," Testimony before the U.S.-China Economic and Security Review Commission, Heritage Foundation, May 20, 2009, http://www.heritage.org/research/testimony/chinas-military-and-security-relation-ship-with-pakistan.

15. Manjit Singh, "Pakistan-Occupied Kashmir—a 'Buffer State' in the Making," *Strategic Analysis* 37, no. 1 (January–February 2013): 1–7.

16. See Jingdong Yuan, "China's Kashmir Policy," *China Brief* 5, no. 19, Jamestown Foundation, http://www.jamestown.org/single/?tx_ttnews%5Btt_news%5D=3893#.VdCLvLKqqko.

17. Ishaan Tharoor, "What China's and Pakistan's Special Friendship Means," *Washington Post*, April 21, 2015, www.washingtonpost.com/news/worldviews/wp/2015/04/21/what-china-and-pakistans-special-friendship-means/.

18. Ibid.

19. Michael Beckley, "China and Pakistan: Fair Weather Friends," *Yale Journal of International Affairs* (March 2012): 1–22, http://yalejournal.org/wp-content/uploads/2012/04/Article-Michael-Beckley.pdf.

20. SyedFazl-e-Haider, "Pakistan and China Prove Powerful Combination in Aviation," *National*, November 25, 2013, http://www.thenational.ae/business/industry-insights/aviation/pakistan-and-china-prove-powerful-combination-in-aviation.

21. R. Jeffrey Smith and Joby Warrick, "Pakistani Nuclear Scientist's Accounts Tell of Chinese Proliferation," *Washington Post*, November 13, 2009, http://www.washingtonpost.com/wp-dyn/content/article/2009/11/12/AR2009111211060.html.

22. R. Jeffrey Smith and Joby Warrick, "Pakistani Nuclear Scientist's Accounts Tell of Chinese Proliferation," *Washington Post*, November 13, 2009, http://www.washingtonpost.com/wp-dyn/content/article/2009/11/12/AR2009111211060.html.

23. Rohan Joshi, "China, Pakistan, and Nuclear Non-Proliferation," *Diplomat*, February 16, 2015, http://thediplomat.com/2015/02/china-pakistan-and-nuclear-non-proliferation/.

24. Ibid.

25. Ibid.

26. Ibid. See also Jonah Blank, "Thank You."

27. "China and Pakistan: Geopolitical Friends."

28. Curtis, "China's Relationship with Pakistan."

29. Blank, "Thank You."

30. Ibid.

31. Diwakar, " China Showing 'Flexibility' on Border Talks with India," *Times of India*, September 29, 2008, http://timesofindia.indiatimes.com/india/China-showing-flexibility-on-border-talks-with-India/articleshow/3537865.cms.

32. Beckley, "China and Pakistan: Fair-Weather Friends," 30.

33. Wajahat S. Khan, "With China, for China," *India Today*, July 10, 2015, http://indiatoday.intoday.in/story/china-investments-in-pakistan-xi-jinping-modi/1/450425.html.

34. Elizabeth Roche, "India Bids to Expand Strategic Footprint in Afghanistan," *Live Mint*, May 2, 2012, http://www.livemint.com/Politics/JTMMoLAFnmVCL6hxMhTMNK/India-bids-to-expand-strategic-footprint-in-Afghanistan.html.

35. Louis Ritzinger, "The China-Pakistan Economic Corridor, Regional Dynamics and China's Geopolitical Ambitions," National Bureau of Asian Research, August 5, 2015, http://www.nbr.org/research/activity.aspx?id=589.

36. "Nawaz's China Visit," *Dawn*, July 30, 2013, http://www.dawn.com/news/1032950.

37. G. Parthasarathy, "India Must Counter China's Aid Games," *Hindu Business Line*, November 2, 2016, http://www.thehindubusinessline.com/opinion/columns/g-parthasarathy/india-must-counter-chinas-aid-games/article9296515.ece.

38. Ritzinger, "China-Pakistan Economic Corridor."

39. Ibid.

Chapter Four

China and the Himalayan States

Forging a New Strategic Understanding

Nepal and Bhutan, situated in the heart of the Himalayas, have emerged over the past decade as a fulcrum of the geopolitical and geostrategic contest between China and India. Sandwiched between the two Asian giants, Kathmandu and Thimpu are faced with a real challenge of maintaining equidistance in their relationship with Beijing and New Delhi. It may be recalled that China's military takeover of Tibet in 1951 created not only a fear psychosis within the ruling circles of Nepal and Bhutan but also misgivings about India's military capability to safeguard their independence and sovereignty vis-à-vis China's overwhelming military prowess. This was one of the overriding reasons that Nepal and Bhutan preferred to maintain neutral in the 1962 Sino-Indian War rather than coming out openly to India's support, morally and diplomatically.

In the twenty-first century, geostrategic atmospheres have vastly altered in the Indian subcontinent, with rapid political and economic development at global and regional levels. First, India and China are coming closer to each other than ever before in every domain of their relationship, including defense and security. This is manifest first from their holding joint military exercises, unthinkable during the Cold War era. Second, the dependency of Nepal and Bhutan on India in foreign, economic, and defense realms has been reduced in large measure. Rather, they are virtually independent and autonomous in conducting relations with China, without India's direct intervention. Bhutan, for example, has held nearly two dozen border talks with China without Indian intervention, even though Thimpu has not yet officially established its diplomatic relations with Beijing. In the past couple of years, the Bhutanese government has been throwing hints to Beijing leadership that it was serious about establishing full diplomatic ties with China. What will be the implications for India? How will India's security interests be jeopardized following the conclusion of the China-Bhutan border treaty? How will a Sino-Bhutanese strategic partnership impact manifold ties between New Delhi and Thimpu? A modest attempt has been made to find answers to these questions in subsequent sections. One thing is still mired in confusion and uncertainty: India's precise policy response to an increasing politically rapprochement between Beijing and Thimpu.

CHINA-NEPAL TIES

China-Nepal relations began on a positive note with the changing political dynamics in Nepal when a Maoist government led by Pushpa Kamal Dahal came to power in August 2008. He publicly pronounced that his government's priority would be to keep equidistant relationships with China and India, which in effect meant that Nepal did not subscribe to the past policy of unilaterally tilting toward India. It may sound palatable that the Maoist government pronounced an evenhanded policy toward China and India. But given its ideological proximity with Communist China, a major policy shift occurred during Dahal's political dispensation. Deviating from the old tradition of visiting India first on the state visit abroad, Prime Minister Dahal headed for his first official trip to China in August 2008. He was accorded red carpet treatment by the party's top cadre. As expected, China pledged to provide economic aid and humanitarian assistance on a massive scale to help rebuild Nepal's ravaged economy as a result of over a decade of Maoist insurgency.

The Nepalese perceive Chinese aid as indispensable for improving its poor infrastructure, while China calculated that its economic aid might act as a catalyst in lessening Nepalese dependence on India. Naturally, New Delhi was seriously alarmed at China's growing political rapprochement with the Maoist government. It also sparked speculation in New Delhi's power corridor that China was firm on weaning Nepal away from Indian influence.

Before evaluating China's soft power tools to cultivate Nepal, it will be a useful exercise to give a succinct overview of the trajectory of China-Nepal relations since the establishment of their diplomatic relations in 1955.

Soon after establishing diplomatic ties, in 1956 China and Nepal signed a historic treaty that replaced the old Treaty of Thapathali. Under the 1956 treaty, Nepal accepted Tibet as an integral part of China. In this context it is important to underline that China managed to make Nepal agree to abrogate its legal claim over Tibet under the 1856 Treaty of Thapathal. The *Tibetan Political Review* writes that "nothing can erase the documented fact that Nepal once recognized Tibet as an independent state at the United Nations in front of the global stage. The Nepalese people should not be bullied into denying their own national history."[1]

The *Tibetan Political Review* further mentions that under Article 3 of the 1956 treaty, "All treaties and documents which existed in the past between China and Nepal including those between the Tibet Region of China and Nepal are hereby abrogated. . . . This provision was an attempt by China to cover its legal bases by getting Nepal to annul its prior treaty commitments with Tibet, including the defense obligation of the 1856 Nepal-Tibet treaty. As a practical and political matter, this cover-up worked. Subsequent Nepalese governments have restated their position that Tibet is part of the PRC."[2] In realpolitik terms, Nepal has had no other option than to accept Chinese sovereignty over Tibet under the 1960 Treaty of Peace and Friendship in the face of China's overwhelming material and military resources. Even India was unable to offer resistance to the Chinese forces that swiftly occupied Tibet.[3]

Nepal tried to maintain a balanced relationship with China and India, though practically speaking Nepal was much closer to India for a host of factors, including deeply rooted age-old social, cultural, and religious ties with India. At times, the Nepalese king played the "China card" to balance off India. In the 1970s King Birendra put forward the proposal of declaring Nepal a Zone of Peace, much to India's anger and disliking, whereas China was supportive of the proposal. With the introduction of a new democratic constitution in Nepal in 1990, the Maoist rebels used democratic freedom to launch a violent insurgent movement in the country in 1996, with a goal to dethrone the monarchy and replace it with a republican nation. Over thirteen thousand people were killed during the Maoist insurgency. The Maoist insurgency ended in 2006, with the signing of a peace agreement between Maoist rebels and an alliance of seven political parties. Thus, the Maoist movement turned into the people's movement, supported by the Seven Party Alliance (SPA) that demanded the abolition of the unpopular monarchy.

The 12-Point Understanding was reached between the SPA and Maoists who intensified the nationwide protest against the authoritarianism of King Gyanendra, forcing him to abdicate the throne in 2008. With this, a 240-year-old institution of monarchy was abolished, and Nepal became a federal democratic republic. In May 2008 elections to the Constituent Assembly were held in which the Communist Party of Nepal (CPN, Maoists) secured the largest number of seats in the assembly. After intensive political deliberations among various political factions, the CPN could manage to form the government in August 2008 under the leadership of Pushpa Kamal Dahal as the country's new prime minister.

As mentioned before, a major shift in Nepal's policy toward India began occurring. Prime Minister Dahal gave unambiguous signals to India that his government was not bound to toe the Indian line on foreign, defense, and diplomatic affairs. Rather, the new dispensation under his leadership began asserting its independent foreign and defense policy. He openly spoke about redundancy of the 1950 India-Nepal Treaty of Peace and Friendship in the changing political and strategic dynamics of the region. Dahal insisted on scrapping the treaty, questioning its legitimacy in the post–Cold War era. While rejecting his idea of scrapping the treaty, India agreed to review, adjust, and update the 1950 treaty.

NEPAL'S RAPPROCHEMENT WITH CHINA

The dynamics of Nepal's relations with China and India under the Maoist government took a U-turn when India's political and economic influence over Nepal began waning and China's began waxing. Since then China has actively been politically hobnobbing with Nepal. This became manifest from high-level political visits of Chinese leaders to Nepal. And they began taking a keen interest in Nepal's internal affairs. These developments forced India to revaluate its ties with Nepal, especially with the floundering of its two-pillar policy—supporting monarchy and promoting democracy in Nepal. One of the core dilemmas before India's foreign policy establishment is whether it should turn a blind eye to Prime Minister K. P. Sharma Oli's growing overtures of friendship to China or convey India's annoyance over Nepal's increasing strategic proximity to China at the cost of India.

Both China and Nepal perceive mutual benefits in forging deeper ties. For instance, China's engagement with Nepal is driven by its economic, trade, and investment interests to outpace India, which in effect is tantamount to denying India a larger political space in the new Nepal. Nepal's interests are two-fold. First, it wants to ensure a free flow of economic and development assistance from China, indispensable for rejuvenating its tethered economy and rebuilding its shattered infrastructure. Second, Nepal desires to reduce its dependency on India in defense, security, and service sectors. But strategic commentators in India assert that given the geographical proximity, Nepal's dependence on India for an uninterrupted supply of essential goods will continue. Apart from this, Nepal's landlocked status makes it inevitably dependent on India for transit facilities to expand its international trade and commerce.

NEPAL'S' DISTANCING AWAY FROM INDIA?

A surging question arises as to whether an upswing in the Beijing-Kathmandu relationship will scuttle the hitherto deeply entrenched ties between New Delhi and Kathmandu or reduce Nepal's dependence on India to a certain extent. The question is valid for an array of reasons. First, there is a widely held perception among Nepalese people, including its ruling class, that India's bullying tactics bruise their national pride. Second, there is a convergence of short-term interests between China and Nepal ever since China employed soft power tools, for instance, opening up the CI at Kathmandu University, Lalitpur, in October 2007. Third, Nepal has been Tibet's largest trading partner since 2006. To further boost bilateral trade, in October 2015 China reopened its border with Nepal at Jilung, which is scarcely 130 kilometers away from Kathmandu. Jilung's strategic importance can be gauged by the fact that if India ever imposes an economic embargo on Nepal, then the border port at Jilung can be easily used to ensure the supply of essential goods to Nepal.

As reported by the *Economic Times*, "Nepalese politicians have been saying that they will turn to China for supplies. China . . . has been providing substantial aid in recent years and has acquired strategic influence in Nepal countering India's support base."[4] In this context, China and Nepal have signed the Memorandum of Understanding (MoU) in Beijing on October 28, 2015, under which China will supply gasoline to Nepal, ending the monopoly of Indian Oil Corporation for over four decades or so. This will further bring Nepal closer to China.

SETTING UP THE CONFUCIUS INSTITUTE

In pursuit of its soft power diplomacy, China established the Confucius Institute at Kathmandu University (CIKU), in collaboration with China's Hebei University of Economics and Business in 2007, to teach Chinese language and spread Chinese culture by organizing cultural activities and events there. This will not only act as a bridge of friendship between China and Nepal but also enhance mutual understanding between them. Furthermore, it has enabled China to strengthen its strategic hold over Nepal despite India's deep-rooted societal and cultural linkages to Nepal. In order to offset Indian influence over Nepal, China has vigorously embarked on establishing a large number of China Study Centers to promote its culture and civilization values among Nepalese people. Thousands of Nepalese students have been attracted to learning the Chinese language and have engaged in educational exchange programs. Dina Nath Sharma, minister for education, while speaking at the celebration of CIKU's fifth anniversary in June 2013, underlined that such events not only strengthen relations between the two countries but also increase contacts at the people-to-people level. The then prime minister Baburam Bhattarai, in his special message on this occasion, stated that "the institute has been tremendously contributing in promoting cultural relations between our two ancient civilizations."[5]

CHINA'S SILK ROAD PROJECT

In order to resurrect the old Silk Road trading route, President Xi Jinping announced in November 2014 a $40 billion infrastructure development project to facilitate swift connectivity to Asia. According to *Xinhua*, the fund will be utilized for jointly building China's Silk Road Economic Belt and the Twenty-First-Century Maritime Silk Road initiative to build roads, railways, ports, and airports across Central Asia and South Asia. This initiative, according to the National Development and Reform Commission of the PRC, "The connectivity projects of the Initiative will help align and coordinate the development strategies of the countries along the Belt and Road, tap market potential in this region, promote investment and consumption, create demands and job opportunities, enhance people-to-people and cultural exchanges, and mutual learning among the peoples of the relevant countries, and enable them to understand, trust and respect each other and live in harmony, peace and prosperity."[6]

But it is a patent fact that China is not funding infrastructure development for any charity purpose. Rather, it is China's well-planned and well-structured geostrategic roadmap aimed at the expansion of its trade and investment. At the same time, China intends to send out the message to its neighbors that it is very serious about helping victims of poverty and underdevelopment through these projects. China is partly concerned about projecting its image as a benign soft power committed to sharing the burden of others. When India's strategic community expressed apprehension about the One Belt, One Road project, Liu Yunshan, the fifth-ranking member of the powerful Standing Committee of the ruling Communist Party of China, said that projects would benefit all those countries that join them.

As reported in *Business Today*, "New Delhi has objected to the $46 billion China-Pakistan Economic Corridor (CPEC) as it goes though the Pakistan-occupied Kashmir (PoK) but is taking part in the Bangladesh, China, India, Myanmar (BCIM) Economic Corridor."[7]

As regards South Asia, reeling under abject poverty and underdevelopment, this ambitious project might be attractive to the small states of the Indian subcontinent that are gripped with tattered economies and poor infrastructure. The project is also aimed at boosting China's economic growth when it is faced with a growth slump. Moreover, China is today internally riddled with social and economic contradictions, spurring domestic unrest following the failure of the government to lift the rural poor out of economic deprivation and social pangs as well as its inability to control scandals by local Chinese entrepreneurs who are indulged in producing bogus receipts.[8] China's central planners are also looking at ways to fight the global recessionary fallout of its economy and also to ensure its economic revival through a consumption-driven growth model.

CHINA-NEPAL SECURITY COOPERATION: REALITY OR FARCE?

China and Nepal share a 650-mile-long border along the Himalayan region. Recently China set up a consulate office in Pokhara, Nepal. Since the Maoists came to power in Nepal in 2008, China seized the initiative to gain influence in this Himalayan state. In fact, China considers the Communist regime led by Maoists well suited to its ideological and strategic interests. Undoubtedly, India always considered Nepal as its natural sphere of influence. Therefore, Nepal loomed large in India's security architecture. In plain terms, there was a kind of tacit alliance between India and Nepal executed through the 1950 Treaty of Peace and Friendship. But with the changing strategic environment in South Asia, Nepal is asserting its independence and autonomy in foreign policy. Kathmandu has made it clear to New Delhi that it no longer wants to remain an appendage of India. For the last couple of years, Nepal has been putting pressure on India to withdraw its troops from the Kalapani region and dismantle its security posts there. This issue has been at the core of the New Delhi–Kathmandu relationship since 2008. China sought to revive it through backdoor channels by inciting ruling leaders in Nepal to assert its sovereignty over the Kalapani. The underlying motive behind the Chinese strategy is to derive maximum political leverage over India. China does miss an opportunity to corner India on contentious issues India has with Nepal.

In light of this analysis, China has endeavored to reset its security relations with Nepal. According to *Xinhua,* Chinese state councilor and minister of public security Guo Shengkun, in his talks with Nepal's then deputy prime minister Bam Dev Gautam in October 2010, reassured him that China was committed to strengthening security cooperation between the two countries. As reported in *Xinhua,* "Hailing the traditional friendship between the two countries and the smooth cooperation between the ministries, Guo said he hopes the two sides will increase personnel interactions, improve mechanisms of cooperation, and boost practical cooperation on Tibet-related affairs, fight against illegal border crossing and drug trafficking to safeguard security and stability of the two countries as well as the region at large to provide a favorable environment for common development."[9]

From that statement it is explicitly clear that China's strategic masterstroke is to garner Nepalese cooperation on Tibet-related affairs to crush anti-China Tibetan protesters on Nepalese soil. What kind of security cooperation does China expect from Nepal? Is it to obviate India's real or imaginary security threat to Nepal? The answer is no. A large majority of strategic analysts opine that China will remain a real threat to Nepal if it fails to fulfill its wish list. By this logical extension, security cooperation between China and Nepal has neither a distinct policy stance nor a well-defined boundary line. Whatever the strategic scenario, China will want to play an assertive role in South Asian affairs as a regional power broker. This scenario demands that India be extremely cautious and vigilant lest Nepal fall into China's booby traps.

A new window of opportunity has been opened recently to intensify security cooperation between Beijing and Kathmandu. Both governments signed the MoU in Kathmandu in November 2014, worth $1.63 million annually from 2014 to 2018. The Chinese aid will be utilized to develop fifteen border districts in Nepal bordering China's Tibet Autonomous Region. Undoubtedly, China's core interest is to construct a security architecture of its vision with Nepalese support. In Nepalese perception also, China's increasing role in Nepal's security affairs will help reduce its security and strategic dependence on India, though no appropriate mechanism has been worked out so far. But for India it is certainly a matter of serious concern that China, under the guise of developing Nepalese border districts, intends to stabilize its strategic presence in Nepal, antithetical to India's security interests. This is likely to sharpen the geopolitical rivalry between China and India. Moreover, for India the dilemma is how to create a peaceful and stable security architecture in the Himalayan region without antagonizing China. At the same time, India should no longer give the illusion that it enjoys leverage over Nepal and Bhutan to dictate its decisions to them.

MILITARY COOPERATION

Military cooperation between China and Nepal has expanded in the form of military exchange programs, supply of hardware, and army training. China's military assistance to Nepal has witnessed an upswing since the Maoist government was installed in August 2008. In September 2008 China pledged military aid worth $1.3 million to train the Nepalese Army. By providing military assistance, China is engaged in upending the strategic environment in South Asia by cutting to size India's strategic space and influence in the region.

Nepalese Army chief Gen. Gaurav Shumsher Rana undertook a ten-day official trip to China in July 2013. China pledged military aid worth $8 million, mainly for border security

to prevent immigrants from entering Nepal. China also agreed to set up two mobile hospitals for the Nepalese Army. General Rana's visit produced positive momentum in China-Nepal military ties. But this should not be construed that Nepal's military ties with India would be adversely affected. Rana made it unambiguously clear during his visit to India in October 2013 that Nepal would stick to its policy of nonalignment. He eulogized the military capabilities of Indian armed forces in giving a strong response to China if the latter ever dared attack India. He discounted any possibility of Sino-

Indian conflict. In an interview given to the *Times of India,* General Rana said, "China is too pre-occupied with the Tibetan issue. And, then there is [the] Xinjiang region facing the separatist movement. The PLA cannot afford to enter India, or for that matter Nepal. Whether it's the mighty Himalayas or the Indo-Gangetic plains, they have no reasons to make incursions into India. There are no provocations."[10]

As reported by *Xinhua* in October2014, Chinese security chief Meng Jianzhu vowed to "crack down on transnational crimes" when he met with Nepal's deputy prime minister and home minister Bam Dev Gautam. Meng, head of the Commission for Political and Legal Affairs of the Communist Party of China Central Committee, "expressed hope that law-enforcement bodies of the two countries will improve their coordination mechanism and expand cooperation in a bid to jointly safeguard security and stability in the region."[11]

Guo Shengkun held diplomatic parleys with Gautam in October 2014, and pledged to "boost security cooperation" between the two countries.

CHINA'S ECONOMIC ENGAGEMENT WITH NEPAL

As an integral component of China's soft power instruments, economic engagement with Nepal has received top priority in China's Nepal policy. The Beijing leadership has embarked on a policy of economic engagement through development assistance and investment in Nepal. To reap strategic dividends, China has quickly responded to the urgency of development aid that has not been forthcoming from multilateral financial institutions like the World Bank and IMF or from giant donor nations. China's role as a leading player in infrastructure development in Nepal, acutely suffering from paucity of resources, has created a positive image of China among Nepalese ruling leaders, academia, and media. At the same time Nepal's policy is to strengthen its economic ties with both China and India in order to take the benefit of their economic aid for developing poor roads and railway networks.

So far as export of Chinese goods to Nepal is concerned, it is done mainly through a sea route via India. Its inland trade with China is conducted through the Khasa-Tatopani border point, covering 25 percent of Nepal's total trade with China. When Nepal was faced with an unofficial Indian economic blockade, Nepal required more trade routes to ensure a supply of essential commodities from China. But due to logistical inroads, China could not prove to be a feasible alternative to fulfill Nepal's essential requirements. The difficult terrain and geographical distance also make it extremely problematic for China to supply essential commodities like petrol, diesel, kerosene, edible oils, food, and medicines to cater to the needs of Nepalese people. At the same time, China has agreed to provide duty-free market access facility to Nepal for its over eight thousand goods. [12]

China is deeply engaged in making heavy investments in Nepal as a tool of its foreign aid to win over the recipient country. It pledged aid worth $35.48 million to Nepal in 2010–2011—a quantum jump from the $140,000 it had offered to Nepal in 2005–2006.

Nepalese prime minister Oli paid a seven-day official visit to China beginning March 20, 2016. His visit raised high hopes in both countries to boost mutual ties between them. It ought to be remembered that the Panchsheel Treaty of 1955 between Nepal and China forms a central basis of their bilateral relationship, based on mutual respect for each other's territorial integrity and sovereignty and noninterference in each other's internal affairs. Oli's main agenda has been economic development of Nepal ever since it was hit by an earthquake in April 2015. It is also important to underline that Nepal has open borders with India on three sides and has, therefore, been dependent on India for a large part of its trade and commerce. Nepal has two dozen transit points with India, whereas it has two open trade points with China, which makes it difficult to free itself from Indian domination. Therefore, Nepal needs more transit points with China and for that a transit and transportation agreement between the two countries is important. Today, Nepal has the facility of only the Kolkata port for its trade with another country. If this agreement is clinched, India's seaport monopoly will end to a great extent. But China will need to ensure that Nepal has sufficient defense capabilities to secure its interest vis-à-vis Tibetan refugees living in Nepal. Nepal shares 1,400 kilometers with Tibet, while China is engaged in connecting Nepal to the One Belt, One Road initiative through the Shigatse Railway Service. [13]

When asked why Nepal failed to establish stronger ties with China so far, Tanka Karki, a former Nepalese ambassador to China replied, "We kept staying away from China in the name of democracy; and we kept a distance from India in the name of nationalism. That was wrong. Countries in today's time are driven by their economic and development needs, not ideology, when they plan their foreign policy. But Nepal always gave its ideologies— democracy and nationalism—undue importance. This needs to change. Our geostrategic location is complicated but we need to maintain cordial relations with both our neighbours and work for our advantage without pitting one against the other." [14]

EXILED TIBETAN COMMUNITY IN NEPAL

Nearly twenty thousand exiled Tibetans have been living in Nepal for decades. The Chinese government has stepped up its efforts to prevent the exodus of Tibetans into Nepal with a close cooperation of law enforcement agencies of the two countries. It may be recalled that with the installation of the Maoist government in Nepal, Kathmandu signed several security and intelligence-sharing agreements with China. At the behest of China, Nepalese police have indulged in using excessive force to arbitrarily detain and torture people in the Tibetan community. For the Chinese fear that anti-China protests by Tibetans living in Nepal may flare up tension in Tibet. Quite often China has put mounting pressure on the Nepalese government to deal with Tibetan refugees with an iron-handed policy if they carry anti-China flags and chant anti-China slogans. Nepalese law enforcing authorities put restrictions on the Tibetan community to celebrate the seventy-sixth birthday of the Dalai Lama in July 2011. Besides this, Tibetans have no freedom to offer prayers on the streets. According to the Human Rights Watch Report "Under China's Shadow: Mistreatment of Tibetans in Nepal," "Tibetan refugee communities in Nepal are now facing a de facto ban on political protests, sharp restrictions on public activities promoting Tibetan culture and religion, and routine abuses by Nepali security forces. These include excessive use of force, arbitrary detention, ill-treatment in detention, threats and intimidation, intrusive surveillance, and arbitrary application of vaguely formulated and overly broad definitions of security offences."[15] These repressive measures for political purposes do not properly fit into China's soft power approach.

INDIAN DISAFFECTION

Anti-India geopsychological impulses flared up in Nepal following India's unofficial blockade of goods in the country. This Indian move was aimed at sympathizing with the Madhesi ethnic group of the Terai region, who were clamoring for an amendment in the newly promulgated constitution in September 2015 to accommodate their political demands. The blockade on the borders caused a severe shortage of fuel and other essential goods and services in the country. More than 1,100 tankers carrying essential commodities were stranded across the Sunauli border. As reported by the *Nepal Times*, "Madhesi parties, unsatisfied with the new constitution, have been blocking the Nepal-India border by staging sit-ins at various points for the last two weeks. And India has not allowed the supply of essential commodities citing the political unrest in Nepal's plains area."[16]

India wanted Nepal to postpone promulgation of the new constitution until a broad-based agreement was arrived at with the Madhesi group to address their legitimate political concerns over delimitation of constituencies. India was in favor of granting more rights to marginalized ethnic groups. But Indian advice was not heeded by the Nepalese government.

As mentioned earlier, India-Nepal relations reached their the lowest ebb on the question of India's economic embargo, termed a "catastrophic episode" in the history of India-Nepal relations. Public opinion and the political environment in Nepal turned deeply hostile to India. The growing anti-India environment in Nepal naturally brought Kathmandu closer to Beijing. One political commentator, Madan Dahal, writes, "The protracted India's economic impasse imposed against Nepal, the third in a series during the last forty five years is not only an inhuman, immoral and censurable action but also the unilateral declaration of strategic war against a neighbouring landlocked country with age-old ties resulting in untold misery and sufferings in a sacred land—the birth place of Lord Buddha."[17]

It may be recalled that during the past decade or so, a vast geopolitical transformation has taken place in the region. Nepal has emerged as a new focal point in the India-China rivalry. China's strategy is not to miss out on an opportunity to trigger differences between New Delhi and Kathmandu through its proactive commercial diplomacy to achieve its strategic objectives in South Asia. China has considerably succeeded in limiting the Indian role in the Himalayan region through its economic aid diplomacy.[18]

Furthermore, the Beijing leadership's political gambit is to exploit India's naive handling of domestic politics in Nepal. It should be recalled that Indian diplomacy had a serious setback when Nepalese parliament elected Khadga Prasad Oli as the new prime minister, much to India's chagrin and disapproval. Without mincing any words, New Delhi's protracted efforts failed to ensure Oli's exit from the prime ministerial race. Undoubtedly, New Delhi was fully aware of Oli's strong nationalistic credentials as well as his political leaning toward China. But in Nepalese circles, Oli's election was viewed as the victory of the people who felt deeply humiliated by India's economic blockade. The common perception among the government and people of Nepal is that India is part of problem, deeply involved in interfering with its domestic politics. Their deep-seated agony and anger over their belief that Nepal has been shabbily treated by India as its protectorate, making it forcibly dependent on India's senseless whims of heartless fanatics in New Delhi. Thus, anti-India geopsychology clearly reverberates in Nepalese hearts and minds.

However, Oli reiterated that his government's priority would be to normalize relations with India. His government reassured New Delhi that it would make the best efforts to rebalance its relations with two powerful neighbors—China and India. Nevertheless, New Delhi perceived Oli as being much closer to China than India. His public utterances amply reflected his priority to respect Nepalese people's pride and wishes in mind while conducting Nepal's relations with Beijing and New Delhi. In this context, M. K. Bhadrakumar observes:

Beijing looks forward with optimism that the new political dispensation under the leadership of Khadga Prashad Oli as Nepal's new prime minister augurs well for an intensification of the bilateral cooperation. It is a fresh beginning insofar as Nepal is returning to constitutional rule. . . . First and foremost, Beijing knows it can depend on Oli to do everything possible to ensure that Nepal's territory is not used by Tibetan exiles in India to infiltrate the Chinese region and destabilize it. . . . To be sure, Oli's top priority will still be to mend fences with India, because in the ultimate analysis Nepal, a landlocked country, cannot do without India's goodwill and will be sensitive to India's vital interests and concerns. Suffice it to say, it is far from the case that China fails to understand India's special interests in Nepal.[19]

Bhadrakumar further notes, "China's comfort level with Oli's leadership becomes self-evident—the quiet confidence that China can hope to enjoy a level playing field in Kathmandu, thanks to the staunchly nationalistic leadership of Oli, which will not countenance Indian attempts to dictate to him his government's China policies. . . . Paradoxically, the Modi government unwittingly created a dream wicket in Kathmandu for Chinese diplomacy. It can do with some serious introspection as to the root causes why this situation came about."[20]

Though India lifted the blockade on October 3, 2015, it sparked fresh anti-India protests throughout Nepal, refreshing the bitter memories of the 1989 crisis when India had refused to renew the Trade and Transit Treaty. At that time also, China had derived a full political advantage from India's mishandling of the situation. India's bizarre diplomacy was exposed when it unnecessarily antagonized Nepal by refusing to renew the treaty simply on the untenable ground that Nepal had imported military arms and equipment from China in the 1980s.

The Modi government, however, tried to inject new energy into India's relations with Nepal when he went to Kathmandu in August 2014. During this visit, three MoUs were signed, including one on a 5,600-megawatt hydropower project on Mahakali River. He also pledged $1 billion for reconstruction after the devastating earthquake that hit Nepal in April 2015. While treading on the line of the United Progressive Alliance government, the Modi government also promised to revise the 1950 Treaty of Peace and Friendship. A group of eminent representatives from both countries has already been set up to reexamine the controversial clauses in the 1950 Treaty. It is yet to be seen when and to what extent the treaty will be revised and reviewed or if it will keep national interests of both countries intact.

The Modi government is called on to redefine India's relations with Nepal. There is strong pro-China sentiment in Nepal. During a book launch in Kathmandu on January 24, 2016, deputy prime minister and foreign minister Kemal Thapa said, "[the] Nepal-China relation is time-tested and multi-dimensional with strong cooperation in economic, political and social fields.

We are grateful with China for helping Nepal in socio-economic development."[21] Nepal's former prime minister Kirtinidhi Bista expressed a similar sentiment during the book release ceremony. He said, "China has remained our non-interfering and generous neighbour. I stress that Nepal must work toward enhancing the bilateral relationship into a new high so as to achieving benefits through rapid progress and economic development of northern neighbour China."[22]

The Modi government in New Delhi also needs to read between the lines of China's offer to start a transit treaty with Nepal. India might take cudgels against China's new transit treaty signed with Nepal during Oli's visit to China in March 2016. The reality is that most of Nepal's third-country trade will continue to be conducted through India. However the treaty has long-term implications for India in political and strategic terms. First, the treaty has brought China and Nepal much closer than ever before. Second, there is a symbolic value of the treaty that China is a reliable friend of Nepal. Third, the treaty confers much psychological confidence onto Nepal. Finally, the Nepalese people feel much obliged to China that it always comes forward to bail out Nepal in catastrophic situations. Moreover, political commentators perceive the Treaty as a big diplomatic jolt to India. Biswas Baral, a journalist from Nepal, writes, "Oli signed a number of bilateral agreements, most notably one on transit facilities through China, thereby ending India's monopoly over Nepal's third-country trade. This is being seen in Kathmandu as meaningful as the common perception thus far was that given Nepal's precarious geopolitical position, it had no option but to rely on India—its unpredictable 'big brother' next-door."[23]

Apart from the transit treaty, China and Nepal have signed a number of agreements: "China has agreed to upgrade two road links between Nepal and Tibet, pledged financial support to build an international airport at the tourist hub of Pokhara, agreed to extend the Chinese railway to Kathmandu and then to Lumbini, and given its nod to a long-term commercial oil deal. Up until now Nepal has imported all its fuel from India."[24] Transit facilities offered by China will surely help boost Nepal's trade with China and other countries. But this does not mean its dependence on India for transit facilities will end. The new government under Prime Minister Dahal will tread on the path with foresightedness to maintain equidistance in Nepal's relations with China and India. But Nepalese diplomacy under the leadership of Dahal since August 2016 will be driven by playing its China card against India, although with extreme caution and pragmatism.

CHINA'S RELIEF AID TO NEPAL: IS IT A
SOFT POWER APPROACH?

China provided massive relief aid to Nepal following an unprecedented earthquake there in April 2015. According to the *Xinhua* news agency, China dispatched "a total of 1,088 military personnel and members of armed police forces to help with disaster relief in Nepal . . . the biggest group the People's Liberation Army (PLA) and armed police forces have sent to foreign soil for humanitarian aid missions since New China was founded in 1949. . . . The PLA Air Force had deployed eight transport planes to carry a total of 416 tonnes of relief supplies to Nepal."[25]

Commentators did raise the question whether such massive aid has had any hidden political agenda. It would be naive to call it purely a hidden agenda since it is the well-established practice in international relations that neighbors quite often offer relief aid to mitigate the burden from natural calamities. But the way the Chinese government took a special interest, moving swiftly to ensure disaster assistance worth $3.3 million—three times that of the United States—it was assumed that China considered Nepal a part of the New Silk Road project to connect Asia with Europe. Apart from this, the Nepalese government has been quelling anti-China protests by Tibetan refugees living in Nepal.[26]

The other view is that Nepal felt much obliged to India's swifter and quicker relief aid to the earthquake victims, compared to that of China. Walter Andersen, director of the South Asia Studies program at the John Hopkins University, said, "Prime minister Modi has taken a much more public call for assistance than his Chinese counterpart in part because India has a much closer relationship. My guess is that India's generosity will have a positive impact on Nepali views regarding India and may make it easier to work out the problems that have delayed projects."[27]

CHINA AND BHUTAN

Bhutan is a landlocked Himalayan state sandwiched between two Asian giants—China and India. China and Bhutan share 470 kilometers of border, proximate to the Siliguri corridor (known as the chicken's neck) in the state of West Bengal, that connects India's northeastern states with the rest of the country. It serves as a "buffer having a strategic importance to the Siliguri corridor. . . . The corridor is considered a vulnerable bottleneck for India's national security. Delhi worries that China will send troops to the corridor if a China-Indian military clash breaks out."[28]

The annexation of Tibet by China in 1951 sounded a warning to Bhutan that its independence and sovereignty might be in jeopardy. The situation turned alarming when China's cross-border incursions became quite frequent. Bhutan, being a tiny Himalayan kingdom in size and resources, has had to depend on India. In China's perception, Indian influence over Bhutan is a stumbling block in resolving the Bhutan boundary dispute, whose certain parts of traditional borders between China and Bhutan were shown in Chinese maps as part of China. Over the past several decades, China has reiterated that it desires a "fair and reasonable" boundary agreement with Bhutan, though it is not precisely defined what those reasonable parameters are. Nevertheless, the Four Cardinal Principles of 1988 and 1996 are often invoked as the main basis of resolving the boundary dispute to maintain peace and tranquility on the borders.

China's foreign policy toward its periphery countries is mainly guided by the principle of benign softness to win over their goodwill. This is equally true of Bhutan, which forms one of five fingers of China's palm theory. The palm theory, sponsored by Mao, has been notorious in two respects. First, through this doctrine, China attempted to provoke its neighbors into accepting Chinese terms and conditions on artificially generated border disputes. Second, under this theory, China lay its historical claims over neighboring territories. This became crystal clear when the PRC rushed its forces into Tibet in 1950 and occupied it under its palm theory. India was then neither in a position to deter Chinese threat nor possessed military capabilities to push Chinese forces back from Tibet. This emboldened China's Communist leaders to frighten Bhutan. Being geographically contiguous to Bhutan, over six thousand Tibetans fled to Bhutan. They were granted political asylum by the Bhutanese monarchy.

The royal government of Bhutan, having sensed the Chinese threat to its territorial integrity, became closer to India and virtually became dependent on India for its internal and external security. When Bhutan became a member of the UN in 1971, it began articulating its independent policy, even though Bhutan remained completely dependent on India for its economic development, as India contributed 25 percent of financial resources to Bhutan's Five-Year Plan. It should be recalled that Bhutan's first two Five-Year Plans were 100 percent financed by India. Thus, India and Bhutan enjoyed very warm and cordial relations. Bhutan was the only country in South Asia that sided with India to abstain from voting on the Comprehensive Test Ban Treaty at the UN General Assembly in September 1998.

Since Bhutan was under British suzerainty during British imperialism in the Indian subcontinent, China had no legal claims over Bhutanese territory. However, China felt offended when Bhutan sided with Britain in the latter's war with Tibet. After the withdrawal of the British Empire from the subcontinent, Bhutan's relations with China began deteriorating over their shared borders of 470 kilometers. Bhutan's borders with China were never officially demarcated. Hence, Chinese forces took the advantage of undefined borders with Bhutan and began making intrusions into Bhutanese territory. Bhutan was worried whether India would be able to defend its borders against China's impending threat. This question still looms large in the Bhutanese psyche. So far twenty-four rounds of border talks have taken place between China and Bhutan until 2016. Though no definite time frame can be set to settle the border dispute, differences over it have been minimized following the report of the Joint Technical Field Survey. The report of the team was endorsed during the twenty-second round of border talks. In this regard, Bhutanese foreign minister Damcho Dorji stated before the National Council in November 2016, "We cannot say that the problem is from their side or from our side. But our intention is to reduce the differences in claims as far as possible."[29]

At a historic meeting between Chinese premier Wen Jiabao and his Bhutanese counterpart L. J. Y. Thinley on the sidelines of the Rio+20 Summit in Rio de Janeiro on June 21, 2012, Wen raised the issue of border demarcation with Thinley and also broached the idea that China was willing to forge diplomatic relations with Bhutan on the basis of five principles of peaceful coexistence, known as Panchsheel. It should be remembered that Bhutan is the only country in South Asia that does not have diplomatic relations with China. But with the ceasing of the protectorate status of Bhutan in 2007, Bhutan is free to pursue an independent foreign policy, although still with certain reservations about sensitive issues like the border settlement with China.

Bhutan, being dependent on India for border maps and also its economic development, remains warily sensitive about India's security concerns and interest vis-à-vis China. Thimpu would not undertake a strategic move to settle the border dispute with China without taking India into confidence. While recognizing Bhutan's strategic value, China deploys its soft power resources to win it over rather than to bully or coerce it into concluding the border agreement on Chinese terms and conditions.[30]

In order to take the border settlement issue forward, Chinese vice foreign minister Fu Ying, leading an eight-member delegation, arrived in Thimpu in August 2012 to hold the twentieth round of boundary talks with Bhutan. Fu eulogized Bhutan's development model of gross national happiness (GNH) and said that this model is admired in China and was becoming popular—part of a soft power diplomacy to admire others' achievements and models of development to win favor and become acceptable.

CHINA-BHUTAN BORDER TALKS

Since the early 1980s China and Bhutan have been holding border talks to reduce tension and maintain tranquility on the borders. At the twenty-fourth round of boundary talks, in 2016, both sides emphasized reducing differences on the dispute inherited from long traditional claims. As mentioned before, both sides conducted the Joint Technical Field Survey of Bayul Pasamlung in September 2013.The first round of the Expert Group Meeting was held in Thimpu in October 2014. At the twenty-second boundary talks, held in Beijing in July 2014, China conveyed its clear-cut message to Bhutan's then foreign minister, Rinzin Dorji, that Beijing was in favor of reaching "a fair, reasonable solution" to the border settlement, acceptable to both sides. Moreover, China expressed a sense of optimism that an early settlement would push their bilateral relations to new heights. The second round of the Expert Group Meeting was held in Beijing in March 2015. And soon thereafter, the twenty-third round of talks was held in August 2015 in Thimpu between Bhutan's foreign minister Damcho Dorji and China's foreign affairs vice minister, Liu Zhenmin. But the talks remained inclusive. At the twenty-fourth round of boundary talks, held in Beijing in August 2016, Dorji and Chinese vice president Li Yuan expressed the hope to establish diplomatic relations between the two countries once the border dispute is amicably settled at an early date.

Interestingly, Bhutan, a tiny country with a population of over seven hundred thousand, has no air force. It is dependent on India and Nepal for helicopters. According the *Diplomat*:

> The checkpoints are near a region of Bhutan that Beijing says is its territory, in addition to the claims it has made on Bhutan's northern border. Bhutanese soldiers report that their usual task on the frontier is to intercept smugglers, but that the Chinese military sometimes crosses into Bhutanese territory via roads China has recently built all the way to the western Bhutanese border. . . . From the disputed western China-Bhutan border, China could easily strike India's geographic "chicken neck"—a narrow band of land, the Siliguri Corridor, that connects the main body of India with its northeastern states, home to 45 million people. [31]

Bhutan is strategically vulnerable to China. India's army chief visited Bhutan in November 2014. A two-day state visit to Bhutan by President Pranab Mukherjee on November 7, 2014, was a historic one since he was the first Indian president to visit Bhutan in twenty-six years. President Mukherjee made it clear that his visit had nothing to do with China-Bhutan boundary talks. He, however, pointed out that "India-Bhutan relations stand on their own with great potential for us to scale new heights in the future." [32]

After the president held talks with King Jigme Khesar Namgyel Wangchuck, the then Indian foreign secretary Sujatha Singh was asked whether India was worried over China-Bhutan border talks. She replied, "If you have a border with a country, it is logical that you will have border talks. We also have a border with China and we also have border talks with China. Bhutan is a sovereign and independent country under the very wise leadership of its monarchy and its government. We have absolutely no doubt that Bhutan will deal with this issue in a manner that is in the best interest of both Bhutan and India."[33]

Singh did not disclose this fact that Indian national security advisers and top bureaucrats from the south block in New Delhi had been advising the Bhutanese government on how to handle border talks with China and take the benefit of India's experience with China's "negotiation tactics on a sensitive border issue."[34] Given the sensitivity of the issue, New Delhi keeps close vigilance over deliberations and communiqués issued at the end of China-Bhutan border talks since they involve serious repercussions for India and its border talks with China. As reported in an article in the *Global Times* that for India, China's advances in the Doklam area is a "strategic threat" to the Siliguri corridor.[35]

As reported by Sherpem Sherpa, "the Bhutan-China border talks are intimately related to [India's] own border conflicts with China. India is particularly concerned with the territory in Doklam near the contentious Chumbi valley—strategically located at the corner where Bhutan, India, and China intersect. If Bhutan agrees to China's offer of territory in the disputed Jakarlung and Pasamlung areas in the north, it could mean that India's Siliguri corridor, the 12 mile wide and 120 mile long corridor surrounded by Nepal, Burma, Bangladesh, and Bhutan, would be threatened."[36]

THE INDIA FACTOR

It merits a mention that under Article 2 of the 1949 India-Bhutan treaty, Bhutan had agreed "to be guided by the advice of India" in conducting its foreign policy. But Bhutan has been insisting for so long that it will be guided by its own independent foreign policy since it is not India's protectorate. Ultimately, with India's acquiescence, both sides signed a new Friendship Treaty in 2007, replacing the old provisions on foreign and defense matters. Under the 2007 treaty, India and Bhutan have a collective responsibility not to allow each country's territory to be used "for activities harmful to the national security and interests of the other." This was exemplified by the crackdown of Bhutanese armed forces on the United Liberation Front of Assam (ULFA) insurgents who were carrying out insurgent activities against India in Bhutanese soil. It was a rare example of cooperative security in the region when Bhutan assisted in flushing out ULFA insurgents, which further consolidated India-Bhutan ties.

As said earlier, under the dispensation of the new treaty, Bhutan has been given more freedom and autonomy to conduct and manage its external relations on its own. Furthermore, in 2008, Bhutan's monarch paved the way for democratic governance in the country by transferring his powers and authority to the elected government at the center—the prime minister at the helm of affairs. The Bhutanese monarch is now a titular head. While respecting the sensitivities of the Bhutanese people, India made the important decision to open sixteen entry and exit points. Apart from this, India is engaged in Bhutan's development and economic modernization. For this India pledged 50 billion rupees to help implement Bhutan's eleventh Five-Year Plan. India is Bhutan's largest trading partner. It helps sustains Bhutanese economy with its 90 percent imports from Bhutan. [37]

CONCLUSION

China's recent expanding footprint in Nepal and Bhutan has enabled Beijing to play a larger strategic role not only in South Asia but also in influencing their domestic politics. Undoubtedly, China's masterful diplomatic stroke in the form of unconditional economic aid for their infrastructure development, economic modernization, and people's welfare has cemented Beijing's strategic bonds with Kathmandu and Thimpu. Though India is not opposed to China's expanding economic and trade ties with the Himalayan states, what worries India more is the negative fallout of China's deepening economic engagement with them on India's national defense and security interests in the Himalayan region.

Without glossing over the geopolitical reality in the changing political and strategic dynamics in South Asia, China's focus is concentrated on upgrading its security and strategic profile in Nepal and Bhutan vis-à-vis India. Moreover, Nepal and Bhutan have realized that since the gravity of power is shifting toward China, they ought not to miss the opportunity to coming closer to China. And China wants to cash in on its economic power projections to allure Himalayan states to come into the strategic fold.

Clearly China has succeeded in its game plan to mitigate India's influence over Kathmandu and Thimpu, even without sharing common religious, cultural, societal, and emotional bonds with them. Indeed, India's diplomatic task to regain the trust and confidence of Himalayan states has become excruciatingly difficult. India will need to redefine and redesign its policy approach toward them and also plug the fault lines both in psychological and strategic terms to win their trust. In geopsychological terms, Nepal feels deeply hurt and neglected by the imperialist attitude of the Indian foreign policy establishment. In strategic terms, India has not yet rejuvenated its policy toward its immediate neighbors in the changing political dynamics of South Asia, while China has a fine blend of both soft and hard power to achieve its strategic objectives in South Asia.

Prime Minister Modi was initially able to create much euphoria and enthusiasm in Kathmandu and Thimpu when he paid official visits to Bhutan and Nepal soon after assuming the office of prime minister in May 2014. But Modi's charisma did not last long. His verbal promises did not deliver. China took the advantage of Modi's mismatched policy toward Nepal. Beijing capitalized on New Delhi's unofficial economic embargo by rescuing Nepal from an acute shortage of essential commodities in the wake of nationwide protests by Madhesis, who were demanding a constitutional amendment to ensure their adequate representation in democratic institutions.

If India needs to revive its political clout with them, New Delhi will need to do extensive homework to locate the core reasons as to why Nepal and Bhutan prefer to keep political distance from India and are excited to strengthen ties with China. Also, India must learn from the success story of China's so-called soft power diplomacy in creating a cache of goodwill among South Asian countries rather than fixating on being paranoid about China.

NOTES

1. "The Forgotten History of Tibet's Role in Nepal's 1949 UN Application," *Tibetan Political Review*, October 14, 2011, https://sites.google.com/site/tibetanpoliticalreview/articles/theforgottenhistoryoftibetsroleinnepals1949unapplication.

2. Ibid.

3. "Nepal-China Relations," *Economic Weekly*, September 3, 1955, http://www.epw.in/system/files/pdf/1955_7/36/nepalchina_relations.pdf

4. "China Reopens Border with Nepal for Goods Movement," *Economic Times*, October 13, 2015, http://economictimes.indiatimes.com/news/international/business/china-reopens-border-with-nepal-for-goods-movement/articleshow/49336061.cms.

5. "Confucius Institute at Kathmandu University: A Bridge of Friendship through Language," *Hanban News*, September 13, 2013, http://english.hanban.org/article/2013-09/13/content_509620.htm.

6. National Development and Reform Commission, People's Republic of China, "Vision and Actions on Jointly Building Silk Road Economic Belt and 21st-Century Maritime Silk Road," March 28, 2015, http://en.ndrc.gov.cn/newsrelease/201503/t20150330_669367.html.

7. V. S. Chandrasekar, "China Dismisses India's Apprehensions on Silk Road Projects," *Business Today*, September 22, 2015, http://www.businesstoday.in/current/economy-politics/china-dismisses-india-apprehensions-on-silk-road-projects/story/224012.html.

8. See John Mauldin, "Can Central Planners Revive China's Economic Miracle?," *Forbes*, June 8, 2014, http://www.forbes.com/sites/johnmauldin/2014/06/08/can-central-planners-revive-chinas-economic-miracle/.

9. "China, Nepal Pledge to Boost Security Cooperation," *Xinhua*, October 17, 2010, http://www.globaltimes.cn/content/886869.shtml.

10. Rohan Dua, "China Can't Afford to Enter India: Nepal Army Chief," *Times of India*, October 4, 2013, http://timesofindia.indiatimes.com/india/China-cant-afford-to-enter-India-Nepal-Army-chief/articleshow/23488581.cms.

11. "China, Nepal Vow to Fight against Cross-Border Crime, October 17, 2014, *Xinhua*, http://news.xinhuanet.com/english/china/2014-10/17/c_133725154.htm.

12. See "Nepal, China Agree to Reopen Khasa-Tatopani Border Points at Earliest Date," *Xinhua*, April 11, 2015, http://news.xinhuanet.com/english/2015-11/04/c_134782637.htm.

13. See "Diversifying Trade with China Is the Need of the Hour," *Kathmandu Post*, March 21, 2016, http://kathmandupost.ekantipur.com/news/2016–03–21/diversifying-trade-with-china-is-the-need-of-the-hour.html.

14. Ibid.

15. Quoted in "Nepal: Increased Pressure from China Threatens Tibetans," Human Rights Watch, April 1, 2014, https://www.hrw.org/news/2014/04/01/nepal-increased-pressure-china-threatens-tibetans.

16. "Call for New Government," *Nepal Times*, October 2, 2015, http://www.nepalitimes.com/blogs/thebrief/2015/10/02/call-for-new-government/.

17. Madan Dahal, e-mail interview with the author, October 29, 2015.

18. Satish Kumar, China's Expanding Footprint in Nepal: Threats to India," *Journal of Defence Studies* 5, no. 2 (April 2011), or alternatively see David Scott, ed. *Handbook of India's International Relations* (New York: Routledge, 2011).

19. M. K. Bhadrakumar, "How China Pipped India at Nepal Post," *Asian Times*, October 17, 2015, http://atimes.com/2015/10/how-china-pipped-india-at-nepal-post/.

20. Ibid.

21. "Book on China-Nepal Relations Released in Nepal," *Xinhua*, January 25, 2016, http://news.xinhuanet.com/english/2016-01/25/c_135042583.htm, accessed April 19, 2016.

22. Ibid.

23. Biswas Baral, "Nepal's Deepening Ties with China Need Not Be Bad News for India," *Wire*, March 28, 2016, http://thewire.in/2016/03/28/nepals-deepening-ties-with-china-need-not-be-bad-news-for-india-26215/.

24. Ibid.

25. "China Sends Record Military Personnel Numbers to Nepal," *Xinhau*, May 7, 2015, http://eng.mod.gov.cn/Database/MOOTW/2015-05/07/content_4583728.htm.

26. See Heather Timmons and Manu Balachandran, "China's and India's Charity in Nepal Has a Hidden Political Agenda," *Quartz India*, April 28, 2015, http://qz.com/392295/chinas-and-indias-charity-in-nepal-has-a-hidden-political-agenda/.

27. Ibid.

28. Claude Arpi, "In Bhutan Too, Chinese Grab Land," *Indian Defence Review*, June 14, 2014, http://www.indiandefencereview.com/news/in-bhutan-too-chinese-grab-land.

29. "Differences in Bhutan-China Border Dispute Minimised," *Kuensel*, November 26, 2016, http://www.kuenselonline.com/differences-in-bhutan-china-border-dispute-minimised/.

30. See Brian Benedictus, "Bhutan and the Great Power Tussle," *Diplomat*, August 2, 2014, http://thediplomat.com/2014/08/bhutan-and-the-great-power-tussle/.

31. Victor Robert Lee, "Bhutan: The Indian Army's Front Line," *Diplomat*, November 6, 2014,http://thediplomat.com/2014/11/bhutan-the-indian-armys-front-line/.

32. "Visit Not Connected to Bhutan-China Border Talks: Pranab Mukherjee," *Economic Times*, November 7, 2014, http://economictimes.indiatimes.com/news/politics-and-nation/visit-not-connected-to-bhutan-china-border-talks-pranab-mukherjee/articleshow/45071177.cms.

33. Ibid.

34. "Ceding Aksai Chin Not an Option for India," *Tribune*, May 19, 2013, http://www.tribuneindia.com/2013/20130519/pers.htm.

35. Claude Arpi, "In Bhutan Too, Chinese Grab Land," *Indian Defence Review*, June 14, 2014, http://www.indiandefencereview.com/news/in-bhutan-too-chinese-grab-land/.

36. Sherpem Sherpa, "Bhutan: Between Two Giants," *World Policy Journal* (Winter 2016), http://www.worldpolicy.org/journal/winter2013/bhutan-between-two-giants.

37. For a comprehensive discussion on various dimensions of China-Bhutan and Bhutan-India relations, see Sherpa, "Bhutan."

Chapter Five

China and the Island States of the Indian Ocean

Geostrategic Imperatives

Sri Lanka and the Maldives, located in the heart of the Indian Ocean, have acquired a geostrategic primacy in international relations over the past decade or so. This has naturally tempted extraregional powers into expanding their strategic presence in the region in order to protect a myriad of their national interests, mainly in economic, trade, and energy sectors. For instance, China has launched the Twenty-First-Century Maritime Silk Road Initiative to expand its economic and trade network across the region, covering over five dozen countries, including those in Southeast and South Asia. It may be pointed out that Sri Lanka is the first country in South Asia to join the multi-billion-dollar China-sponsored project in India's backyard. The Maldives have followed the suit.

Quite significantly, China's increasing naval presence in the Indian Ocean is fundamentally driven by its ambition to play a more assertive and influential role in shaping the emerging security architecture of the Indo-Pacific region. With this goal in mind, China has launched a series of mega-projects, for instance building a vast network of ports and highways in Sri Lanka—a country known as the "Pearl of the Indian Ocean." Unsurprisingly, Sri Lanka became "ever chummier" with China owing to former president Rajapaksa's policy, which tilted heavily toward China. As noted in the *Economic Times*, "China is also developing roads, airports and another port, Hambantota, on Sri Lanka's south coast. Chinese warships have stopped at Colombo on the way to Pakistan and to anti-pirate operations in the Gulf of

Aden."[1] Much to India's discomfiture, Sri Lanka obliged China by permitting its submarines to dock at its ports.

As pointed out earlier, Sri Lanka's strategic primacy in the evolving maritime geopolitics in the Indo-Pacific region has prodded major powers to adopt proactive diplomacy to maintain their spheres of influence in the region. Given China's overt and covert naval activities in the Indian Ocean region, the Obama administration's Pivot to Asia strategy has been vigorously active, although indistinct and ill-defined, to protect and maintain a strategic US stronghold in the Indian Ocean region. This is one of the key reasons that the Obama administration made a renewed effort to engage Colombo in diplomatic parleys. Secretary John Kerry's official visit to Colombo in April 2015 reflected the administration's political mood to initiate political and strategic dialogue with Sri Lanka. His confutations with the new president, Maithripala Sirisena, primarily centered on three important issues. First, expressing the US desire to cultivate its "positive relationship" with Sri Lanka in the altered political regime. Second, apprising the Sirisena regime of US concerns over war crimes committed by Sri Lankan forces during the final phase of their offensive against the Liberation Tigers of Tamil Eelam (LTTE) in 2009. Third, conveying the administration's message to Colombo about the negative fallout from China's incremental strategic engagement with Sri Lanka on US foreign policy and economy.[2]

U-TURN IN CHINA–SRI LANKA TIES?

Sri Lankan president Sirisena's unexpected victory over his political-heavyweight rival, Mahinda Rajapaksa, in the presidential election in January 2015 psychologically upset the Beijing leadership over China's Indian Ocean plans. It might be recalled that Sirisena, during his election campaigns, lambasted President Rajapaksa for making Sri Lanka hopelessly dependent on China economically. With Sirisena's coming to power, China apprehended that the new regime in Colombo might either delay or cancel its several strategically important projects, including the port city project, worth $1.4 billion. It may be recalled that President Xi Jinping managed to secure a nod from Sri Lanka and the Maldives on its Maritime Silk Road project in 2014. But this project had a twin objective of encircling India and controlling the sea lanes that link the Persian Gulf and China in order to ensure hassle-free oil imports into China.

If viewed in hindsight, China was the biggest donor with its supply of sophisticated weapons worth millions of dollars, including a free gift of an F7 fighter aircraft, to Sri Lanka at a time when Sri Lanka was fighting the decisive phase of its military-led offensive against the LTTE. Mahinda Rajapaksa expressed his personal gratitude to China for its massive military aid, which enabled a total decimation of the LTTE in 2009. With this, the civil war, bleeding the country for over two decades, was terminated. Besides that, Beijing went to the extent of exercising its veto power to prevent the Security Council from debating the plight of Tamil civilians in postwar Sri Lanka.

INDIA'S FLIP-FLOP POLICY

India–Sri Lanka relations deteriorated following the Sri Lankan government's failure to fulfill its political commitment on the question of devolution of political power and authority to Sri Lankan Tamils in their majority areas. A broad-based, inclusive reconciliation process was brought to a logical conclusion by the Colombo government headed by President Rajapaksa for one decade. Had he displayed an unconstrained political vision, the country could have been saved from civilian minority community unrest, communities including Muslims in Sri Lanka. Rajapaksa's parochial and purblind approach to the ethnic conflict flared up the identity crisis more intensively, which further complicated the cultural symbiosis and synthesis for internal peace and ethnic harmony. Instead, Rajapaksa resorted to resolving the ethnic conflict by exercising a military option—a myopic view.

History is a guiding star that shows the path out of dark and thick woods. Few politicians or military dictators ever make even mild attempts to learn from the past follies and foibles committed by their predecessors. So was the case with Rajapaksa. His apathetic and adamant attitude toward Indian political leaders at the helm of power cost him politically. If Rajapaksa was firm on resolving the ethnic civil war through military means with Chinese military aid and cooperation, India was equally adamant about not providing an iota of military aid to Sri Lanka to defeat the LTTE—a dreaded terrorist organization. The point I wish to hammer out is that China did not jump into the fray of Sri Lankan domestic affairs so abruptly. Initially there was no sign of Chinese involvement in Sri Lanka's internal security structures. It was a well-designed and well-calculated strategic move on the part of Rajapaksa to bring extraregional influence into South Asia by inviting China into its backyard to transfer deadly weapons to Sri Lanka to eliminate the LTTE.

Having sensed Sri Lanka's indispensable defense requirements, China did not entertain any inhibitions to provide it with lethal weapons on a massive scale without taking Indian sensitivity into account on such a sensitive issue. Rather, China soberly took strategic advantage of the widening political chasm between New Delhi and Colombo on India's blatant refusal to provide Sri Lanka with military hardware. As such, China was eagerly looking forward to seizing the opportunity to expand its arms market in South Asia by exploiting the irritant between New Delhi and Colombo. Pitiably, India failed to properly articulate its resentment against China's overt and covert inter-

vention in South Asian affairs. That gave the Beijing leadership an easy
political handle to interfere in South Asian strategic and security affairs,
obviously detrimental to India's manifold national interests. In fact, India's
flip-flop diplomacy toward Sri Lanka was responsible for not only China's
expanding strategic role in Sri Lanka but also consolidating a strategic alliance between them.[3]

President Rajapaksa was overflowing with good cheer at the end of the
over two-decade-long civil war. He publicly acknowledged that without Chinese military assistance, in the form of sophisticated military hardware, Sri
Lanka could have never won the toughest war in its history against the well-
trained and disciplined military cadre of the LTTE. To repay the debt, President Rajapaksa was determined to do anything for China under his presidential executive powers. Colombo's heavy tilt toward China was clearly perceptible. The Rajapaksa administration took a momentous decision to make
Colombo a major part of China's Maritime Silk Road initiative. This will, in
Colombo's perception, pave the way for China–Sri Lanka mutual cooperation in the development of ports as well as in maritime security and maritime
resource management.

POLICY PARADIGM SHIFT

A major policy shift occurred in the Beijing-Colombo relationship under the
Sirisena regime. President Sirisena threw distinct hints to China that his
government would review all those projects that were previously sanctioned
to it under the Rajapaksa regime. Given this, it is important to examine the
underlying reasons that drove President Sirisena to make a geopolitical swing
toward India. There are underlying reasons behind it.

First, Sirisena felt that President Rajapaksa's pro-China credentials unnecessarily antagonized India—a neighbor indispensable for Sri Lanka's political stability and economic development. Sirisena did not subscribe to his
approach of heavily leaning on China for military and economic aid by
glossing over the stark geopolitical reality that India was a preeminent power
in South Asia. Second, in Sirisena's perception, Rajapaksa made Sri Lanka
economically overly dependent on China, making it virtually impossible to
get out of China's investment booby-trap at the cost of Sri Lanka's economic
health. Third, China's "string of pearls" strategy in the Indian Ocean was
motivated by its power projection in the region to advance and consolidate its
economic and trade interests to replace India as Sri Lanka's largest trade
partner. Third, in the Sirisena administration's perception, China's growing
maritime activities in the Indian Ocean region might trigger a big-power
conflict in the region with negative fallout for Sri Lanka's political stability
and economic development. Fourth, to rebuild Sri Lankan ties with India,

Sirisena embarked on a cautious but prudent policy path while dealing with New Delhi and Beijing.

SIRISENA'S VISIT TO CHINA

President Sirisena's first state visit to China in March 2015 came at a time when Sino–Sri Lankan relations were clouded with uncertainty. Naturally, his visit evoked great awe and interest in Beijing and New Delhi pertaining to the visit's net outcome and political ramifications, if any, for both capitals. While according a grand welcome to Sirisena, President Xi in his opening remark stated that China always perceived Sri Lanka as a "strategic partner" and wanted to "promote and elevate the China–Sri Lanka relationship to fulfil an important purpose."[4]

President Xi, although apparently nervous, gave the impression to President Sirisena that China was committed to fulfilling its past promises by renegotiating more than $5.3 billion worth of Chinese deals signed during Rajapaksa's leadership. It was reported by the *Mail Online* that "the $1.4 billion 'port city' land reclamation scheme in Colombo suspended by Sirisena was also considered a security risk by neighbouring India."[5] In his meeting with Xi, Sirisena made clear that the people of Sri Lanka gave him a political mandate to restore good governance, transparency, and rule of law in the country. Both countries signed five MoUs for cooperation with special aid in public health, development of water treatment methods, and technologies in kidney disease treatment, research and development of the coconut industry, and refurbishment of the Superior Courts Complex in Sri Lanka.[6]

Given this background, this chapter will examine the policy shift in Sri Lanka's China policy with the takeover of the Sirisena regime and its implications for India in general and for South Asia in particular. What have been the driving forces behind Sri Lanka's new take on China? What is the future of the Beijing-Colombo relationship under the new dispensation of Sirisena? Will China's soft power instruments entice Sri Lanka? Will India be able to scuttle China's security and strategic roles in Sri Lanka?

These questions demand dispassionate answers in order to better understand the logic behind China's offer of soft loans and infrastructure development aid for constructing bridges, airports, and high-tech theaters. Or China may set up academies or institutes to promote Chinese language and culture—important components of its soft power diplomacy.

POLITICAL DYNAMICS

Renewed Ties with India

Sirisena's landmark visit to India in February 2015 signaled a positive move toward refurbishing the ties between two countries. Modi described Sri Lanka as India's "closest neighbor and friend" and expressed a desire to take bilateral relations to a "new level." As expected, four agreements were signed between two countries. Of them, the most important was related to nuclear cooperation. Under this, India agreed to assist Sri Lanka in developing infrastructure of its nuclear technology, including the "exchange of knowledge and expertise, sharing of resources, capacity building and training of personnel in peaceful uses of nuclear energy."[7] In addition, both countries agreed to expand defense and security cooperation. These pragmatic measures were intended to reset the ties between New Delhi and Colombo, which frayed during the presidency of Rajapaksa, especially in the last phase of the war between Sri Lankan forces and the LTTE in early 2009.

Sri Lankan power and energy minister Champika Ranawaka, accompanying President Sirisena, in a *Daily Mirror* interview on February 23, 2015, accused Rajapaksa of making "a mistake by allowing the Colombo Port to be used for docking Chinese submarines and other military activities."[8] He also claimed to adhere to a nonaligned foreign policy. It should be remembered that ever since China established its strategic presence in the island nation, it dispatched its submarines to visit Colombo, something India strongly objected to. Also, Modi urged President Sirisena to address legitimate concerns of Sri Lankan Tamils, who were still the worst victims of discrimination in the country and were alienated from the national mainstream.

With the warming up of relations between the two countries, China proposed a trilateral cooperation among India, China, and Sri Lanka, with the objective to dissuade India from becoming part of the US Pivot to Asia policy to contain China. But India does not see any merit in the Chinese proposal. Nor is India going to dilute its strategic partnership with the United States. But for sure, if the new government in Colombo cooperates with India, New Delhi is optimistic about maintaining regional peace and stability, although China and Pakistan continue to create a political rift between India and Sri Lanka. The unfolding political dynamics clearly show that India has enormous opportunities to revitalize its hitherto weakened ties with Sri Lanka. It ought to be noted that the Sirisena administration flatly refused to grant permission to China to dock its vessels in Sri Lanka. Apart from this, Colombo took a bold "decision to suspend Chinese-led development of the port in Colombo. That decision was a significant blow to Beijing's plans for a 'Maritime Silk Road' and its One Belt, One Road policy that would improve connectivity in South Asia."[9] In view of the deepening political and strategic differences between China and Sri Lanka, the Beijing leadership devised a face-saving plan by announcing $46 billion energy and infrastructure investment in Pakistan.

China–Sri Lanka Security Ties

Especially since the heydays of the Rajapaksa regime (2005–2014), Chinese diplomacy has been structured on two principal pillars. First, China wants to woo the Sri Lanka by offering it incentives for rebuilding Sri Lanka's infrastructure that got destroyed during the ethnic conflict. China did not miss the opportunity to come closer to Sri Lanka when it discovered that the Sri Lankan ruling class was distancing itself from India, mainly on account of India's flat refusal to supply military hardware to fight the LTTE. Second, the Rajapaksa regime was extremely favorable to serve China's long-term security and economic interests in the Indian Ocean region. The strategic cooperative partnership between China and the Maldives has gone a long way in helping China implement its Maritime Silk Road project in South Asia. The project will serve their maritime security and economic and trade interests. Maritime cooperation between Beijing and Male has paved the way for joint naval exercises. In continuation of increasing security ties between China and Sri Lanka, they conducted a second set of joint military exercises in June and July 2015. From the Chinese side, the forty-three members of the PLA participated. This has naturally caused serious concern in New Delhi, which interpreted the growing security relationship between Beijing and Colombo as an attempt at its encirclement.

If seen from a realistic perspective, there was no rationale behind carrying out such exercises, since the LTTE was already defeated, with the aid of Chinese offensive military equipment. India may work that Sri Lanka entertains future plans to utilize against India the experience gained during joint exercises. This is not even a distant possibility though. Apparently it is China's game plan to keep close surveillance over Indian strategic assets and naval activities offshore in the Indian Ocean.

Keeping the centrality of its objective, China successfully managed to come closer strategically. Chinese president Xi visited Sri Lanka in September 2014.He was accorded red carpet treatment by President Rajapaksa. During this visit, an agreement on action plan was reached to strengthen the strategic cooperative partnership between the two countries. In continuation of the first China–Sri Lanka defense cooperation dialogue, Chinese defense minister Chang Wanquan's Sri Lanka visit in June 2015 carried political and strategic importance. Chang said, "China is willing to make full use of the dialogue, expand cooperation and exchanges in various fields and levels, and maintain the smooth development of military-to-military ties."[10]

It is important to note that China's defense minister's visit to Sri Lanka, beginning June 7, 2015, synchronized with that of Pakistan's chief of army staff general Raheel Sharif in June 2015. Sharif met with President Sirisena and discussed bilateral cooperation between their two countries on regional security issues. India has been keeping a close watch over the possible implications of trilateral defense and security cooperation among China, Sri Lanka, and Pakistan.

Though Sirisena had previously decided to review earlier contracts with China, he seems to have given this a second thought and begun soft-peddling Sri Lanka's China policy. He favors pursuing a balanced policy toward China and India in the emerging Asian security order. At the same time, Sirisena is also aware of the complexities of domestic politics in which it is possible that Rajapaksa may become prime minister. In that eventuality, Rajapaksa will be capable enough to renegotiate with China. The latter eagerly awaits this, to balance out Sirisena's positive tilt toward India.

China–Sri Lanka Economic and Trade Ties

The recent Sino–Sri Lankan comprehensive economic partnership is rooted in their shared national interests and identical views on regional affairs. In fact, President Rajapaksa has turned Sri Lanka into a global maritime logistics and world-class harbor center. In his perception this would change the face of the Sri Lankan economy and boost the country's development profile.

Their economic links are traceable to the signing of the first agreement on economic and technological cooperation in 1962. In 1982 they signed an agreement regarding a Joint Trade Committee. In 2009 an investment facilitation agreement was signed between the China Development Bank and the Central Bank of Sri Lanka. This has further boosted economic and trade ties between the two countries.[11]

According to the Central Bank of Sri Lanka's 2008 annual report, Sri Lanka's exports to China were worth $46.8 million, while China's exports to Sri Lanka stood at a huge trade imbalance ($1044.7). In 2012 a huge trade deficit against Sri Lanka grew to the size of $2554 million, which naturally caused much worrying in Colombo as to how to narrow this gap.[12] For this China is considering a free-trade agreement—a means to provide some relief to Sri Lanka on the front of the widening trade imbalance. "At present trade is worth US$3.1 billion between Sri Lanka and China, out of which $2.9 billion worth of goods and services are imported by Sri Lanka. Sri Lanka exports only $200 million worth of goods and services to China."[13]

It may be noted that "Sri Lanka's major exports to China include raw coconut coir, apparel items, tea—whether or not flavoured, natural rubber, diamonds and other precious stones, titanium ores and concentrates and bicycles and other cycles. . . . Sri Lanka's major imports from China include electrical machinery and equipment, boilers and machinery and other parts, cotton, iron or steel and its articles, man-made staple fibres, knitted or crocheted fabrics, fertilizers, railway locomotives and inorganic chemicals."[14] China has become a major investor in Sri Lanka. Those Chinese entrepreneurs who invest a minimum of $25 million are provided Sri Lankan passports, or "second home" passports.

Most important, China has emerged as a major donor to Sri Lanka, replacing Japan. In 2008 it provided Sri Lanka with about $1 billion, including humanitarian assistance for those who had suffered during the ethnic conflict. It undertook several projects in tsunami-affected areas. In addition, the China National Petroleum Cooperation has begun oil exploration in Sri Lanka. They have launched a joint car project. In fact, China offers a huge market to Sri Lanka with China's growing economic strength and also is a potential economic partner for foreign direct investment in Sri Lanka. One Sri Lankan scholar comments, "The China–Sri Lanka relationship is an excellent instance of 'big nation-small nation relations' with mutual benefits experienced by both nations. With so many 'missed opportunities,' Sri Lanka should make up for past failures by making use of this emerging opportunity properly."[15]

It is reported that projects of fourteen Chinese companies registered at the Board of Investment of Sri Lanka have generated more than 2,500 local jobs. But at what cost? If perceived from realistic grounds, China has crippled the Sri Lankan economy. How? China's nearly 70 percent investment in Sri Lanka's infrastructure projects developed and funded by China during the Rajapaksa regime has tripled the debt that Sri Lanka now owes to China. Sri Lanka's mounting foreign debt amounted to 90 percent of its gross domestic product in 2014–2015. That is why the Sri Lankan finance minister, Ravi Karunanayake, had to urge China to relax the "immerse foreign debt" to help ease Sri Lanka's crippled economy. In an exclusive interview with the *South China Morning Post*, Karunanayake said, "I urge China to put the acrimony of the past behind us and come and help us by adjusting the terms of the loans to make them more viable." He further added, "Chinese loans are a big part of our problem. . . . A bulk of the government expenditure goes into servicing them."[16]

When Sirisena came to power, Chinese projects were halted, creating tense relations between Beijing and Colombo. The Chinese leadership has made it clear in absolute terms that unless the issue of pending Chinese-funded projects worth billions of dollars is resolved, "none of the much-needed foreign direct investment (FDI) to salvage Sri Lanka's economy will be forthcoming."[17] The Sirisena administration has blamed predecessors for creating a chaotic economic situation in the country. But this does not convince the Sri Lankan people who want that the new administration to deliver and help the country's economy. It must be noted that there has been a policy shift in the Sirisena administration. President Sirisena and his prime minister, Ranil Wickremesinghe, have been arguing that to keep the country's economic health in good shape, Sri Lanka must cooperate with India and pursue a nonaligned policy. In effect, Sri Lanka has realized its strategic error in overwhelmingly depending on China, a move that has left its economy in a shambles.

Politics and diplomacy are fluid. Sri Lanka has managed to repair its relations with China on controversial issues of corruption and irregularities in approving the Chinese-funded megaprojects. As reported by Shannon Tiezzi of *Diplomat*, "a Chinese mega-project in Sri Lanka is set to recommence, after the Sri Lankan government announced that its concerns regarding the project 'have been resolved.' . . . Sri Lankan Minister of International Trade Malik Samarawickrema gave the green light for the $1.4 billion project to construct "Port City" near the Colombo Harbor."[18]

As mentioned before, Chinese projects were suspended by the Sirisena administration in March 2015. After a year, intensive deliberations were held on how to get the Sri Lankan economy back on track, crippled as it was by the massive debt to China following China's heavy investment in it. In his *South China Morning Post* interview, Karunanayake made a passionate appeal to China to help tide over the economic crisis Sri Lanka was wading through: "I urge China to put the acrimony of the past behind us and come and help us by adjusting the terms of the loans to make them more viable."[19] He further said, "Chinese loans are a big part of our problem. . . . A bulk of the government expenditure goes into servicing them."[20] At the same time, Karunanayake acknowledged that China, with "rapidly growing Asian superpower's status," had been "a key stakeholder in Sri Lanka's faltering economy." He said, "We are serious about putting our relationship [with China] on the right path and mending the pathetic finances we have inherited from a corrupt regime."[21]

Sri Lanka knew well that India was not going to salvage its crisis-ridden economy. A serious rethinking prodded the administration to resolve the outstanding issues with China amicably. The Sri Lankan government realized that the development of the port city would be an important hub for China's One Belt, One Road initiative.[22]

CHINA-MALDIVES RELATIONS

The island nation of the Maldives is located south of India. Because of its strategic location in the heart of the Indian Ocean, it has recently caught the attention of China. It should be noted that being a hub of trade, hundreds of cargo ships from the east and west pass through the Maldivian territorial waters every year. China has launched the Maritime Silk Route initiative to expand east-west trade through maritime cooperation with the Maldives. Although the latter has traditionally been part of India's sphere of influence, China has been actively engaged in political hobnobbing with the Male government in the past couple of years to cement its ties with it. Toward that end, China has been attempting to lure the Maldives into its development strategy of agriculture and infrastructure development. The Beijing government has undertaken projects to build houses, roads, and bridges in the Maldives. China has already committed to construct a bridge connecting the airport island with the capital, Male. In this part of our analysis, the focus will be on four critical areas in which China and the Maldives can enhance mutual cooperation. They are strategic partnership, the new government and new land law, economic and trade cooperation, and tourism.

Strategic Partnership

It sounds paradoxical that there can be a strategic partnership between China and the Maldives given the unparalleled asymmetries between these two countries in terms of population size and military, industrial, and technological capabilities. Why has China begun evincing strategic interest in the Maldives? The simple answer lies in the strategic location of the Maldives in the Indian Ocean, which has become a hotbed of China's growing activities for its energy security, and the dynamic of its ambition to project itself as a global power. From this angle, China launched the Maritime Silk Road project, which was endorsed by the Male government.

Chinese military elites have drawn up a road map for China's long term-plan to set up a military base in the Maldives. The Chinese establishment anticipates that the United States may set up a naval base on the Maldives' southernmost island of Gan. This apprehension has acquired some credence on the basis of China's perception that the US naval facility at Diego Garcia might facilitate further US expansion to the Maldives, though no evidence is there that supports this right now. However, China's apprehension, though it may be a misplaced one, has firmed up the country's resolve to solidify its defense cooperation with the Maldives, with an intent to kill two birds with one stone. First, the evolving strategic partnership between Beijing and Male might obviate India's strategic closeness with the Maldives, especially when President Abdulla Yameen's pro-China tilt is evident.

Second, China's growing defense ties with the Maldives is expected to preempt the future US plan to build up a military base in the Maldives. But such an assessment may not be true. It will depend on the political and strategic environment in China and the Maldives. Whatever China's apprehensions or wild calculations, India has made it crystal clear to the Beijing leadership that New Delhi will not tolerate its ongoing sensitive strategic activities in the Maldives that involve India's security interests. New Delhi has clearly signaled that "it would continue providing the island's security. India offered the Maldives a state-of-the-art 260-ton fast-attack craft to aid in guarding coastal waters, in addition to providing other defence equipment and setting up of radar systems on all 26 Maldivian atolls."[23]

But the Male government, according to *Voice of America*, has reassured India that "it will not allow China to set up military bases on its territory. . . . Maldivian President Abdulla Yameen conveyed the assurance the Maldives will remain a 'demilitarized zone' in a letter given to Indian Foreign Minister Sushma Swaraj in New Delhi by the country's foreign secretary Ali Naseer."[24] But such assurance will not deter China from consolidating its position in the Indian Ocean. India needs to keep tight vigilance over China's sensitive strategic activities in the Maldives. In this regard, India's foreign secretary, Subrahmanyan Jaishankar, during his visit to the Maldives in August 2015, expressed concerns "about a new law that allows foreigners to own land in the country if they invest $1 billion and reclaim 70 percent of the land from the sea. . . . India fears this law will pave the way for China to establish its military presence in the Maldives, a string of 1,200 islands located south of India along major shipping routes in the Indian Ocean."[25] But the Maldivian government clarified that the law was meant only to attract foreign investors to establish special economic zones, such as that in Dubai, giving an economic boost and reducing the Maldives' "reliance on tourism."

New Government and the New Land Law in the Maldives

After a three decade of autocratic rule in the country, free elections were held in the Maldives in 2008. The results of the election heralded a change in Maldivian foreign policy. Political instability and terror threats in the past couple of years have been seen as common phenomena in Maldivian politics. In 2012 President Nasheed was jailed for thirteen years. In 2015 President Yameen declared a state of emergency to ensure the "safety and security of every citizen."[26] Yameen clearly maintained that his government was committed to attracting foreign investment in the country. For which, he argued, his government passed legislation that would allow "foreign ownership of land" for the first time in Sri Lankan history. This naturally triggered concern in Delhi over China's opportunity to extend its reach in the Indian Ocean. China's "growing footprints" in the Maldives caused some serious anxiety in India over what was happening in its backyard. "Alarm bells rang in New Delhi when President Yameen announced in July that foreigners who invest more than $1bn in the island could own land in perpetuity, provided 70 percent of it is reclaimed from the sea."[27] China has "expertise in churning sand from the ocean bed has been recently well demonstrated in the South

China Sea. It also has deep pockets."[28] This will certainly strengthen China's naval presence in the Indian Ocean.

Apart from this, China is overtly engaged in the expansion of its maritime activities in Colombo. It may be pointed out that China had docked submarines at the port of Colombo. Also, it was reported that "Chinese nuclear submarines carried out patrols in the Bay of Bengal. The possible presence of Chinese nuclear missiles so close to its coastline was a matter of utmost concern to India's nuclear deterrence."[29] Therefore, India lodged a strong protest that China's deeper penetration into the Indian Ocean region would undermine India's economic and security interests. But Indian protests are meaningless unless Indian policy elites carve out a pragmatic strategy in sync with implementation mechanisms to thwart China's impending potential threat to India's maritime, trade, and security stakes in the region.

Economic and Trade Cooperation

The Maldivian government's model of free trade is aimed at attracting federal direct investment in the country. President Yameen, while announcing his policy stance in 2014, defended the rationale behind assigning priority to forging economic cooperation with China. In the Maldivian government's perception, economic and trade collaboration with China does not constitute a threat to the Maldives' Islamic identity. During President Yameen's official visit to China, the Chinese government "pledged 100 million Yuan (approximately MVR 250 million) in free financial aid to cover a huge part of the cost for the Male'-Hulhule' Bridge Project as well as expressing interest in investing in several other major development projects."[30]

Fishery is another sector in which Chinese enterprises have made investments in the Maldives. According to Chinese ambassador Wang Fukang, "In recent years, in order to support the development of Maldivian fisheries and agricultural sector, the Chinese government has invited the Maldivian side to attend training programs in China and has developed and implemented small-scale cooperation projects with the Maldivian government."[31]

Apart from this, China's soft power strategy in the Maldives is driven by the special needs of its people, which include building houses under concessional loans. According to Ambassador Wang, "China has carried out housing projects with 1,000 flats under concessional loans, in order to assist Maldives in achieving sustainable development. The project is welcomed by the Maldivian people and who, as sign of gratitude, named the project as the China town."[32]

Tourism

China's ties with the Maldives have strengthened over the past decade through the instrumentality of its soft power initiative in the form of boosting tourism. Chinese tourists form the largest number of the Maldivian tourism industry. According to Ambassador Wang, "Since 2010, China has remained the largest source of tourist arrivals in the Maldives. In 2013 alone, more than 330,000 Chinese tourists visited Maldives. In the future, both sides could encourage more Chinese tourists to visit Maldives. Maldives could attract potential Chinese companies to invest in the tourism sector of the country."[33]

President Xi's visit to the Maldives in September 2014 carries manifold implications. First, Xi wanted to give the impression to the Male government that China, without any ulterior motive, was eager to make investments in its infrastructure development, including housing projects. According to the *Times of India*, The Maldives signed a deal "with a Chinese company to upgrade its international airport after cancelling a $511 million deal with India's GMR Infrastructure in 2012."[34]

China's relations with the Maldives became stronger and friendlier with the Yameen government's pro-China stance. The arrest of former president Nasheed at the behest of his political foe Yameen raised eyebrows in the capitals of New Delhi and Washington and led to political turmoil in the country. But Beijing has unambiguously made clear its commitment to the policy of noninterference in domestic affairs, which has morally emboldened President Yameen.

India's lackluster policy is responsible for bringing Chinese influence to the Maldives. New Delhi failed to handle domestic affairs of the Maldives with caution and prudence. Moreover, India's confused and indistinct approach to the political crisis–ridden Maldives landed New Delhi in a political dilemma. China took advantage of this bizarre situation. It may be recalled that the Maldives' former foreign minister Ahmed Naseem, during his visit to New Delhi, urged India to play a "stabilizing role" in the Maldives, and balance out China's increasing presence there. He stated, "For Maldives it is imperative to stand together with India to balance Indian Ocean security and protect the interests of the Maldives in a growing gamble for power in the Indian Ocean."[35] Recall that India's relations with the Maldives in comparison to China have been friendly and peaceful. India generously contributed to the Maldives' political stability and economic development. In 1988 the Rajiv Gandhi government came to Male's rescue when a handful of militants belonging to People's Liberation Organisation of Tamil Eelam, attempted a coup to dislodge President Maumoon Abdul Gayoom. For that Gayoom expressed his deep gratitude to Prime Minister Gandhi on behalf of the nation.[36]

India's cooperative security approach toward Sri Lanka and the Maldives paid dividends. New Delhi's maritime strategy of addressing nonmilitary issues and threats in the region led to trilateral cooperation in the region. Bilateral defense cooperation between India and the Maldives focused on

> joint surveillance, search and rescue operations, training and capacity building of MNDF and Maldives Coast Guard Officers. The Government of India "responded to request of the government of Maldives and provided the first Advanced Light Helicopter (ALH) renamed "Kurangi." It was commissioned by the MNDF in April 2010 and positioned in Gan. The second ALH was given in December 2013. However, access to EEZs in Sri Lanka is restricted for India, even though the agreement provides for surveillance in and around EEZ. On the other hand, China has better access in the EEZ of Sri Lanka. [37]

CONCLUSION

China's soft power projection through burgeoning economic and trade ties with Sri Lanka has richly delivered the goods. By providing soft loans to and investment in Sri Lanka China has created much goodwill and appreciation. The Colombo regime, irrespective of the party in power, has been grateful to China for its investment in Sri Lanka. In Sri Lanka, Beijing's soft power initiatives of launching major infrastructure projects, such as developing ports, airfields, and roads, have paid it rich dividends. Currently China is the largest investor in and second-largest trading partner with Sri Lanka, which has revved up its strategic leverage over Sri Lanka. These developments are worrisome to India. One important component of China's soft power strategy is addressing the dire needs of people by way of offering specific foreign aid, for instance, building houses for the poor, to win over the recipient government's trust.

China's typical soft power approach is to win back goodwill and trust when China encounters opposition to its development projects from the internal voices of the country. For example, when China's most trustworthy and closest friend Rajapaksa lost to Sirisena in the presidential elections, the new regime in Colombo ordered China to stop implementing the projects approved by President Rajapaksa. At that time, it was dubbed a great setback to China. But the Beijing leadership redeployed its soft power tools to strike rapprochement with Sirisena and Wickremesinghe, convincing them that China was their reliable friend. As a result, over $1 billion worth of projects were revived. India needs to learn from Chinese diplomacy rather than creating enemies or adversaries by displaying its arrogance in dealing with small neighboring countries.

India's Sri Lanka policy needs to be evaluated within the parameters of converging their mutual interests in order to boost economic, trade, and strategic ties that better suit their respective long-term national interests. It will be fatuous to expect the new leadership in Sri Lanka will alter the basics of the country's fundamental national interests, although atmospheric changes in Sri Lanka's India policy are in sight. I do not think the Modi government's diplomacy will be able to create strategic ripples between Colombo and Beijing to derive strategic gains for India. It is too early to judge whether Indian diplomacy will succeed in eroding Chinese influence in the Indian Ocean region in general and in the island nations in particular. Indian policy makers must understand the dynamics of China's subtle and nuanced diplomacy, conducted with patience, prudence, and foresightedness to deal with friends and foes, rivals and competitors efficaciously.

As regards China's soft power projections in the Maldives, China enjoys the upper hand over India, though India is equally proactive in capacity-building programs in the Maldives. India's soft power initiatives in the Maldives—for example, in the form of offering scholarships to its students under various schemes such as the Indian Council of Cultural Relations, the South Asian Association of Regional Cooperation (SAARC) Chair Fellowship, and medical scholarships—have created a positive image of India among Maldivians. The Indian government's $5.30 million project the Technology Adoption Programme in Education Sector in Maldives has been very popular there. In addition, Hindi television series and music have fascinated Maldivians. Though these may sound palatable, the underlying reality is that China has been able to outpace India geopolitically and geopsychologically. The Indian Ocean states that have fallen under the spell of the Chinese charm offensive.

While setting national priorities to advance the political agendas, Maldivian ruling elites want to ensure that their country's political, economic, trade, and investment interests remain intact without souring relations with both China and India. It is yet to be seen whether the Yameen government will pursue a pro-China policy or favor an evenhanded policy to maintain equal relations with both neighbors. However, given the geographical proximity between India and the Maldives, it is natural that political gyrations in their relationship will occur.

NOTES

1. "The New Masters and Commanders," *Economist*, June 8, 2013, http://www.economist.com/news/international/21579039-chinas-growing-empire-ports-abroad-mainly-about-trade-not-aggression-new-masters; see also Darshana M. Baruah, "Modi's Trip and China's Islands: The Battle for the Indian Ocean," *Diplomat*, March 11, 2015.

2. See Nilanthi Samaranayake, "India's Key to Sri Lanka: Maritime Infrastructure Development," *Diplomat*, March 31, 2015, http://thediplomat.com/2015/03/indias-key-to-sri-lanka-maritime-infrastructure-development/.

3. See Sandra Destradi, "Domestic Politics and Regional Hegemony: India's Approach to Sri Lanka," *International Relations*, January 14, 2104, http://www.e-ir.info/2014/01/14/domestic-politics-and-regional-hegemony-indias-approach-to-sri-lanka/.

4. "Sri Lanka Seeks Improved Relations with China," *Al Jazeera*, March 26, 2015, http://www.aljazeera.com/news/2015/03/sri-lanka-china-150326081156090.html.

5. Agence France-Presse, "China Offers Sri Lanka Olive Branch and Warnings," *Daily Mail*, March 26, 2015, http://www.dailymail.co.uk/wires/afp/article-3012377/China-offers-Sri-Lanka-olive-branch-warnings.html.

6. See "President Sirisena Completes Successful State Visit to China," *DailyFT*, March 27, 2015, http://www.ft.lk/2015/03/27/president-sirisena-completes-successful-state-visit-to-china/#sthash.ZvgTrVN4.dpuf.

7. Deepal Jayasekera, "Sri Lankan President's Visit to India Highlights Foreign Policy Shift," *World Socialist Web Site*, February 25, 2015, https://www.wsws.org/en/articles/2015/02/25/siri-f25.html.

8. Ibid.

9. Peshan Gunaratne and J. Berkshire Miller, "Sri Lanka: Balancing Ties between China and the West," *Diplomat*, May 26, 2015, http://thediplomat.com/2015/05/sri-lanka-balancing-ties-between-china-and-the-west/.

10. "China, Sri Lanka Pledge to Strengthen Military Cooperation," *Xinhua*, June 9, 2015, http://news.xinhuanet.com/english/2015-06/09/c_134311558.htm.

11. See Ariyaratthna Herath, "China–Sri Lanka Economic Affiliations: Trends and Opportunities," *DailyFT*, September 17, 2014, http://www.ft.lk/2014/09/17/china-sri-lanka-economic-affiliations-trends-and opportunities/#sthash.cNXWkG2N.dpuf.

12. Saman Kelegama, "China-Sri Lanka Economic Relations: An Overview, China Report, May 5, 2014, http://www.ips.lk/staff/ed/publications_ed/international/china_srilanka_economic/china_sl_economics.pdf.

13. "Sri Lanka and China FTA Go Ahead to Re-Balance Ties with Beijing," *Sunday Times*, March 22, 2015, http://www.sundaytimes.lk/150322/business-times/sri-lanka-and-china-fta-go-ahead-to-re-balance-ties-with-beijing-140528.html.

14. Saman Kaligama, "China–Sri Lanka Economic Relations," presentation to the Sri Lanka–China Forum, September 25, 2009, 8, http://www.ips.lk/news/newsarchive/2009/20_9_9_china_business/china_presentation.pdf.

15. Herath, "China–Sri Lanka Economic Affiliations."

16. Rishi Iyengar, "Sri Lanka Attempts to Repair Relations with China amid an Escalating Financial Crisis," *Time*, October 19, 2015, http://time.com/4077757/sri-lanka-china-financial-crisis-ravi-karunanayake-interview/.

17. Ibid.

18. Shannon Tiezzi, "China's $1.4 Billion Port City in Sri Lanka Gets the Green Light," *Diplomat*, March 12, 2016, http://thediplomat.com/2016/03/chinas-1-4-billion-port-city-in-sri-lanka-gets-the-green-light/.

19. Iyengar, "Sri Lanka Attempts."

20. Ibid.

21. Ibid.

22. See Peter Popham, "Sri Lanka Is Welcoming China—and Its Money—Once More," *Independent,* December 11, 2015, http://www.independent.co.uk/voices/sri-lanka-is-welcoming-china-and-its-money-once-more-a6770201.html.

23. Asma Masood, "India—Maldives—China: Strategic Relations," Chennai Centre for China Studies, January 7, 2015, http://www.c3sindia.org/uncategorized/4753 .

24. Anjana Pasricha, "Maldives Reassures India, Says 'No' to Chinese Bases," *Voice of America*, August 10, 2015, http://www.voanews.com/content/maldives-says-no-to-chinese-bases/2910908.html.

25. Ibid.

26. "Maldives Declares State of Emergency ahead of Protest Rally," *Aljazeera America*, November 4, 2015, http://america.aljazeera.com/articles/2015/11/4/maldives-declares-state-of-emergency.html; "Maldives President Abdulla Yameen Declares State of Emergency," *Deccan*

Chronicle, November 4, 2015, http://www.deccanchronicle.com/151104/world-asia/article/maldives-declares-state-emergency-official.

27. Seema Guha, "India Keeps Cautious Vigil as Abdullah Yameen Snuffs Out Democracy in Maldives," *Firstpost*, November 7, 2015, http://www.firstpost.com/world/india-keeps-a-cautious-vigil-as-abdulla-yameen-snuff-out-democracy-in-maldives-2499036.html.

28. Ibid.

29. Sunil Gupta, "Indian Ocean—Checkmating China," June 22, 2015, http://drsunilgupta.com/indian-ocean-checkmating-china/.

30. Adele Verdier-Ali, "Chinese Investment in Global Hospitality Sector Soars, Maldives Strengthens Ties," *Hotelier Maldives*, June 7, 2015, http://www.hoteliermaldives.com/chinese-investment-in-global-hospitality-sector-soars-maldives-strengthens-ties/; see also C. Srikanth Kondapalli, "Maritime Silk Road: Increasing Chinese Inroads into the Maldives," Institute of Peace and Conflict Studies, November 13, 2014, http://www.ipcs.org/article/china/maritime-silk-road-increasing-chinese-inroads-into-the-maldives-4735.html.

31. Huang Haimin, "News Analysis: Chinese Envoy Sees Expanded China-Maldives Economic Cooperation," *Xinhua*, July 21, 2014, http://news.xinhuanet.com/english/indepth/2014-07/21/c_133500267.htm.

32. Ibid.

33. Ibid.

34. Ben Blanchard, "China Says Not Planning Military Bases in the Maldives," July 28, 2015, http://www.reuters.com/article/us-china-maldives-idUSKCN0Q20IU20150728.

35. Baruah, "Modi's Trip."

36. For details, see M. Samatha, "India, Sri Lanka and Maldives Trilateral Maritime Security Cooperation: Political and Economic Constraints in Implementation," policy brief, Indian Council of World Affairs, New Delhi, July 8, 2015, http://www.icwa.in/pdfs/PB/2014/IndiaSri-LankaMaldivesPB08072015.pdf.

37. Ibid., 4.

Chapter Six

China-Bangladesh Relations

From Strangers to Intimate Friends

Over the past four decades, Sino-Bangladeshi relations have undergone a phenomenal transformation. Since the establishment of diplomatic relations in October 1975, their bilateral relations have steadily flourished from strength to strength, except for a brief interregnum when China adopted an anti-Bangladesh stance. It may sound paradoxical that despite fundamental contradictions in terms of history, ideology, ethnicity, and culture both countries have been able to maintain warm and friendly ties. Why and how? In realistic terms, Bangladesh looms large in China's regional and global geopolitical and geostrategic framework. To Bangladesh, Chinese economic and military aid is indispensable for its infrastructure development and fulfillment of its defense requirements. China's relations with Bangladesh are primarily driven by its trade, investment, and energy interests. China is currently the largest trade partner of Bangladesh, with an annual turnover of approximately $10 billion.

Over the past couple decades, the trajectory of domestic politics in Bangladesh has been a critical variable in shaping and articulating its foreign policy and relations. If viewed in a historical context, it is important to know about a fundamental shift in the Beijing-Dhaka relationship since the post–Sheikh Mujibur Rahman leadership. Both countries have come much closer to each other due to a host of intermeshing factors, including shared strategic perceptions and common economic and trade interests. More significant, in the strategic prism of Beijing and Dhaka, India is a regional hegemon in South Asia, as reflected in New Delhi making unilateral decisions without taking note of the region's small states' sensitivities.

   The recent political phenomenon in Bangladesh suggests that irrespective of the political party in power, Bangladesh has displayed pragmatism to strengthen relations with China. The political dispensation in Bangladesh is chiefly guided by the hardboiled reality that China is a potential factor in the country's fast economic development and political stability. What can China offer vis-à-vis India? China's phenomenal economic rise in world politics has convinced the ruling class in Bangladesh that it will be in the larger interest of the country to pursue the policy of a positive tilt toward China. There is a host of overriding reasons for this. First, Bangladesh perceives China as a principal source of economic aid, indispensable for the country's economic development and prosperity. Second, there is a growing perception among Bangladeshis that China is friendlier and more accommodating than India. Third, China is perceived as a noninterventionist in their domestic and foreign affairs. The streak of realism in the foreign policy of Bangladesh was manifest from Prime Minister Sheikh Hasina Wazed's public acknowledgment during her visit to China in 2014, when she said that Bangladesh had pledged to become "an active partner" of the "China-led century."[1] Hasina is widely known as a confirmed pro-India. She wanted to send a clear signal to India that China remains critically important in the development process of Bangladesh in its fast-changing political and economic dynamics, globally and regionally.

   Given this backdrop, hits chapter discusses the multifaceted relation between China and Bangladesh from a holistic/historical perspective. It will also examine whether or not China's strategy of drawing Bangladesh into its orbit of influence through its soft power diplomacy, and concomitantly weakening the Dhaka–New Delhi ties, has met with success given the shared historical legacy and ethnocultural affinity between Bangladesh and India.

   China is at a crossroads in its foreign policy and diplomacy. In an attempt to craft short- and long-term strategies to promote its global and regional interests, President Xi called on his entire party cadre, including Chinese diaspora, to propagate and promote China's cultural soft power, which will help project China's image as a peaceful an responsible nation. Also, Xi's revisiting the Marxist-Maoist ideology is aimed at preventing Western liberal democratic values from taking root in China.

   In China's perception, political pluralism and liberal democratic values do not suit its political system. Its monolithic political structure is based on the belief that embracing Western-style democratic liberalism will not only lead to political chaos and anarchy in the country but also reverse the economic gains achieved so far. China's meteoric economic rise has emboldened the fifth generation of leadership in China and confirmed its belief that it is poised to become a superpower fully capable of breaking the monopoly of the United Sates as the only superpower in the international system. With China's GDP at $10.4 trillion in 2014, its economy is likely to surpass the US economy in 2028. Toward that end, China is frantically engaged in gaining access to energy-rich countries and regions such as Bangladesh, Myanmar, Central Asia, and the Middle East and Gulf countries. Therefore, Xi's ideology-based approach is partly aimed at sustaining peaceful conditions at home, something indispensable for maintaining political stability, economic growth, and societal harmony.

So far as Xi's South Asia policy is concerned, it is guided by three main pillars. First, China will continue to accelerate and consolidate its historic ties with Pakistan, which came to its rescue when China was internationally isolated in the 1960s and early 1970s. Second, Xi has inaugurated the One Road, One Belt (OROB) policy to attract South Asian countries to join it. Bangladesh is one of the parties to the OROB. Third, Xi's energy diplomacy is focused on the vast energy and mineral resources of Bangladesh.

Before we discuss China's political economic, military, and cultural relations with Bangladesh, it is important to see how their relations have evolved and flourished since China's recognition of Bangladesh on October 4, 1975. We will also see what prompted Xi to expand cultural exchanges with Bangladesh as part of China's soft power diplomacy.

HISTORICAL PERSPECTIVE

It is a profound irony that India's pivotal role in the Bangladesh Liberation War in December 1971 has been virtually erased from the memory of ruling elites in Bangladesh. Moralistic pronouncements like indebtedness, gratitude, or obligation have, practically speaking, no value or meaning in international politics. However, the supreme sacrifices the Indian Army made during the Bangladesh Liberation War cannot be set aside easily. In this context, it may be added that the Dhaka government awarded the Bangladesh Liberation War Honour to former Indian prime minister Atal Bihari Vajpayee for his "active role" in the struggle of Bangladesh for independence. The award was received by Prime Minister Narendra Modi on behalf of Vajpayee during his maiden visit to Bangladesh in June 2015.[2] Strangely enough, recognition of this kind is missing in the state-to-state relationship.

To India's great dismay, the newly independent Bangladesh swiftly began cultivating friendly ties with China, which had not only opposed the independence of Bangladesh but also vetoed its admission into the UN in August 1972. Cooperation between the two countries grew smoothly, with both having identical views on international and regional issues. Thus, flowering relations between Beijing and Dhaka were basically guided by Pakistan—an all-weather friend of China. It should be remembered that China accorded recognition to Bangladesh in October 1975 following Pakistan's in 1974.

This shows that Pakistan leveraged its friendship with China in the latter's opposition to the independence of Bangladesh and cultural nationalism.

In hindsight, the political honeymoon period between India and Bangladesh lasted for nearly four years. Prime Minister Indira Gandhi's historic state visit to Bangladesh in March 1972 resulted in a further consolidation of friendly ties between India and Bangladesh. Both the leaders signed a historic Treaty of Peace and Friendship, which committed both countries not to interfere in each other's internal and external affairs. They reaffirmed their unflinching faith in the policy of nonalignment. But the conservative lobby in Bangladesh was unhappy with Sheikh Mujibur Rahman's policy of nonalignment, socialism, and secularism. Hard-core Bangladeshi Muslims disapproved of his policies and called him "India's satellite."

A great tragedy struck Bangladesh when, in a premeditated military coup hatched by a group of junior army officers, Sheikh Mujib, along with his family, was assassinated on August 15, 1975. The country was plunged into political turmoil. During the interregnum, the reign of the country was temporarily in the hands of President Khandakar Mushtaq. After his death, a series of coups and countercoups occurred in the country. Amid the murky domestic condition, army chief general Ziaur Rahman restored internal law and order in the country and declared himself president of the country in 1978. He did three things. First, while exercising his presidential authority, he granted immunity to all those officers who were involved in the assassination of Sheik Mujib and his family. Second, he outright rejected Sheikh Mujib's policies of socialism and secularism. Third, in the foreign policy realm, he tilted toward Pakistan and China.

It was by accident that after the assassination of Sheikh Mujib China got an opportunity to open a new chapter in its relationship with Bangladesh. It opened a diplomatic mission in Bangladesh in October 1975. Top Chinese leaders began befriending Bangladesh by cultivating personal rapport with Bangladesh's military brass—General Ziaur Rahman and General H. M. Ershad. Not surprisingly, the military regime in Bangladesh, which lasted for nearly fifteen years (1976–1990), had better suited China. The latter managed to develop stronger and deeper political ties with Dhaka through the instrumentality of aid diplomacy. The psychological effect on Bangladesh was overwhelmingly conspicuous. Through diplomacy China was able to persuade Bangladesh to pursue an independent foreign policy rather than to toe India's policies.

In order to build some sturdy political rapport with Chinese leaders, Bangladeshi military rulers undertook frequent high-level visits to China, which helped boost bilateral ties in various sectors of mutual concern and interest. Ziaur Rahman, the chief martial law administrator, and the chief of army staff of Bangladesh, paid an official visit to China January 2–6, 1977. Rahman met with Chinese premier Hua Kuo-feng. The visit was reported to be "highly successful." "During the visit, Vice-Premier Li Hsien-nien and Major General Ziaur Rahman exchanged views on the international situation, the strengthening of relations between the two countries and other questions of common concern, thus enhancing their mutual understanding and trust. An economic and technical cooperation agreement and a trade and payment agreement between the Governments of China and Bangladesh were signed in Peking."[3]

Rahman showered praise on China "for supporting Bangladesh to safeguard its national independence and on the issue of the sharing of Ganges water. The two governments signed the Agreement of Economic and Technological Cooperation and the Agreement of Trade Payment."[4] In March 1978 Chinese vice president Li paid a state visit to Bangladesh. During this visit, the two countries signed an agreement of cooperation in economy, science, and technology. President Ziaur Rahman visited China in August 1980. The two governments signed the Agreement of Loans and the Agreement of Aviation Transportation.

Since his Jatiya Party came to power in March 1983, President H. M. Ershad assigned top priority to cultivating relations with China. He paid five visits to China in November 1982, July 1985, July 1987, November 1988, and in June 1990. Ershad stated that relations between China and Bangladesh "had most solid foundation since both the countries enjoyed common targets and interests. The Chinese side stressed that the Sino-Bangladesh relationship was that of mutual trust and cooperation. China welcomed Dhaka government's principled stand on adhering to 'one China' policy—having no official ties with Taiwan. Both the countries signed the Agreement of Cooperation in Science and Technology and the Agreement of Establishing Meeting System between Officials of the two Foreign Ministries."[5]

For his part, as president Li Xiannian visited Bangladesh in March 1986. According to the Chinese Embassy in Bangladesh, "Both sides expressed the determination to further strengthen the traditional friendship and expand cooperation so as to promote the bilateral relations to a higher level."[6] While President Ershad admired China as "a friend of Bangladesh that could stand up to all kinds of tests, President Xiannian appreciated Bangladesh's efforts in enhancing good-neighboring friendship among South Asian countries and promoting regional cooperation in South Asia and its positive contributions to safeguarding peace and stability in the region of South Asia and Asia as a whole."[7]

In November 1989 Chinese premier Li Peng visited Bangladesh. Both countries signed a couple of agreements, covering trade and mutual exemption of visas. During Prime Minister Sheikh Hasina's visit to China in September 1996, agreements on avoidance of double taxation and prevention of tax evasion were signed. In January 2002 Chinese premier Zhu Rongji paid an official visit to Bangladesh. He met with Bangladeshi president A. Q. M.

Badruddoza Chowdhury. Both leaders exchanged views on peace, security, and stability in South Asia. President Chowdhury underlined that both the countries enjoyed "a history of long-standing friendship." Zhu expressed his gratitude to "Bangladesh for its understanding of and support for China over the issues concerning Chinese sovereignty and national feelings such as the issues of Taiwan, Tibet and human rights."[8]

In December 2002 Bangladeshi prime minister Begum Khaleda Zia visited China. Both sides inked four agreements. Exchange of visits by Zhu Rongji and Khaleda Zia in the same year were milestones in the development of Sino-Bangladeshi relations. A key outcome of her visit was the signing of a Defence Cooperation Agreement between the two countries for the first time in the history of their relationship. Under the agreement, China would fulfill the requirements of Bangladesh's defense forces. Some commentators perceived that the defense agreement gave an impression that there existed an Indian threat to the national security of Bangladesh. It is believed that Dhaka's threat perception was created by Pakistani general Pervez Musharraf when he visited Bangladesh in October 2002. In Musharraf's estimation, Bangladesh's defense agreement with China might help divert India's attention from the "West to the East," which would ease pressure on Pakistan. But Bangladeshi's foreign minister clarified that this "defence umbrella agreement" was "not directed against any country and would not affect Bangladesh's relations with India"[9]

Nevertheless, the agreement has long-term strategic implications for India. In India's perception, the defense agreement not only brought China's strategic expansion into India's eastern flank in Bangladesh but also contributed to fulfilling China's game plan to develop the Chittagong Naval Base as it did in Pakistan's Gwadar port. More important, Bangladesh is likely to fall into China's booby-trap, converting Dhaka into Beijing's client state permanently. Without concealing facts, Bangladesh's air force and navy are virtually dependent on Bangladesh since it imports Chinese frigates, boats, and combat aircraft from China. The question still remains to be answered who the enemy is that these weapons would be used against.

In April 2005 Chinese premier Wen Jiabao visited Bangladesh. The two countries established a comprehensive cooperative partnership featuring long-term friendship, equality, and mutual benefit. Both sides also declared the year 2005 as the "Year of China-Bangladesh Friendship" to celebrate the 30th anniversary of diplomatic relations.[10]

Moreover, China's increasing global influence in the 1980s and 1990s onward garnered the attention of the ruling class in Bangladesh, which came to perceive China as an alternative source to India for economic development aid, water management, and maritime security. China did not miss the opportunity to utilize the pro-China image within ruling circles in Bangladesh. For that China came forward with massive economic aid, grants, and soft loans to

Bangladesh, which in the latter's perception would help strengthen its economy and build its infrastructure, apart from boosting cultural exchanges between the two countries.

CHINESE MOTIVATION

As pointed out before, China has vigorously embarked on soft power diplomacy through the instrumentality of foreign aid. This has made it much easier for the Beijing leadership to influence domestic and foreign policies of small nations of South Asia. As China focuses on investment in infrastructure development of Bangladesh, including providing soft loans, it obfuscates the question whether it is politically correct to apply soft power to win the confidence and trust of its neighbors.

In the past couple years China has been pursuing proactive diplomacy in security, defense, and strategic sectors. Without exaggeration, the Beijing leadership under President Xi Jinping is ruthlessly engaged in multipronged diplomacy to encircle India through a sophisticated strategy of offering massive economic aid to win over countries like Nepal and Bangladesh, which harbor anti-India biases for various reasons, notably India's role as a regional hegemon rather than a benign superpower of the region.

Realistically speaking, Beijing-Dhaka relations have neither been structured on geographical proximity nor on solid historical, societal, and cultural linkages. Nor do they share common ideological or ethnic affinity. What then explains the much-hyped all-weather friendship rhetoric"? The answer will be offered in succeeding sections. In brief, however, the Beijing-Dhaka relationship is based on a common agenda of preventing India from becoming a sole regional hegemon. In this context, it ought to be remembered that the foundation of the China-Pakistan relationship was laid on the same understanding when Beijing and Islamabad signed a border agreement in March 1963, under which Pakistan illegally ceded the Shaksgam Valley, around 5,180 square kilometer, to China. In an endeavor to demonstrate the long-surviving, deepening friendship between Beijing and Dhaka, China built six friendship bridges over its rivers—a symbol of depth in their bilateral ties—a 180-degree turn around.

Another attraction that Bangladesh holds for China is its strategic location, which helps serve China's regional goals. Shariful Islam writes, "Bangladesh matters to China in multiple dimensions, such as security, geostrategy and economy. In fact, the geostrategic location of Bangladesh, as a gateway for connectivity between Southeast Asia and South Asia, and as a littoral state on the border of the Bay of Bengal that provides an easy access to and from Myanmar and to China's south-eastern belly, makes the country particularly important."[11]

POLITICAL ORIENTATION

In retrospect, China's cold-shouldered policy toward the Mujib regime from 1972 to 1975 was a manifestation of its dislike for and frustration with Sheikh Mujib's "pro-India" policy and his secular credentials. But soon after his assassination in the military coup on August 15, 1975, the political scenario underwent a huge change. The post-Mujib leadership represented by the military junta's Bangladesh Nationalist Party (1978) and Jatiya Party (1986), led by H. M Ershad, adopted an anti-India stance, while Pakistan and China had prominently figured in their foreign policy approach. First, it gave a political advantage to China to utilize the opportunity to prop up an anti-India constituency in Bangladesh, represented by conservative and extremist elements who had formed a favorable image of China. Second, China did not carry the historic baggage of border conflicts with Bangladesh, unlike India. This also helped China to carve out its new political and strategic role in the post-Mujib era. Third, Bangladesh's geographical proximity to India did not prove to be an asset. Rather, it was a big liability that resulted in tension between Dhaka and New Delhi on many and varied issues, such as distribution of the Ganges water, illegal migration and insurgency across the borders, border security management, and drug- and people-trafficking. In contrast, the absence of geographical contiguity between China and Bangladesh proved a catalyst agent in generating a friendly political environment both internally and externally in the power corridors of Bangladesh.

With the emergence of an assertive Islamic identity in Bangladesh during the political regimes of Ziaur Rahman and General Ershad, India's historical, cultural, and political affinity with Bangladesh had virtually vanished. Rather, Bangladesh viewed China as an alternative source of economic and military aid. From 1975 until the rise of Sheikh Hasina of the Awami League in early 1990s, relations of Bangladesh with India remained tense and chaotic over complex bilateral issues such as the Tin Bigha Corridor, Chakma refugees, and the distribution of water resources left out by the legacy of the partition of India and further fueled by the disintegration of Pakistan in 1971. China was closely watching these developments. For China, it was much easier to forge friendly relations with Bangladesh since there was no direct clash of interests in terms of territory or unresolved bilateral issues. Moreover, China had another advantage. Radical Islamists in Bangladesh had no reservations about cultivating a friendship with China, unlike India. Rather, they openly supported friendship with China as a counterweight to the secular India and its hegemonic designs in the region. In a temptation to use the anti-India political environment in the country, the post-Mujib leadership sent clear signals to the Beijing leadership that Bangladesh wanted to forge closer ties with China, politically, militarily, and strategically.

In the changing political equations over time, China did not face any problem in cultivating friendly relations with Bangladesh Nationalist Party leader Khaleda Zia or Awami League chief Sheikh Hasina—these two women alternatively held the prime ministerial position in the governance of Bangladesh since 1991.

During Prime Minister Sheikh Hasina's official visit to China in March 2010, both countries agreed to establish the Closer Comprehensive Partnership of Cooperation Agreement. They also agreed to enhance economic and technical cooperation between the two countries in addition to from forging rail and road links to facilitate bilateral trade. According to a joint statement, the Bangladesh government welcomed "the active involvement of Chinese enterprises in the energy, communication, transportation, industry and infrastructure sectors in Bangladesh."[12] What was more important for China was to deepen its cooperation in oil and gas sectors, as was manifest from the signing of the Memorandum of Understanding on Cooperation in the Oil and Gas Sector between the two countries.

MILITARY AND SECURITY TIES

China has emerged as the largest supplier of military hardware to Bangladesh. Its military and security cooperation with Bangladesh is perceived by the Dhaka government as a "security hedge" against India, though falsely propagated by China. According to a Swedish International Peace Research Institute (SIPRI) fact sheet from March 2015, "Chinese exports of major arms increased by 143 per cent between 2005–2009 and 2010–14, and China's share of global arms exports increased from 3 to 5 per cent. China became the third largest supplier in 2010–14, slightly ahead of Germany and France. China supplied major arms to 35 states in 2010–14. A significant percentage (just over 68 per cent) of Chinese exports went to three countries: Pakistan, Bangladesh and Myanmar."[13] According to Al Jazeera, there is "continuing scourge of weapons-smuggling from China into South Asia," notably originating from Bangladesh. Bangladesh is the main destination of China's smuggled weapons.[14]

Slowly but steadily, China has emerged as a major arms supplier, including transferring small arms like AK-47 rifles to Bangladesh. It remains, however, ambivalent as to against whom Chinese weapons will be used. Even in its wild imagination, India scarcely entertains the idea of threatening the national security of Bangladesh. There is no evidence available so far to suggest that India ever threatened Bangladesh. But the Beijing leadership has been engaged in projecting India as a potential threat to Bangladesh. Arguably, China has been pleading with the Dhaka government that there is imperative need for beefing up its security with Chinese military assistance.

It has already supplied missiles, heavy guns, and tanks (T-59) to Bangladesh. In addition, Chinese strategic designs are aimed at encouraging its maritime presence in Bangladesh.

China has been active since 2002 to help build Bangladesh's military capabilities. It has emerged as a major supplier of military hardware to Bangladesh, including the transfer of two Ming-class submarines in 2014. It has also been reported that a missile launchpad near the Port of Chittagong was set up with Chinese assistance in 2008. As Asma Masood asserts:

> These developments make it clear that Bangladesh fears perceived Indian hegemony. However Sheikh Hasina has reassured Delhi that her state will not be a base for anti-Indian maneuvers. Such traditional military threats do not exist, but there are non-traditional threats towards India. These include terrorist outfits operating from Bangladeshi soil. This is one reason for which Bangladesh is keen to have strong military alliance with China, apart from counter-insurgency cooperation with India. It helps maintain the small state's internal security. It also addresses China's call for peace in Bangladesh for smooth development. Besides, a strong military setup adds a perception of stability in the eyes of international community which is observing constant political turmoil in Bangladesh. In Beijing's and Dhaka's view, such perceptions will help prevent hegemonic tendencies from greater powers such as India and U.S.A [15]

Sino-Bangladeshi relations got a further boost when Wen Jiabao paid an official visit to Bangladesh in April 2005. During this visit, the two countries initialed nine agreements, of which the most important pertained to the peaceful use of nuclear energy. The increasing strategic cooperation between Beijing and Dhaka clearly suggested that India ought to have resurrected and rejuvenated its ties with Bangladesh to deny China a large strategic space in South Asia.

Contrary to the views of some Indian strategic analysts, it is incorrect to say that Dhaka has come closer to Beijing, emotionally or spontaneously. The reality is that China has managed to not only produce an anti-India lobby in Bangladesh by providing the country with modern military hardware on a massive scale but also instill fear into the minds of the ruling class and radical elements in Bangladesh that India is the real enemy of Bangladesh while China is its friend.

As mentioned before, China's air and naval buildup has brought the country strategically closer to Bangladesh. Chinese ships have the freedom to access Bangladesh's Chittagong port. Apart from this, China agreed to transfer two Ming-class submarines to Bangladesh in 2013 at a cost of $203 million. Four military agreements were signed between Bangladesh and China in May 2014 to enhance Dhaka's "defence capabilities." "Under the agreements, Chinese military would provide military support to Bangladesh armed forces and provide training to military personnel. They will also help setting up a language laboratory under the agreement at Bangladesh University of Professionals." [16]

According to the SIPRI report, Bangladesh purchased "anti-ship missiles, tanks, fighter aircrafts and other arms from China between 2008 and 2012." Bangladesh finds Chinese arms much cheaper compared to the international arms bazar, including India, and therefore Chinese arms are "lucrative" for it. [17]

It should be noted that China is the biggest arms supplier to Bangladesh. [18] This was testified to by Prime Minister Sheikh Hasina when she confirmed that China and Bangladesh have had strong naval cooperation, as was evident from the decision of inducting two Chinese submarines into the Bangladeshi navy to build it into a three-dimensional force. According to the Chinese ambassador in Dhaka, Li Jun, the submarines would help Bangladesh bring "stability in the region." [19] Apart from this, Bangladesh procured two new frigates, *Abu Bakar* and *Ali Haider*, from China in March 2015.

Bangladesh's chief of army staff Abu Belal Muhammad Shafiul Huq visited Beijing on December 3, 2015. He met with Wang Jianping, deputy chief of general staff of the PLA. Both sides eulogized the increasing military relations between China and Bangladesh and pledged "deeper cooperation" in the future. "Gen. Wang expressed satisfaction with the decades-long sound mil-to-mil relations between the two countries as evidenced by the pragmatic and efficient cooperation in many areas, hoping that the two militaries can keep enhancing high-level exchange of visits, communication between military academies and cooperation in technologies and personnel training." [20]

According to Nurul Islam Hasib, "The two countries have built up a solid military relationship, thanks largely to the fact that China is Bangladesh's largest supplier of military equipment. Since 2010, Beijing has supplied Dhaka with five maritime patrol vessels, two corvettes, 44 tanks, and 16 fighter jets, as well as surface-to-air and anti-ship missiles, according to the Stockholm International Peace Research Institute. That's in addition to new Ming-class submarines Bangladesh ordered from China in 2013, which are expected to enter the Bangladeshi fleet in 2016, according to Prime Minister Sheikh Hasina." [21] As expected by the Hasina government, Bangladesh took delivery of its first-ever submarines from China in November 2016. The *Times of India* said, "The two diesel-electric submarines handed over to Bangladesh Navy chief Admiral Mohammed Nizamuddin Ahmed at the Dalian seaport of Liaoning province in China, is a big indicator of the extensive military ties forged between Dhaka and Beijing." [22] The *Times of India* noted that during President Xi's first-ever visit to Bangladesh in thirty years, twenty-seven deals worth a total of $25 billion were signed and then went on to say, "India, of course, can neither match China's economic muscle nor its domestic defence industrial base." [23]

SINO-BANGLADESHI TRADE AND INVESTMENT TIES

Since the emergence of Bangladesh as an independent nation in 1971, India has been its largest trading partner. In the early 1990s, India's exports to Bangladesh were 150 times bigger than China's exports to Bangladesh. But China surpassed India with faster speed in the early twenty-first century. A host of factors were responsible for the growing decline in India's trade with Bangladesh. First, structural changes in global and regional economies facilitated relations among nations in economic, trade, and investment realms. Second, the establishment of the WTO provided enormous opportunities to countries like China to expand their trade market globally and regionally. Third, infrastructure connectivity through sea trade made it much easier for China to rev up its trade and commerce with Bangladesh. Fourth, contrary to India's nontariff barriers, like bureaucratic bottlenecks and visa encumbrances, Bangladeshi traders find a hassle-free and friendlier environment when doing business with China. In addition, China's development assistance and soft project loans have created goodwill for China among the people of Bangladesh. In cumulative terms, China has emerged as Bangladesh's largest trading partner. There has been a phenomenal increase in the bilateral trade from just $900 million in 2000 to $14.7 billion in 2015. The number is expected to touch the mark of $30 billion by 2020. Apart from this, Bangladesh has endorsed China's initiatives of "One Belt and One Road" and the Bangladesh-China-India-Myanmar economic corridor.

During Prime Minister Sheikh Hasina's visit to China in June 2014 a series of agreements and MoUs were signed, which included a joint venture to establish a 1,320-megawatt coal-fired power plant. Hasina is poised to deepen economic and trade engagement with China as a rebuff to the United States and European Union, who together dubbed the January 2014 national elections "not credible," doubting the legitimacy of the Hasina government. China, Russia, and Japan kept mum on this.

As reported by Al Jazeera, "The two countries signed a memorandum of understanding on the creation of a Chinese economic and investment zone in Chittagong, Bangladesh's main deep-sea port, and discussed construction of a highly anticipated second port at Sonadia, a tiny island in the Bay of Bengal sea. . . . Sonadia may emerge as a major regional trade hub as it provides sea access to China's Yunnan province, India's landlocked north-eastern states, the Himalayan nation of Nepal, and Bhutan."[24] But India felt much relief when the Hasina government scrapped the Sonadia deep-sea port project in early 2016. It was a big jolt to the dragon.

It should also be noted that China was neither a major donor nor a significant aid contributor to Bangladesh until 2009–1010. Though China has become Bangladesh's biggest trading partner, its imports from Bangladesh are increasingly on decline.[25] Bangladesh suffers a heavy trade deficit vis-à-vis

China. "The bilateral trade deficit between Bangladesh and China stood at $9,112 million in 2013." In fiscal year 2014–2015 (July 2014–June 2015), it surged 45.97 percent to about $10 billion. In order to "address the growing trade imbalance, Beijing . . . offered duty-free access for 4,721 Bangladeshi products."[26]

Despite China's duty-free access to Bangladeshi goods, its trade deficit did not narrow. As reported in *Xinhua*, Bangladeshi officials said "remittances from nearly nine million Bangladeshis, living and working abroad, helped offset the impact of the trade shortfall and kept the overall balance of payments in surplus. The BB (Bangladesh Bank) data showed in the 2014–15 financial year, inflow of remittances stood at nearly 14.23 billion U.S. dollars."[27] Also, China is a major investor in Bangladesh's key sectors such as agriculture, energy, industry and infrastructure. In 2014 China invested $43 million in Bangladesh. Ambassador Li Jun expressed a sense of optimism that China's investment in Bangladesh would increase, which would help narrow trade deficit of Bangladesh vis-à-vis China. He stated, "It is for sure that the establishment of CIZ [Chinese Industry Zone] will attract more Chinese investment, especially in the labour intensive industries. Hopefully, with more Chinese investment, Bangladesh export to China will get notable increase and the bilateral trade will be more balanced."[28]

Be that as it may, China's soft power tools in Bangladesh have produced mixed results. In fact, China's increasing influence over Bangladesh has prompted Beijing's top leadership to assign priority to Bangladesh through high-level political visits. President Xi's visit to Bangladesh in October 2016 "set new milestones" in their relationship with his commitment to provide Bangladesh with soft loans worth $25 billion for over two dozen projects. The real motivation of XI's visit was to elevate China's relations with Bangladesh to the level of strategic partnership between two countries. Bangladesh also realized that Xi's visit to Bangladesh opened up vast avenues not only to promote its "geo-economic interests" but also to elevate its "geopolitical standing" in the region.[29]

However, it is yet to be seen how China's soft power diplomacy works by committing soft loans for its various projects. In this context, it is important to remember that during the Rajapaksa regime in Sri Lanka, China heavily invested in developing its ports, including the Hambantota port and the Colombo port city. Initially, they looked very attractive to Sri Lanka. But now Sri Lanka is facing a terrible debt burden. China has been insisting on repayment of outstanding debt. Surprisingly, over of 90 percent Sri Lanka's revenue goes to foreign debt repayment. From the Sri Lankan experience, Bangladesh needs to be extremely cautious, lest it fall into China's debt trap of the unsustainable debt servicing ratio, before it proceeds further to conclude projects with China. In other words, Bangladesh ought to carefully study the feasibility and relevance of projects in cost-effective terms and from a long-term perspective.

PEOPLE-TO-PEOPLE CONTACT

As an integral part of its soft power strategy, the Chinese government laid emphasis on promoting the exchange of visits from people on both sides. Importantly, China has introduced the scheme of various scholarships to Bangladeshi students, including for young Bangladeshi diplomats. During Prime Minister Hasina's visit to China in 2010, it was agreed that "the two sides will actively expand exchanges and cooperation in culture, press, health, sports and tourism and promote contacts between the media organizations, think tanks, scholars, friendship groups, women's groups, cultural troupes, athletes and youths."[30]

In pursuit of promoting its positive image, China is poised to boost people-to-people contact between the two countries through educational and cultural exchange program. Chinese vice premier Liu Yandon, during her visit to Dhaka in May 2015, announced, "China will offer 100 scholarships for Bangladeshi students in the next three years, donate 1 million RMB [renminbi] (160,000 U.S. dollars) in education equipment to the China Studies Centre of the Dhaka University, and invite 100 Bangladeshi university students to take part in the "Chinese Bridge" summer camp in China this year."[31] In 2015 more than four hundred Bangladeshis went to China for studying various courses, including in the medical field, under the sponsorship of the Beijing government. No doubt, China has emerged as an attractive destination for Bangladeshi youth, who have immeasurably contributed to not only producing China's positive image within the country but also creating a large political constituency that favors prioritizing Dhaka's relationship with Beijing.

CONCLUSION

China has been able to strengthen and deepen its ties with Bangladesh through various soft power tools such as development assistance, scholarships, promotion of tourism and media contacts, exchanges between think tanks and scholars, performances of cultural troupes and social groups to project its image as a soft power practitioner. China's noninterference in Bangladesh's internal and external affairs on the one hand and Bangladesh's acceptance of the one-China doctrine on the other hand have contributed to easy relations between the two countries. Apart from this, they share common perceptions on global and regional affairs, which might go a long way in consolidating their bilateral ties. I share the widely accepted view of the strategic community that China's increasing influence in Bangladesh might transform "Chittagong into Gwadar East."[32] It is true that conservative lobbies in Dhaka prefer China's engagement with Bangladesh. China's soft loans and grants to Bangladesh under the banner of soft power policy have been welcomed, although with some reservations. It is true that Bangladesh has become economically more dependent on China than ever before. It suffers from a huge trade deficit vis-à-vis China. In spite of that, Bangladesh does not discount China's constructive role in its economic and infrastructure development, apart from its role in building Bangladesh's defense capabilities. A kind of anti-India lobby is working in Bangladesh under a nuanced and subtle Chinese initiative while the South Block in New Delhi is not proactive to counter China's canards against India. Moreover, the Indian ruling class has diplomatically failed to weaken China's strategic grip over Bangladesh. In fact, China has been relentlessly engaged in anti-India propaganda by projecting India's image as a regional hegemon in South Asia. Therefore, India needs to sensitize Bangladesh to the fact that China has been creating artificial threat perceptions to spoil relations between New Delhi and Dhaka. From a geopsychological perspective, Bangladesh needs to learn a bitter lesson from the Indian experience that China's strategic culture is fundamentally rooted in expanding its strategic footprint while simultaneously chanting the mantra of peaceful coexistence. Keeping this centrality of argument in mind, Bangladesh needs to recalibrate its ties with China, informed by a mix of pragmatism and prudence.

It is unfortunate that Modi's minions and party spokespersons on various TV channels have been projecting him as India's messiah to save the country from the dragon's bullying. The underlying reality is that the Modi government has not yet precisely crafted India's foreign policy to effectively meet the myriad Chinese challenges to Indian interests in Bangladesh, except for its occasionally harping on China's "strategic and expansionist" motive in Bangladesh. The situation is likely to further complicate India's long-term strategic interest if China expands its naval arm in the Bay of Bengal, and further upgrades its access to the Indian Ocean.

NOTES

1. Syed Tashfin Chowdhury, "Bangladesh Woos China in Snub to West," *Aljazeera*, June 23, 2014, http://www.aljazeera.com/indepth/features/2014/06/bangladesh-woos-china-snub-west-20146236549759339.html; "India-Bangladesh Ties: Dhaka Must Show Intent to Improve Relations, Build Confidence," *Times of India*, September 3, 2014, http://timesofindia.indiatimes.com/india/India-Bangladesh-ties-Dhaka-must-show-intent-to-improve-relations-build-confidence/articleshow/41628396.cms.

2. Press Trust of India, "Bangladesh Confers Award of Liberation War Honour on Atal Bihari Vajpayee," *Indian Express*, June 7, 2015, http://indianexpress.com/article/india/india-others/bangladesh-confers-award-of-liberation-war-honour-on-atal-bihari-vajpayee/.

3. "New Developments in China-Bangladesh Relations," *Peking Review* 2, no. 2 (January 7, 1977): 4, https://www.marxists.org/subject/china/peking-review/1977/PR1977-02.pdf.

4. "China-Bangladesh Relations," Economic and Commercial Counsellor's Office of the Embassy of the People's Republic of China in the People's Republic of Bangladesh, May 16, 2007,   http://bd2.mofcom.gov.cn/article/bilateralcooperation/inbrief/200705/20070504675608.shtml.

5. Ibid.

6. Ibid.

7. Ibid.

8. "Chinese PM Meets Bangladeshi President," *Xinhua*, January 12, 2002, http://news.xinhuanet.com/english/2002-01/12/content_235890.htm.

9. Subhash Kapila, "Bangladesh-China Defence Cooperation's Strategic Implications: An Analysis," South Asia Analysis Group, paper 582, January 14, 2003, http://www.southasiaanalysis.org/paper582.

10. "Major Events in Sino-Bangladeshi Relations," *China Radio International(CRI English)*, June 14, 2010, http://english.cri.cn/6909/2010/06/14/1361s576666.htmhttp://english.cri.cn/6909/2010/06/14/1361s576666.htm.

11. Shariful Islam, "China-Bangladesh Relations," *Global Times*, September 27, 2015, http://www.globaltimes.cn/content/944756.shtml.

12. "Joint Statement between the People's Republic of China and the People's Republic of Bangladesh," Embassy of the People's Republic of China in the People's Republic of Bangladesh, http://bd.china-embassy.org/eng/zmgx/zywj/t697175.htm.

13. Pieter D. Wezeman and Siemon T. Wezeman, "Trends in International Arms Transfers, 2014," SIPRI Fact Sheet, Stockholm International Peace Research Institute, March 2015, http://books.sipri.org/files/FS/SIPRIFS1503.pdf.

14. Subir Bhaumik, "Smuggling of China-Made Weapons in Focus," *Asia Pacific,* February 4, 2014, http://www.aljazeera.com/news/asia-pacific/2014/02/smuggling-china-made-weapons-focus-20142463722679830.html.

15. Asma Masood, "India-Bangladesh-China Relations: A Complex Triangle," Chennai Centre for China Studies, March 2, 2015, http://www.c3sindia.org/india/4860.

16. Nurul Islam Hasib, "4 Military Agreements Signed with China," bnnews24.com, May 12, 2014, http://bdnews24.com/bangladesh/2014/05/12/4-military-agreements-signed-with-china.

17. Ibid.

18. See Wezeman and Wezeman, "Trends in International Arms."

19. Sheikh Shahariar Zaman, "Chinese Submarines in Bangladesh to Help Bring Stability in the Region," *Dhaka Tribune*, March 7, 2014, http://archive.dhakatribune.com/law-amp-rights/2014/mar/07/chinese-submarines-bangladesh-help-bring-stability-region#sthash.HpVHjHka.dpuf.

20. "China, Bangladesh Cement Bilateral Military Relations," *China Military Online*, December 3, 2015, http://english.chinamil.com.cn/news-channels/china-military-news/2015-12/03/content_6798961.htm.

21. Hasib, "4 Military Agreements."

22. Rajat Pandit, "To Counter China, Government Rushing Defence Minister Manohar Parrikar to Bangladesh," *Times of India,* November 16, 2016, 7.

23. Ibid.

24. Syed Tashfin Chowdhury, "Bangladesh Woos China in Snub to West," *Al Jazeera,* June 23, 2014, http://www.aljazeera.com/indepth/features/2014/06/bangladesh-woos-china-snub-west-20146236549759339.html.

25. M. Serajul Islam, "Four Decades of Sino-Bangladesh Relations," *Daily Sun*, October 27, 2015, http://www.daily-sun.com/printversion/details/86269/Four-Decades-of-Sino-Bangladesh-Relations.

26. Fahmida Khatun, "Country Illustration Report: Bangladesh," Centre for Policy Dialogue, August 26, 2014, 43, https://ec.europa.eu/europeaid/sites/devco/files/erd5-country-illustration-bangladesh-2015_en.pdf.

27. "Bangladesh's 2014–15 Fiscal Trade Deficit Balloons to 10 bln USD on Import Pick-up," *English.news.cn*, August 12, 2015, http://news.xinhuanet.com/english/2015–08/12/c_134508598.htm.

28. LI Jun, "A New Opportunity for China-Bangladesh Cooperation," *Bangladesh News*, March 12, 2014, http://opinion.bdnews24.com/2014/03/12/a-new-opportunity-for-china-bangladesh-cooperation.

29. Tekendra Parmar, "China's President Xi Jinping Makes 'Historic Visit' to Bangladesh," *Time*, October 14, 2016, http://time.com/4530974/bangladesh-xi-jinping-visit-china/.

30. Ibid.

31. "Chinese Vice Premier Stresses People-to-People Exchanges with Bangladesh," *Xinhua*, May 26, 2015, http://news.xinhuanet.com/english/2015–05/26/c_134271332.htm.

32. Farabi Ahmed, "Trade Relations between China and Bangladesh," Slideshare, August 6, 2015, http://www.slideshare.net/farabii/china-bangladesh-trade-relations.

Conclusion

The central theme of the book is to explore and assess the motivation and rationale behind China's launch of soft power diplomacy in South Asia. Intellectual and political discourse on the theory and practice of the Chinese model of cultural soft power enables one to better grasp the international relations theory offered by the Chinese school of thought in the changing contours of the international system. It, indeed, is an excruciating task to scientifically establish the potency of the Chinese version of soft power. Reasons for this are crystal clear. First, the rise of China as a global power has triggered its political ambition to advance an alternative theory of international relations in order to replace the West-centric world order with a Sino-centric "harmonious" world order. Second, the current fifth generation of Chinese leadership appears to be overenthusiastic about showcasing the country's extraordinary accomplishments in every sector of development to project China's rise as a peaceful and responsible stakeholder in the world order. Third, China's astounding success in managing its economy even in the face of the worst global financial meltdown since the 1930s' economic depression bolstered its morale to expand its political and economic footprints across the globe. South Asia is not an exception.

The book aims to understand the dynamics of China's great game in South Asia in which the triangular relationship of China, India, and Pakistan forms a bedrock to examine the ground reality of China's soft power diplomacy in the region. In the contextual narratives, it is important to examine whether or not the Sino-centric harmonious world, based on China's ancient traditions and cultural values, is practically achievable. Analysis reveals that this may sound good in principle or theory. But in practice, the Chinese brand of a harmonious world order runs counter to China's overt and covert strategic offensives against its neighbors, as reinforced by its flexing of military muscles to bully neighbors on territorial disputes. The South China Sea is a classic case in this regard.

It may be recalled that the top Beijing leadership flatly refused to abide by the Hague-based international arbitration tribunal's ruling of July 2016. The tribunal concluded that there was no legal basis for China's claim to historic rights to resources within the seas. It further observed that China violated the Philippines' sovereign rights in its exclusive economic zone in the South China Sea. On the contrary, President Xi Jinping stated that China's territorial sovereignty and marine rights in the seas would remain intact. In this scenario, how can the ideal goal of a peaceful and stable regional order be achieved? In this regard, the Beijing leadership has been unable to offer any plausible explanation. Notably, Chinese academia and media are resoundingly confused over the modus operandi of establishing linkages between the necessary conditions for using soft power as an instrument of foreign aid on the one hand and geostrategic imperatives to use hard power on the other. In this dilemmatic situation, there is a challenging task to manage a proper combination of hard and soft power, especially when it comes to choosing global norms or strategic expediency.

In light of this backdrop, broad conclusions will be spelled out in the following sections. Though China's normative soft power has triggered an interest among international relations theorists and academia, they remain skeptical about the potency and feasibility of soft power. There is a lurking uncertainty within the ruling circles as to whether China will be able to convert soft power instruments into positive outcomes. In this regard, most scholars hold the view that China's soft power, based on Chinese characteristics, is inconsistent with Joseph S. Nye's notion of soft power. To Nye, soft power is based on "domestic realities," informed by a free, liberal, and democratic society. David Shambaugh also opines that soft power is not a "commodity" to be bought with money; rather it is "earned."[1] In this context, some Sinologists subscribe to the view that the Chinese model of a harmonious world is far from being an exceptional model of a perfect world, of one world and one dream.

In the case of South Asia, a mixed scenario emerges. Despite academia's harangue and pessimism regarding the ability of China's soft power to attract its neighbors, the Chinese influence over smaller countries in the region is conspicuously visible, much to India' s chagrin. So far as strategic rivalry and economic competition between India and China is concerned, it will make it harder for China to sell off its soft power artifacts. The reason is very simple. The past scar of India's humiliating defeat at Chinese hands remains deeply entrenched in the Indian psyche. The continuing impasse, since 1962, between the two countries on the boundary issue does not augur well to build mutual trust between China and India. This has besmirched China's image, in India's perception, as an aggressive and irresponsible power.

Notably, China has managed to win over Sri Lanka, the Maldives, and Nepal and downgrade their traditional high-voltage relationship with India. Though the Narendra Modi government may boast of regaining the trust of most South Asian countries, the fact remains that Indian diplomacy lacks not only clarity and coherence but also a well-calibrated and a well-integrated approach to deal with neighbors. Despite the flawed approach, the much-hyped Indian media has credited Prime Minister Modi with isolating Pakistan among South Asian Association of Regional Cooperation (SAARC) nations on the issue of the terrorist attack on an army camp in Uri sector in Jammu and Kashmir in September 2016 in which seventeen Indian soldiers were killed. It was on India's call for boycott that all SAARC member states, except Pakistan, decided not to participate in the SARRC summit scheduled to be held in Islamabad in November 2016. But this is only the tip of the iceberg that is the so-called isolation of Pakistan—a temporary atmospheric change in South Asian politics. Without losing time, Pakistan delivered a diplomatic punch to India, saying that Pakistan is not bereft of good friends like China, Russia, and US president Donald Trump, who all value Pakistan's geopolitical and strategic value.

Realistically enough, China's soft power diplomacy in South Asia is driven by its strategy to allay the lurking fear and suspicion among South Asian states that China constitutes a threat to their national security and to regional peace and stability. In other words, China has taken a softer tone to convince them of its genuine desire to invest in infrastructure development for jobs and the welfare of their people. But such assurances have not convinced India. Rather, the unresolved territorial dispute with China has, in Indian perception, undermined the credibility of China's soft power initiatives in the region. Therefore, the biggest challenge before Chinese public diplomacy will be muddling through in the face of an annoyed India.

Though China' soft power does not have global appeal, it is attractive and alluring to smaller nations of South Asia, mainly because of incentives behind China's foreign aid to those nations' infrastructure development and economic modernization. China's record on lending money to developing countries in the first decade of the twenty-first century has far exceeded the quantum of aid released by the World Bank. But the sad story is that China's heavy investments has resulted in a mounting debt problem—for instance, in developing ports in Sri Lanka, crippling the Sri Lankan economy. Can this be termed a win-win situation? On the domestic front also, China does not carry the image of a tolerant and rule-abiding nation. China's brutal crackdown on prodemocracy protesters in Tiananmen Square in 1989 and heavy-handed action by the Hong Kong police against student protesters in 2014 are both deeply etched in the people's psyche. Apart from this, the simmering unrest among Tibetans clamoring for cultural autonomy, and the PLA's frequent use of repressive measures against the independence movement of the Uighur Muslim community reinforce Communist China's authoritarian rule. These instances show that China is unable to defend its soft power image.

As regards the China-India soft power equation, there are enormous challenges as well as opportunities. The single biggest challenge to their relationship is the unresolved boundary dispute between the two countries. Frequent encroachments on Indian territory by Chinese armed forces across the LoC have created a warlike situation. Despite nineteen rounds of border talks that have been held, as of April 2016, between SRs of the two governments, no substantial progress has been registered to settle the boundary issue once and for all. This has produced a huge trust deficit between Beijing and New Delhi. In fact, the boundary issue is a litmus test for China as to whether its soft power approach is applicable to India. Despite the border controversy, both countries have many opportunities to work closely together on issues of common interest, such as terrorism, insurgency, drug trafficking, nuclear terrorism, and cyber crimes.

Interestingly, the center-right government led by Prime Minister Modi is trying to ride two horses at once. On the one hand, Modi has displayed an extraordinary penchant for strengthening friendly ties with China in order to benefit from China's experience in infrastructure development in key sectors of its economy. On the other hand, he is singularly engaged in building strategic ties with Japan—China's main adversary. It will be a tough task for Modi to strike a fine balance in India's relationship with China and Japan, and China and the United States. What is more disappointing for New Delhi is that, though Modi called Pakistan the "mothership of terrorism," he failed to persuade President XI to include a reference to Pakistan or its home-grown terrorist outfits such as Lashkar-e-Taiba in the Goa Declaration of the BRICS summit held on Indian soil in October 2016.[2] Rather, President Xi maintained a stoic silence over Modi's remarks. Nor did Xi react to Modi's veiled attempt to accuse China of adopting double standards on terrorism. This is a classic example of China's apathetic and unfriendly attitude toward India and clear-cut preference for Pakistan. Briefly, the Goa summit dealt a big blow to the personal image of Modi. Hence, India should not live in a fool's paradise and believe that China would ever loosen or break off its ties with Pakistan for the sake of its friendship with India.

Furthermore, without glossing over an irreversible reality, Pakistan will remain a permanent cause of trouble in Sino-Indian relations. India understands well that Pakistan will never spare any effort to block India's entry into multilateral organizations, whether it be India's permanent membership to the UN Security Council or its membership to NSG-48 or APEC, by soliciting China's every possible diplomatic succor. For instance, India's flawed diplomacy was manifest from China's twice thwarting India's move at the UN to ban JeM Chief Masood Azhar, the mastermind of the Pathankot terror attack in January 2016. In other words, Pakistan will remain China's preeminent tool in its bid to dilute India's influence in the region. So far as China's soft power initiatives in South Asia are concerned, India is scarcely fascinated by them. For India has been a home of cultural soft power for centuries, well known for a rich culture, spirituality, and yoga as well as for an extraordinary cross-cultural absorptive capacity. Moreover, Indian perception is not favorably disposed toward China on account of its bitter experiences in the past. The historic baggage of mistrust between China and India stems from intermeshing variables, including the unresolved boundary dispute, China's massive assistance to Pakistan's nuclear weapons and missiles program, and its much-hyped geopolitical "string of pearls" doctrine, which is primarily aimed at India's strategic containment. All these instances do not augur well for better returns of China's soft power resources. Arguably, China's rhetoric of soft power initiatives will not substantially contribute to establishing peace, stability, or prosperity in the region.

China's charm offensive may, however, lure smaller countries of the region into its embrace. This will last so long as China's economic and infrastructure aid on nonstringent conditions continues. Its cultural soft power will be appealing so long as China does not overtly or covertly threaten those countries' national security. But once smaller countries such as Nepal, Bhutan, and the Maldives come to realize that the mounting debts they owe to China might cripple their economies, they might consider it imperative to break or loosen their economic and investment ties with China. Alternatively, they will look to India, their old partner in nation building. But at this stage it is difficult to predict precisely whether China will continue to allure new partners in South Asia with its soft power resources.

So far as the all-weather friendship between China and Pakistan is concerned, it is narrowly focused on their common objective of weakening and destabilizing India. Interestingly, China may have strategic solidarity with Pakistan, but it has not offered any blanket security guarantee to Pakistan or entered into a treaty to come to its rescue if India ever threatens Pakistani security. Also, Islamabad should not remain confident that its bonhomie with Beijing will enable it to garner Chinese support in the UN Security Council on the question of holding plebiscite in the Kashmir valley to determine the political wishes of Kashmiris. On numerous occasions in the past, China did not intervene on behalf of Pakistan. It may be recalled that China did not act on Nixon's and Kissinger's repeated pleas to attack India to help defend Pakistan in the 1971 War with India. Nor did China offer military assistance or diplomatic succor to Pakistan in the Kargil conflict in 1999. Much to Pakistan's chagrin, Chinese leaders outright rejected Pakistani request for military intervention in its favor. On the contrary, China feels much embarrassed by Pakistan's overt and covert hand in encouraging or sponsoring terrorist attacks against India. Also, China is inherently fully conscious of its bad image and reputation when it comes across a trenchant criticism from Washington and New Delhi on the issue of transfer of nuclear material and missiles to Pakistan. On numerous occasions, China was failed to defend itself from the violation of Missile Technology Control Regime guidelines when the United States slapped sanctions on it for its alleged transfer of M-11 missiles to Pakistan.

It needs to be underlined that China's public rhetoric of describing its age-old ties with Pakistan as "sweeter than honey" and "higher than Hima-layan heights" has no substantial value. Also, Pakistan needs to cerebrate that China's interests in Pakistan are driven by a host of factors, such as eliciting Pakistani succor in dealing with Uighur separatists in Xinxiang and engaging India at northwestern borders. China's massive investment worth $46 billion in the CPEC project is a component of China's grand strategy to ensure an uninterrupted supply of oil, including a massive slash in shipment costs of oil imports from the Middle East through the Strait of Malacca. It is estimated that China might save approximately $2 billion every year. But this project is likely to undermine the interests of the people of Baluchistan in terms of employment, infrastructure development, and economic prosperity.

Moreover, the geopolitical reality cannot be brushed aside that China and India are carrying out joint military exercises; both are mutually cooperating on regional and global issues. Perhaps China will not undertake any such misadventures that might jeopardize its relations with India. As a hard core pragmatist, President Xi will not risk putting Sino-Indian relations on the back burner. Given the current security and strategic environment at global and regional levels, characterized by uncertainty and unpredictability, China will avoid forging an alliance with Pakistan based on the US pattern. One thing is certain that China will not support: Pakistan's costly proposals, such as deployment of Chinese forces in the PoK against India or directly jumping into a war with India on its behalf.

Yet India needs to be wary of Chinese designs in South Asia, which are narrowly focused on restricting, limiting, and diluting India's role and influ-ence, directly or indirectly, through a calibrated network of strategic partner-ships with South Asian countries, such as Pakistan, Bangladesh, Nepal, and Sri Lanka. But regarding Pakistan, the applicability of China's soft power diplomacy has neither relevance nor value since Pakistan—its old strategic partner—has been a top recipient of China's massive military and economic aid. In other words, China need not indulge in a charm offensive to attract Pakistan and draw it into its political and strategic fold.

So far as China's soft power diplomacy toward Himalayan states is con-cerned, it has succeeded in expanding its footprint there, enabling Beijing to play a larger strategic role impacting not only their external affairs but also their domestic politics. Under the garb of providing economic aid and grants for infrastructure development, Beijing has managed to come closer to Kathmandu and Thimpu. Though India is not opposed to China's growing economic and trade ties with them, what worries it most is that China's increasing political and strategic hobnobbing with Nepal and Bhutan would incite them against India. In that scenario, it will have a direct negative effect on India's national defense and security interests—perhaps much more serious and dangerous than what India suffered in the 1962 Sino-Indian War.

Given the fast-altering political and strategic dynamics in South Asia, China will not miss any opportunity to upgrade its security and strategic profile in Nepal and Bhutan vis-à-vis India. In that scenario, India's defense and security leverage over Nepal and Bhutan will be greatly undermined. To China's good political fortune, the ruling class in Kathmandu, under the Maoist regime, has taken initiatives to come closer to China while realizing that the gravity of power is fast shifting toward China.

Thus, the Beijing leadership is endeavoring to derive maximum political mileage from its soft power initiatives to mitigate India's influence over Kathmandu and Thimpu. In response, New Delhi has increased the quantum of its economic aid to Nepal and Bhutan. This has accentuated competition between China and India for not only investment in and aid to Nepal and Bhutan but also access to their abundant hydropower resources. Given this, Nepal and Bhutan would benefit from a Sino-Indian rivalry for power and influence in the Himalayan region.

Studies suggest that China has enormously benefitted from its soft power mechanisms and has strengthened its political and security ties with Kathmandu and Thimpu, even though China does not have common religious, cultural, societal, or emotional bonds with them. Indeed, India's diplomatic task of regaining the trust and confidence of Himalayan states has become much tougher. It will need to redefine and redesign its policy approach as well as repair the fault lines both in psychological and strategic terms to earn the trust and confidence of smaller South Asian countries. Nepal's distancing away from India reflects New Delhi's geopsychological neglect of and disrespect to it. In strategic terms, India has not yet rejuvenated its policy toward its immediate neighbors in the changing political dynamics of South Asia.

Initially, Prime Minister Modi was able to create much euphoria and enthusiasm in the capitals of Kathmandu and Bhutan by paying them official visits soon after taking the oath of office in May 2014. But his charisma did not last. Instead, China took advantage of his mismatched policy following his failure to translate his verbal promises to Himalayan states into reality. To cite a case study, China promptly came forward to Nepal's rescue by supplying essential commodities when India imposed an unofficial economic embargo on Nepal during a nationwide protest by the Madhesi group in 2015. The Madhesi community was demanding a constitutional amendment to provide them adequate representation in Nepalese political institutions. The national mood and anger in Nepal is still against India's unannounced economic embargo. India thus gave an unnecessary political opportunity to China to exploit the situation by displaying its political and emotional solidarity with Nepal and winning the hearts of Nepalese people.

If India needs to revive and rejuvenate its lost political clout with Himalayan states, New Delhi will need to address their legitimate concerns and interests. Indian diplomats posted in Kathmandu and Thimpu and the foreign policy establishment in the South Block of New Delhi will have to locate the core reasons for Himalayan states' gradual alienation from India and concomitantly their strengthening ties with China. Also, India must learn from the success story of China's so-called soft power diplomacy in creating a cache of goodwill among South Asian countries. This is reinforced from Nepal's direct endorsement of China's full membership of the SAARC. The question remains to be answered as to why Nepal is urging China to play a more meaningful role in SAARC affairs.

China's Sri Lanka policy is dictated by its geopolitical and geostrategic ambitions in the Indian Ocean, which has emerged as a hub of maritime interests among major powers. Sri Lanka, known as the swing state, is situated in the heart of the Indian Ocean, which became a zone of the superpower rivalry in the Cold War era. Since the end of the Cold War, China has been frantically engaged in expanding its naval presence in the Indian Ocean. Being strategically located, Sri Lanka can play a central role in fulfilling China's strategic ambitions in the Indian Ocean region. As Indian influence petered out following its policy of noninterference in Sri Lanka's domestic and external affairs, especially after the assassination of former prime minister Rajiv Gandhi by the LTTE in May 1991, China began entertaining the political ambition of replacing India's role in Sri Lankan affairs. The Colombo regime, under President Mahinda Rajapaksa, also felt the imperative need for Chinese arms to defeat the LTTE, one of the most dreaded terrorist organizations, to end the ethnic war that had enveloped Sri Lanka for over two decades. Moreover, India's blanket refusal to provide military aid to Sri Lanka to eliminate the LTTE provided China with the opportunity to come forward with a huge offer of military hardware. This enabled Sri Lankan forces to finish off the LTTE and its founder, Velupillai Prabhakaran, in 2009.

In the postethnic war scenario, India found itself helpless to keep the levers of geopolitics in its control. Sri Lankan president Rajapakse reciprocated China's generosity by inviting it to launch infrastructure projects, such as development of ports, airfields, and roads. Gradually, China emerged as Sri Lanka's trustworthy partner, manifest from its heavy investment in Sri Lanka. Moreover, Chinese economic engagement in Sri Lanka produced goodwill and a positive image for China among Sri Lankans. Currently China is the largest investor in and second-largest trading partner with Sri Lanka, a situation that has revved up China's strategic leverage over Sri Lanka. China has invested nearly $5 billion in Sri Lanka with the singular motivation of turning it into a pivot point for the Maritime Silk Road initiative. These developments are naturally worrisome to India.

However, the departure of Rajapaksa's pro-China government and the arrival of Maithripala Sirisena as Sri Lanka's new president brought a flicker of hope to New Delhi by bringing India–Sri Lanka relations back on track. President Sirisena and Prime Minister Ranil Wickremesinghe tried to recalibrate Sri Lanka's relations with China in order to rejuvenate Colombo's ties with New Delhi. Sirisena also ordered investigations into corruption charges against the China-aided projects, which gave at least a temporary setback to China. Without losing further time, the Beijing leadership redeployed its soft power tools to convince Sirisena and his prime minister that China was their most reliable friend. This facilitated a revival of over $1 billion worth of projects.

If viewed through a realistic prism, Sri Lanka did not have real and tangible options except to mollify China when Sri Lankan authorities urged it to complete its past projects. However, the underlying reality is that the Sri Lankan economy has been hit hard by its debt repayment problem. Therefore, it is constrained to give maximum concessions to Chinese projects. But China's insistence on repayment of debt has made Sri Lanka realize that India was a better option to help develop its dilapidated infrastructure.

Furthermore, China's motivation to acquire naval bases in the Maldives following the passage of a Maldivian constitutional amendment allowing foreign countries to own land has produced some consternation in the Modi-led government. To assuage New Delhi's apprehension, President Abdulla Yameen reassured Prime Minister Modi that there was neither any move nor any intention to allow China to build a naval base in India's backyard. India has also undertaken measures like capacity-building programs in the Maldives, including scholarships to Maldivian students under various cultural programs. Moreover, one can scarcely ignore the reality that China has been able to outpace India geopolitically and geopsychologically so far as Sri Lanka and the Maldives are concerned.

China has been able to foster and sustain friendly relations with Bangladesh with the aid of its soft power tools, such as providing infrastructure development assistance, offering scholarships, promoting tourism and media contacts, and forging cooperation between think tanks, including exchanging cultural troupes to project its image as a soft power practitioner. More important, China's policy of noninterference in the internal and external affairs of Bangladesh on the one hand and the latter's acceptance of the one-China theory on the other hand have squarely contributed to tension-free relations between the two countries. Unlike China and India, China and Bangladesh have no clash of interests on global and regional affairs. At the same time, it is feared that China's increasing strategic leverage over Bangladesh might transform its Chittagong into Gwadar. Moreover, the conservative lobby in Bangladesh prefers China's engagement with Bangladesh.

China has increasingly provided soft loans and grants to Bangladesh. How? First, China's expanding economic engagement with Bangladesh over the past couple of years has made the latter more dependent on China than ever before. Second, Bangladesh suffers from a huge trade deficit vis-à-vis China, and no opportunities seem to lie ahead for its reduction in the near future. Third, China has been largely successful in its strategy of beefing up defense sales to Bangladesh by politically brainwashing Dhaka into believing that New Delhi is a source of potential threat to its national security. This situation has resulted from inflexibility and languor on the part of the Indian ruling class, which has diplomatically failed to weaken China's strategic grip over Bangladesh. Rather, China has been relentlessly engaged in anti-India propaganda by projecting India's image as a regional hegemon in South Asia. At the same time, Chinese leaders, academia, and thinks tanks have largely succeeded in creating an uneasy relationship between New Delhi and Dhaka by overplaying the landlocked status of Bangladesh.

But interestingly, Prime Minister Sheikh Hasina's momentous decision to shelve the Sonadia deep-sea project sent shock waves through China, even though it remained Bangladesh's largest weapons supplier after Pakistan and also its largest trading partner. This was a pragmatic geopolitical move of Bangladesh to keep in mind the sensitivity and strategic concerns of India, the United States, and Japan in the Indian Ocean. Also, research findings suggest that the Dhaka government is profoundly circumspect about the terms and conditions of China's investment in infrastructure projects, lest it might not become a victim of crippling debt liability, as experienced by Sri Lanka. The Modi administration's diplomacy needs to gear up. It ought to cash in on the lurking fear among smaller South Asian countries of a negative fallout due to the mounting debt burden to China.

Growing Sino-Bangladeshi ties need to be evaluated given the apparent shift from geopolitics to geopsychology, which helps in understanding nuances and complexities of the bilateral relationship. From the geopsychological perspective, Bangladesh needs to learn a bitter lesson from the Indian experience: that China's strategic culture is fundamentally rooted in expanding its strategic footprint while simultaneously chanting the mantra of peaceful coexistence. That was exposed in the 1962 Sino-Indian War. Keeping this centrality of argument in mind, Bangladesh needs to recalibrate its ties with China, informed by a mix of pragmatism and prudence. Be that as it may, South Asian states like Nepal, Bhutan, and the Maldives must understand that their romance with China may not last. Realistically speaking, India is the real culprit pushing them into China's lap. It is an open secret that India's top bureaucratic and intellectual hawks are responsible for alienating its neighbors by patently ignoring their geopsychological impulses, expecting India to treat them with dignity and equality. Their sensitivity is bruised due to the arrogance and apathy displayed by India's diplomatic community in confabulations with its counterparts. China's case is just the reverse. It displays a warm and friendly diplomatic demeanor while engaging its counterparts in a dialogue. India needs to learn from the Chinese style of conducting diplomacy.

The following inferences can be drawn from preceding discussions to better appraise China's soft power diplomacy in both conceptual and pragmatic terms. First, though China has borrowed the soft power notion from Joseph S. Nye, it does not subscribe to it in practice. At times it is rather intriguing to substantiate Chinese claims that their soft power is based on ancient traditions, social norms, and cultural and civilizational values. There is no controversy surrounding the importance of China's great civilization and Confucius thought. But the ruling leadership and academia have not been able to convince the West and the rest of the world of the relevance of establishing a linkage between the primacy of Maoist thought and the imperative of its soft power resources. Does it mean that the Xi leadership is all set to revive Maoist thought as a guiding star while simultaneously embracing state-centric capitalism without political liberalism?

Second, conceptually, the identical meaning of "coercion" and "attraction" in China's notion of soft power is neither logical nor convincing.

Third, it is a myth that China can transform its traditional culture into universally desirable values. No tangible explanation has been offered by its leadership, academia, or think tanks to defend and justify this contention.

Fourth, it is a myth that the Chinese notion of a harmonious world order, without offering an adequate or a logical explanation, will be able to attract a large constituency across the globe to embrace it. This is why its model of a harmonious world order, conceived in terms of a perfect world and of one world and one dream, is not comprehensible.

Fifth, in a larger context, China's soft power resources have not proved adequate at producing desirable outcomes in cost-effective terms, because of inherent contradictions in China's theory of soft power and its practice. For instance, China's record on compliance with international laws and treaties is scarcely impressive. Regarding global issues, China deviates from the practice of supporting democratic voices and antiterror causes. For instance, China's twice blocking the Indian move at the UN to designate Masood Azhar as a terrorist has exposed its true colors. How can China's doublespeak on global terror evoke respect for its claim of being a responsible and peaceful stakeholder in the international system?

An overall scenario that emerges from this study suggests that China's economic and military assistance to smaller countries of the region—such as Nepal, Sri Lanka, and Bangladesh—has been a catalyst in China's gaining a strong strategic foothold and concomitantly undermining India's traditional role and influence in the region. It is also true that India is unable to match the quantum of aid that China can afford to offer South Asian states. But what India can do is educate and sensitize them to be extra cautious about loan repayment liabilities, lest they should fall into China's booby-trap of liberal and lucrative aid offers. Be that as it may, China's soft power resources mixed with coercive diplomacy have produced strategic gains for China. If perceived from a broad perspective, India and the United States will be unable to checkmate Chinese influence in South Asian and Indian Ocean regions given the emerging triangular strategic nexus of China, Russia, and Pakistan. In that eventuality, options before India will be precariously limited to meet the Chinese challenge in the region.

NOTES

1. Joseph Nye, "Why China Is Weak on Soft Power," *New York Times*, January 17, 2012, http://www.nytimes.com/2012/01/18/opinion/why-china-is-weak-on-soft-power.html; David Shambaugh, *China Goes Global: The Partial Power* (New York: Oxford University Presss, 2013), 267.

2. "China Defends Pakistan after Modi's 'Mothership' Remark, Says It's against Linking Terrorism with Ethnicity or Religion," *Indian Express*, October 17, 2016, http://indianexpress.com/article/india/india-news-india/china-pakistan-modi-terrorism-mothership-terror-brics/.

Bibliography

Acharya, Amitav. *Rethinking Power, Institutions and Ideas in World Politics.* London: Routledge, 2014.

Ambekar, G. V., and V. D. Divekar, eds. *Documents on China's Relations with South and Southeast Asia, 1949–1962.* Bombay: Allied, 1964.

Baruah, Darshana M. "Modi's Trip and China's Islands: The Battle for the Indian Ocean." *Diplomat,* March 11, 2015.

Beckley, Michael. "China and Pakistan: Fair-Weather Friends." *Yale Journal of International Affairs* 8, no. 1 (March 2012): 9–22.

Berger, Samuel R. "A Foreign Policy for the Global Age." *Foreign Affairs* (November/December 2000):22–39.

Billioud, Sébastien. "Confucianism, 'Cultural Tradition' and Official Discourse in China at the Start of the New Century." In *China Orders the World,* Callahan and Barabantseva, 231.

Blank, Jonah, "Thank You for Being a Friend: Pakistan and China's Almost Alliance." *Foreign Affairs,* October 15, 2015. https://www.foreignaffairs.com/articles/china/2015-10-15/thank-you-being-friend.

Blazevic, Jason J. "Defensive Realism in the Indian Ocean: Oil, Sea Lanes and the Security Dilemma." *China Security* 5, no.3 (2009): 59–71.

Brzezinski, Zbigniew. "The Cold War and Its Aftermath." *Foreign Affairs* (Fall 1992): 31–49.

Buzan, Barry. "China in International Society: Is 'Peaceful Rise' Possible?" *Chinese Journal of International Politics* 3, no. 1 (2010): 5–36.

Cabestan, Jean-Pierre. "The Many Facets of Chinese Nationalism." *China Perspectives* 59 (May–June 2005): 26–40.

Callahan, William A. "Chinese Vision of World Order: Post-Hegemonic or New Hegemony." *International Studies Review* 10, no. 4 (2008): 749–61.

———. "Conclusion: World Harmony or Harmonizing the World?" In *China Orders the World,* Callahan and Barabantseva.

———. "Introduction: Tradition, Modernity and Foreign Policy in China." In *China Orders the World,* Callahan and Barabantseva.

Callahan, William A., and Elena Barabantseva. *China Orders the World: Normative Soft Power and Foreign Policy.* Washington, DC: Woodrow Wilson Center Press, 2011.

Chan, Steve. *China, the U.S., and the Power-Transition Theory: A Critique.* London: Routledge, 2008.

Chatterji, Manas, and B. M. Jain, eds. *Conflict and Peace in South Asia.* London: Emerald Group, 2008.

Chellaney, Brahma. "India's Growing China Angst." *Far Eastern Economic Review* 172, no.7 (2009): 31–35.

———. "Why Tibet Remains the Core Issue in China-India Relations." *Forbes*, November 27, 2014.

Kelvin C. K. Cheung, "Appropriating Confucianism: Soft Power, Primordial Sentiment, and Authoritarianism." In *China's Rise to Power*, Lee, Nedilsky, and Cheung.

Cho,Young Nam, and Jong Ho Jeong. "China Soft Power: Discussion, Resources, and Prospects. *Asia Survey* 48, no. 3 (May–June 2008): 453—72

Chung, Tan. "Chinese Civilization: Resilience and Challenges. *China Report* 41, no. 2 (April–June 2005): 113–30.

Curtis, Lisa. "China's Military and Security Relationship with Pakistan." Testimony before the U.S.-China Economic and Security Review Commission, Heritage Foundation, May 20, 2009. http://www.heritage.org/research/testimony/chinas-military-and-security-relationship-with-pakistan.

Dasgupta, Sunil, and Stephen P. Cohen. "Is India Ending Its Strategic Restraint Doctrine." *Washington Quarterly* (Spring 2011):163–177.

Destradi, Sandra. "Domestic Politics and Regional Hegemony: India's Approach to Sri Lanka." *International Relations*, January 14, 2104. http://www.e-ir.info/2014/01/14/domestic-politics-and-regional-hegemony-indias-approach-to-sri-lanka/.

Detsch, Jack. "China's Grand Plan for Pakistan's Infrastructure." *Diplomat*, April 21, 2015. http://thediplomat.com/2015/04/chinas-grand-plan-for-pakistans-infrastructure/.

Freidberg, Aaron L. "Compromise or Conflict? China the United States, and Stability in Asia." *International Security* 30, no. 2 (Fall 2005): 7–45.

Gaddis, John Lewis. "Toward the Post-Cold War World." *Foreign Affairs* 70, no. 2 (Spring 1991): 102–22.

Ganguly, Sumit, and Brandon Miliate. "India Pushes Nepal into China's Arm." *Foreign Policy*, October 23, 2015. http://foreignpolicy.com/2015/10/23/india-pushes-nepal-into-chinas-arms/#.

Gill, Bates and Yanzhong Huang. "Sources and Limits of China's Soft Power." *Survival* 48, no. 2 (Summer 2006): 17–36.

Glaser, Bonnie S. and Melissa E. Murphy. "Soft Power with Chinese Characteristics, the Ongoing Debate." In *Chinese Soft Power and Its Implications for the United States: Chinese Soft Power and Its Implications for the United States*, edited by Carola McGiffert, 10–26. Washington, DC: Center for Strategic and International Studies, 2009. http://csis.org/files/media/csis/pubs/090310_chinesesoftpower__chap2.pdf.

Gries, Peter Hays. *China's New Nationalism: Pride, Politics, and Diplomacy*. Berkeley: University of California Press, 2004.

Guihong, Zhang. "China's Peaceful Rise and Sino-Indian Relations." *China Report* 41, no. 2 (April–June 2005): 159–71.

Garver, John. "The China-India-U.S. Triangle: Strategic Relations in the Post-Cold War Era." *NBR Analysis* 13, no. 5 (October 2002): 6–11.

———. "Sino-Indian Rapprochement and the Sino-Pakistan Entente." *Political Science Quarterly* 111, no. 2 (Summer 1996): 326–33

Green, Michael J., and Andrew Shearer. "Defining U.S. Indian Ocean Strategy." *Washington Quarterly* (Spring 2012): 175–89.

Gunaratne, Peshan, and J. Berkshire Miller. "Sri Lanka: Balancing Ties between China and the West." *Diplomat*, May 26, 2015. http://thediplomat.com/2015/05/sri-lanka-balancing-ties-between-china-and-the-west/.

Gungwu, Wang, and Zheng Yongnian, eds. *China and the New International Order*. Princeton, NJ: Princeton University Press, 2008.

Guo, Sujian, ed. *China's "Peaceful Rise" in the 21st Century: Domestic and International Conditions*. Surrey, UK: Ashgate, 2006.

Hagerty, Devin T. "China and Pakistan: Strains in the Relationship." *Current History* 101, no. 656 (September 2002): 288–90.

Harder, Anton. "Not at the Cost of China: India and the United Nations Security Council, 1950." Cold War International Project. Washington DC: Woodrow Wilson Center, 2015.

Hu, Weixing, Gerald Chan, and Daojiong Zha, eds. *China's International Relations in the 21st Century: Dynamics of Paradigm Shift*. Lanham, MD: University Press of America, 2000.

Islam, Shariful. "China-Bangladesh Relations." *Global Times* (September 2015). http://www.globaltimes.cn/content/944756.shtml

Iyengar, Rishi. "Sri Lanka Attempts to Repair Relations with China Amid an Escalating Financial Crisis." *Time*, October 19, 2015. http://time.com/4077757/sri-lanka-china-financial-crisis-ravi-karunanayake-interview/.

Jacques, Martin. *When China Rules the world*. London: Allen Lane, 2009.

Jain, B. M. *Global Power: India's Foreign Policy, 1947–2006*. Lanham, MD: Lexington Books, 2008.

————. "India-China Relations: Issues and Emerging Trends." *Round Table* 93, no. 374 (April 2004): 253–69.

————. *India-US Relations, 1961–1963*. London: Sangam, 1987.

————. "Regional Security in South Asia." in *Challenges to Global Security: Geopolitics and Power in an Age of Transition*, edited by Hussein Solomon. London: I.B. Tauris, 2008.

————. *India in the New South Asia: Strategic, Military and Economic Concerns in the Age of Nuclear Diplomacy*. London: I.B. Tauris, 2010.

Jha, Prem Shankar. *India and China: The Battle between Soft and Hard Power* (New Delhi: Penguin Books, 2010).

Johnston, Alastair Iain. *Cultural Realism: Strategic Culture and Grand Strategy in Chinese History*. Princeton, NJ: Princeton University Press, 1995.

Joshi, Rohan. "China, Pakistan, and Nuclear Non-Proliferation." *Diplomat*, February 16, 2015. http://thediplomat.com/2015/02/china-pakistan-and-nuclear-non-proliferation/.

Kaligama, Saman. "China–Sri Lanka Economic Relations." Presentation to the Sri Lanka–China Forum, September 25, 2009. http://www.ips.lk/news/newsarchive/2009/20_9_9_china_business/china_presentation.pdf.

Kardon, Isaac B. "China and Pakistan: Emerging Strains in the Entente Cordiale." Report. Arlington, VA: Project 2049 Institute, March 2011.

Keefer, Edward C. *The Nixon Administration and the United Nations: "It's a Damned Debating Society."* http://www.diplomatie.gouv.fr/fr/IMG/pdf/ONU_edward_keefer.pdf.

Keohane, Robert O., and Joseph Nye. *Power and Interdependence*. New York: Longman, 2012.

Khatun, Fahmida. "Country Illustration Report: Bangladesh." Centre for Policy Dialogue, August 26, 2014. https://ec.europa.eu/europeaid/sites/devco/files/erd5-country-illustration-bangladesh-2015_en.pdf.

Kim, Samuel S., ed. *China and the World: Chinese Foreign Relations in the Post-Cold War Era*. Boulder: Westview, 1994.

Kissinger, Henry. *On China*. 2nd ed. New York: Penguin, 2012.

Kondapalli, C. Srikanth. "Maritime Silk Road: Increasing Chinese Inroads into the Maldives." Institute of Peace and Conflict Studies, November 13, 2014. http://www.ipcs.org/article/china/maritime-silk-road-increasing-chinese-inroads-into-the-maldives-4735.html.

Kothari, Rajni. *Transformation and Survival: In Search of a Humane Order*. 2nd ed. New Delhi: Ajanta, 1990.

Kumar, Satish. China's Expanding Footprint in Nepal: Threats to India." *Journal of Defence Studies* 5, no. 2 (April 2011).

Kurlantzick, Joshua. *Charm Offensive: How China's Soft Power Is Transforming the World*. New Haven, CT: Yale University Press, 2007.

Lai, Hongyi, and Yiyi Lu., eds. *China's Soft Power and International Relations*. New York: Routledge, 2012.

Lampton, David M. *Same Bed, Different Dreams: Managing U.S.-China Relations, 1989–2000*. Berkeley: University of California Press, 2001.

Lee, Joseph Tse-Hei, Lida V. Nedlisky, and Siu-Keung Cheung, eds. *China's Rise to Power: Conceptions of State Governance*. New York: Palgrave Macmillan, 2012.

Leonard, Mark. *What Does China Think?* New York: Public Affairs, 2008.

Liu, Sidney Y. "Harmonious Online Society: The China Model in the Information Age." In *China's Rise to Power*, Lee, Nedilsky, and Cheung, 94.

Malik, V. P., and Jorg Schultz, eds. *The Rise of China: Perspectives from Asia and Europe*. New Delhi: Pentagon, 2008.

Masood, Asma. "India-Bangladesh-China Relations: A Complex Triangle." Chennai Centre for China Studies, March 2, 2015. http://www.c3sindia.org/india/4860.

Mauldin, John. "Can Central Planners Revive China's Economic Miracle?" *Forbes*, June 8, 2014. http://www.forbes.com/sites/johnmauldin/2014/06/08/can-central-planners-revive-chinas-economic-miracle/.

Mearsheimer, John J. *The Tragedy of Great Power Politics.* New York: W. W. Norton, 2014.

Medeiros, Evan S., and M. Taylor Frave. "China's New Diplomacy." *Foreign Affairs* 82, no. 6 (November/December 2003). https://www.foreignaffairs.com/articles/asia/2003-11-01/china-new-diplomacy.

Mehta, Pratap Bhanu. "Still under Nehru's Shadow? The Absence of Foreign Policy Frameworks in India." *Indian Review* 8, no. 3 (July–September 2009): 209–33.

Menon, Shivshankar. *Choices: Inside the Making of India's Foreign Policy.* New Delhi: Brookings India, 2016.

Nehru, Jawaharlal. *The Discovery of India.* 4th ed. New Delhi: Jawaharlal Nehru Memorial Fund, 1985.

———. "In the Lok Sabha: White Paper on India and China." Motion on India-China Relations, November 25, 1959, Lok Sabha Debates, 2nd series, 35, cos 1680–1708. *Selected Works of Jawaharlal Nehru* 54 (November 1–30, 1959). http://www.claudearpi.net/maintenance/uploaded_pics/SW54.pdf.

Noorani, A. G. *India-China Boundary Problem, 1846–1947: History and Diplomacy.* New Delhi: Oxford University Press, 2011.

Nye, Joseph S. *Bound to Lead: The Changing Nature of American Power.* New York: Basic Books, 1990.

———. *The Future of Power.* New York: Public Affairs, 2011.

———. "The Information Revolution and Soft Power." *Current History* 113, no. 759 (January 2014): 19–22. http://dash.harvard.edu/bitstream/handle/1/11738398/Nye-InformationRevolution.pdf?se.

———. "Limits of American Power." *Political Science Quarterly* 117, no. 4 (2002–2003): 545–59.

———. "The Pakistan Thorn in China-India-U.S. Relations." *Washington Quarterly* (Winter 2012): 83–95.

———. *The Paradox of American Power: Why the World's Only Superpower Can't Go It Alone.* New York: Oxford University Press, 2003.

———. "Redefining the National Interest." *Foreign Affairs* (July–August 1999): 22–35.

———. *Soft Power: The Means to Success in World Politics.* New York: Public Affairs, 2004.

Pant, Harsh. *The China Syndrome: Grappling with an Uneasy Relationship.* London: HarperCollins, 2010.

Osnos, Evan. "The Next Reincarnation." *New Yorker*, October 4, 2010.

Pan, Esther. "The Promise and Pitfalls of China's Peaceful Rise." Council on Foreign Relations, April 14, 2006. http://www.cfr.org/china/promise-pitfalls-chinas-peaceful-rise/p10446.

Pant, Harsh. *The China Syndrome: Grappling with an Uneasy Relationship.* London: HarperCollins, 2010.

———. "The Pakistan Thorn in China-India-U.S. Relations." *Washington Quarterly* (Winter 2012): 83–95.

Parashar, Sachin. "China using Nepal Study Centers for Spying.?" *Economic Times*, October 1, 2009.

Pocha, Jehangir S. "China and India on Verge of Nuclear Deal." *Boston Globe*, November 20, 2006.

Riedel, Bruce. "One Year of Modi Government: Us versus Them." Brookings Institution, May 25, 2015. https://www.brookings.edu/opinions/one-year-of-modi-government-us-versus-them/.

Ritzinger, Louis. "The China-Pakistan Economic Corridor, Regional Dynamics and China's Geopolitical Ambitions." National Bureau of Asian Research, August 2015. http://www.nbr.org/research/activity.aspx?id=589)

Samaranayake, Nilanthi. "India's Key to Sri Lanka: Maritime Infrastructure Development." *Diplomat,* March 31, 2015. http://thediplomat.com/2015/03/indias-key-to-sri-lanka-maritime-infrastructure-development/.

Samatha, M. "India, Sri Lanka and Maldives Trilateral Maritime Security Cooperation: Political and Economic Constraints in Implementation." Policy brief, Indian Council of World Affairs, New Delhi, July 8, 2015. http://www.icwa.in/pdfs/PB/2014/IndiaSriLankaMaldivesPB08072015.pdf.

Shambaugh, David. *China Goes Global: The Partial Power.* Oxford: Oxford University Press, 2013.

———. *China's Future.* Cambridge: Polity, 2016.

———. "China's Soft-Power Push: The Search for Respect." *Foreign Affairs* (July/August 2015). https://www.foreignaffairs.com/articles/china/2015-06-16/china-s-soft-power-push.

———. *Is China Unstable?* London: M.E. Sharpe, 2000.

Sharma, Shalendra D. *China and India in the Age of Globalization: A Comparative Political Economy.* New York: Cambridge University Press, 2009.

Shirk, Susan. *China: Fragile Superpower.* New York: Oxford University Press, 2007

Singh, Jaswant. *Defending India.* New York: Macmillan, 1999.

Singh, Manjit. " Pakistan-Occupied Kashmir—a "Buffer State' in the Making." *Strategic Analysis* 37, no. 1 (January–February 2013): 1–7.

Singh Sidhu, W., Yuan, J. "Resolving the Sino-Indian Border Dispute: Building Confidence through Cooperative Monitoring." *Asian Survey* 41, no.2 (2001): 351–376.

Small, Andrew. *The China-Pakistan Axis: Asia's New Geopolitics.* London: C. Hurst & Co, 2015.

Sinha, Nirmal. "The Simla Convention 1914: A Chinese Puzzle." *Presidency College Magazine: Diamond Jubilee Number* (1974): 35–39. http://himalaya.socanth.cam.ac.uk/collections/journals/bot/pdf/bot_1977_01_05.pdf.

Small, Andrew. "China's Caution on Afghanistan-Pakistan." *Washington Quarterly* 33, no.3, June 24, 2010.

Tellis, Ashley. "Report on Balancing without Containment: An American Strategy for Managing China." Washington, DC: Carnegie Endowment, 2014.

Tiezzi, Shannon. "China's $1.4 Billion Port City in Sri Lanka Gets the Green Light." *Diplomat,* March 12, 2016. http://thediplomat.com/2016/03/chinas-1-4-billion-port-city-in-sri-lanka-gets-the-green-light/.

Tow, William T. *Asia-Pacific Relations: Seeking Convergent Security.* New York: Cambridge University Press, 2001.

Tse-Hei Lee, Joseph, Lida V. Nedilsky, and Siu-Keung Cheung, eds. *China's Rise to Power: Conception of State Governance.* New York: Palgrave Macmillan, 2012.

Twinning, Daniel. "A Chinese Charm Offensive Will Work Better Than a Military One." *Foreign Policy,* February 23, 2016. http://foreignpolicy.com/2016/02/23/a-chinese-charm-offensive-would-work-better-than-a-military-one/.

Van Eekelen, W. F. *Indian Foreign Policy and the Border Dispute with China.* The Hague: Martinus Nihoff, 1967.

Wang, Hongying and James N. Rosenau. "China's Global Governance." *Asian Perspective* 33, no. 3 (2009): 5–39.

Wang, Qingxin. "Cultural Norms and the Conduct of Chinese Foreign Policy." In *China's International Relations,* Hu, Chan, and Zhopp, 143–69.

Wei, Wei. "China's New Neighbourhood Diplomacy Will Have Positive Impact on Its Relations with India." *News From China* 26, no. 2 (February 2014): 15

Wezeman, Pieter D., and Siemon T. Wezeman. "Trends in International Arms Transfers, 2014." SIPRI Fact Sheet, Stockholm International Peace Research Institute, March 2015. http://books.sipri.org/files/FS/SIPRIFS1503.pdf.

Wuthnow, Joel. "The Concept of Soft Power in China's Strategic Discourse." *Issues and Studies* 44, no. 2 (June 2008): 1–28.

Yong, Deng, and Fei-ling Wang, eds. *China Rising: Power and Motivation in Chinese Foreign Policy.* Lanham: Rowman & Littlefield, 2005.

Yuan, Jingdong. "China's Kashmir Policy." *China Brief* 5, no. 19 (2005), Jamestown Founda-
    tion.   http://www.jamestown.org/single/
    ?tx_ttnews%5Btt_news%5D=3893#.VdCLvLKqqko.
Yucheng, Le. "China-India Relations: Soaring to New Heights." *News from China* 27, no. 10
    (October 2015): 34–35.
Zhonghe Zhu. "China's Perception of India's New Government." Academia. https://
    www.academia.edu/8621880/China_s_perception_of_India_s_new_government.
Zhu, Zhiqun. *China's New Diplomacy: Rational, Strategies and Significance*. 2nd ed. Surrey,
    UK: Ashgate, 2013.

Index

About the Author

B. M. Jain, a former visiting professor in the Department of Political Science at Cleveland State University, Ohio, is editor in chief of the *Indian Journal of Asian Affairs*.

www.ingramcontent.com/pod-product-compliance
Lightning Source LLC
Chambersburg PA
CBHW021819270326
41932CB00007B/257